THE SAINTS IN THE LIVES OF ITALIAN-AMERICANS

AN INTERDISCIPLINARY INVESTIGATION

 Filibrary Series, No. 14

1999

Filibrary Series

M. Ricciardelli, General Editor

Giacomo Leopardi: Proceedings of the Congress Held at the
University of California, Los Angeles, November 10-11, 1988,
edited by Giovanni Cecchetti

THE SAINTS IN THE LIVES OF ITALIAN-AMERICANS

AN INTERDISCIPLINARY INVESTIGATION

Co-Edited by:
Joseph A. Varacalli
Salvatore Primeggia
Salvatore J. LaGumina
Donald J. D'Elia

Foreword by:
Mario B. Mignone

FORUM ITALICUM   *SUPPLEMENT*

FILIBRARY NO. 14   ISBN 1-893127-14-1   1999

FILIBRARY publishes the monographic supplements to
FORUM ITALICUM

FILIBRARY pubblica i supplementi monografici di
FORUM ITALICUM

FILIBRARY is the forum for prospective guest editors. Any
inquiries or manuscripts should be submitted to:

FORUM ITALICUM
Center for Italian Studies
State University of New York at Stony Brook
Stony Brook, NY 11794-3358
USA

Library of Congress Cataloging-in-Publication Data
ISBN 1-893127-14-1
1. Christian Saints, 2. Cults, 3. Saints and Society, 4. Italian-American
Studies.

TABLE OF CONTENTS

PART V: THE SAINTS MARCH ON

FOREWORD

Why focus a study on the veneration of saints by an ethnic group at a moment when rock stars such as Madonna or other popular idols have taken their places? Is it justifiable to give much importance to a kind of veneration that has progressively waned in the last thirty years? The answer is very simple. By understanding this change we will definitely understand one of the most profound changes in the lives of the Italian-Americans. After all, their veneration of saints, in all its dimensions, reflects one of the most important parts of their personal and collective lives up to the 1970s and defines both their brand of Catholicism and their identity as an ethnic group. Religious feasts and individual and collective manifestations of veneration to saints, simultaneously ethnic and religious events, represent a strong and important aspect in which the specific ethnic identity of Italian-Americans is both manifested and reinforced. Now that Italian-Americans have come to the foreground in the United States in various arenas (politics, the sciences, economics, culture), it becomes increasingly provocative and important to understand the meaning of their ethnic and cultural identity.

The Saints in the Lives of Italian-Americans, through an interdisciplinary approach, accomplishes fully what many other scholarly works have dealt with only superficially or sectorally. And it does so by anchoring the investigation of the subject matter in southern Italy, the areas from where the largest number of Italians emigrated. The authors of *The Saints* have provided many explanations not just on the religious practices of Italian-Americans, but also on the differences of past and present religious behavior between Italian-American and Irish-American Catholics, on religious pattern changes in the acculturation process, and, on the other hand, the enduring religious traits as the most revealing characteristics in the preservation of an ethnic identity. By learning about the religious practices of southern Italians, we will learn that the difference in confidence or trust in the clergy by Irish and Italian-American Catholics is not just due to differences in education or socio-economic conditions, or even to historical reasons, but also to the centrality of saints in the religious belief of Italian-

Americans. In Italy, before the secularization of society, which took place especially in the 70s and 80s with the rise of industrialization and economic development, the authority of the Church was very strong and Catholicism formed a profound and natural part of the social fabric of the nation permeating every aspect of Italian cultural life. Catholicism had a position of overwhelming dominance within Italy and generated an enormous variety of cultural forms. Catholic values had played, both anthropologically and culturally, a decisive role in shaping individual lives and collective behavior. For the average citizen, church ceremonies were both social and religious events, and the profession of faith was still felt with strong passion.

The Church's presence in the life of the citizens was strong at every social and cultural level, including education and welfare activities. The parish priest was the center of community life–he was lawyer, adviser, teacher, psychologist, and social and spiritual healer. Church teaching provided many of the basic conceptions in a cosmology of ideas about spirituality, natural forces, fortune, and misfortune. Being a Catholic meant also to be shaped by certain specific social practices that generated an identity. Since most Italians were abiding Catholics, they were all baptized and received a baptismal name that was chosen from the calendar of saints, and that saint's name day (*onomastico*) was celebrated by everybody carrying that name. Catholic identity also expanded to forms of identity based on territory. In many parts of Italy people had and still have a very strong sense of pride and identification with the town or village of birth; there are names and stereotypes for these regional and local identities, and in a number of areas it was the Church that provided the focus for many of the large-scale activities that brought a village together as a collective entity. The village patron saint, with its statue, cult, and processions, provided one way in which a village's collective identity was articulated.

However, although the priest was endowed with authority to assure the authentic practice of religion, people developed particular practices and beliefs (from baptism to the invocation and veneration of saints) that show clearly that religion could be a very personal and continual process. God's grace, invoked when the priest made the annual blessing of all the houses of his parishioners and the fields of the village before Easter, was viewed as having the same magic power of a whole range of practices that grew up to deal with misfortune, from the ringing of church bells to avert storms, to exorcism, or to the invocation of particular saints specializing in help with bodily illness. In the pragmatic culture of the peasants, the blessed olive branches on Palm Sunday and other objects blessed on other occasions were as significant as religious formulas and imagery used in private acts of divination and curing by laity faced with misfortune. The celebration of the mass was no more or less important than the use of a religious amulet as protection against the evil eye. In part the folk religiosity slipped out of the control of the clergy. Even the veneration of saints assumed magical practices.

Indeed, saints found in southern Italian worship appear neither in the Bible nor in the writings of the early Christian fathers, but were folk substitutes for Greek and Roman gods and spirits of the forests, rivers, and mountains. Certainly there are parallels between these practices and those of non-Catholic peasantries; some have their roots in a pre-Christian culture that the Church was either unable to eradicate or desired to transform. Far from being pagan oddities, some of these magical practices show a fundamental continuity with central tenets of Catholic theology, for example with the rite of exorcism that is part of baptism. Even the adoration of a host of local saints was practiced in a widely diffused pagan religiosity.

No one questions the fervor and the genuine devotion that people felt and displayed towards saints. I still remember the acts of profound faith manifested during pilgrimages to shrines of Madonnas and saints when I was a youngster. It was a passionate faith. Saints offered, especially to the peasants, a sustaining refuge from the harsh realities of life. Belief in saints, professed through pagan style worshiping and Catholic devotion, must be understood as a need to anchor one's faith in the concrete, in the palpable, to the accessible. Being human and having the superhuman power of miracles, saints abolished the distance between the cosmic grandiosity of God and his human earthly manifestations. Therefore, saints were not just viewed as intercessors, but as the most important religious agents in favor of the needy. In a world where life was very precarious, man-made evils abounded, and natural disasters (droughts, floods, earthquakes) and diseases struck without warning and without logic, the causes were attributed to forces and powers of superhuman agents. In making sense of a senseless and dangerous world, the undeserving affliction brought on by superhuman powers could only be mitigated or even prevented with the protection of superhuman benevolent agents. Because state agencies were not providing security or support, saints were entrusted with their domain over specific areas of life on a basis of human relationships that were both very personal and collective. Therefore, they were worshiped through masses, novenas, and feasts, but they were also prayed to and implored for specific personal needs and against inner-fears.

Illness and remedies were bound closely to a blend of religion and pagan superstition that varied somewhat from place to place. Christianity had come to cities long before the countryside, where pagan deities continued to hold the attention of peasants. Consequently, in the more agrarian southern society, Catholicism was blended with traditions and customs of pagan origin and reliance upon superstition and magic remained especially strong. Preservation of health was tied closely to worship of individual saints. Saint Rocco protected devotees against illness, Saint Lucy guarded their eyesight, and Saint Anna helped women during their pregnancy, Saint Antonio was the patron saint of animals, Saint Biagio protected the throat. No human activity went uncovered.

Southern Italians often attributed illness to the influence of one who had the *iettatura* or *malocchio* (evil eye), a belief that had no basis in Roman Catholic theology and which the Church never succeeded in supplanting. The old pagan polytheism became Christianized as a whole panoply of saints was passed into service to fulfill the functions of the gods they supplanted. And so, the power of many saints whose names, images, and relics were venerated in countless churches and chapels throughout the country was invoked for myriad reasons.

Processions carrying statues of saints on their feast day were, and to a certain extent still are, an important part of Italian religious practice, especially in the South. These processions are an enactment of relations between the human and the divine and at the same time establish various social identities. Pinning money to a religious icon is part of a transaction with the divine, or may also reflect competition for social status within the village.

This world changed profoundly in the course of two decades or so. By the mid-1970s, with the rapid secularization of Italian society and the profound changes within the Church following the Second Vatican Council, the presence of the Church in society diminished rapidly and the ways

vii

people practiced religion changed as rapidly. Vatican II, besides reducing the distance between laity and clergy (e.g., the use of lay deacons), also changed the prevalent conception of God as a remote figure. Emphasis shifted from God the judging Father to God the loving Son who makes himself available to us through the sacraments and can be approached through prayer and good deeds. This also involved a reminder of Christ's commandments to love one's neighbor and that a Christian life is lived not just through private acts of devotion and the sacraments, but in acts of love, charity, and fellowship with other human beings. These shifts of emphasis to the teaching of Jesus Christ and his sacrifice, which are at the core of religious life, have been called Christocentric. In the process, there was the devaluation of the external cults that focused on the power of the mediating figures, Mary and the saints. Local clergy also began to withdraw their support from many popular forms of celebration, including the procession with the saint's statue or other religious images, which often included a great deal of locally generated ritual and symbolism. There was a concern among Church leaders that parishioners were participating in the events more out of social convention and tradition than for the spiritual significance. Nevertheless, these kinds of celebrations lost much of their significance for people who migrated because the village collectivity that provided the bounded and stable community did not exist anymore. Therefore, forms of Catholicism that had permeated and shaped many social identities and that had operated through ritual acts and symbolic forms, lost their resonance and were replaced by a view of religion that was concerned essentially with the spiritual aspect. There was a general shift away from traditions, which were embedded in particular social contexts whose existence was normally unquestioned, to a more universalistic ethos based on individual conscience. These kinds of changes in religious practice also found better reception with middle-class values.

These changes were paralleled by changes in the way Italian-Americans professed their religion. However, even though public feasts and other collective manifestation in honor of saints have waned, they constitute one of the few remaining opportunities for Italian-Americans as a group and community to maintain a sense of social cohesion and ethnic identity. The feast of the *Giglio* in Brooklyn is an example of a totalizing festival involving people on various levels: ethno-cultural, religious, economic, and in terms of community initiation for the younger generation, of social control, and of continuity with their origin (because it kept rooted in the town of Nola in Avellino). There are few moments like the ethnic feast (so central to the Italian-American experience) in which ethnic identity can be so positively affirmed and socially reinforced.

The Saints in the Lives of Italian-Americans: An Interdisciplinary Investigation not only informs us on a wide range of religious customs and strong faiths in the saints, it also helps us understand the meaning of the ethnic identity of Italian-Americans. It helps us to better understand the problems and issues related to ethnic origins and identity on a wider level: the Italian-Americans, being rooted in the Mezzogiorno, are culturally attached to the deep Mediterranean culture, and consequently, to the ancient Greeks and Moslems. While providing us with a deep understanding of the culture that shaped the *contadini* pragmatic approach in the choosing of witches and saints, doctors and priests, as well as spells, incantations, and magic potions, it sheds light on the misunderstood paradox of passionate Italian-American belief in Catholicism and their stubborn individualism concerning doctrinal interpretation and faith.

MARIO B. MIGNONE
UNIVERSITY AT STONY BROOK

CO-EDITORS' INTRODUCTION

The Saints in the Lives of Italian-Americans: An Interdisciplinary Investigation is notable in several respects. First of all, as the subtitle indicates, the study is truly interdisciplinary, consisting of essays that come from sociological, historical, psychological, philosophical, and theological perspectives or some combination of the above. Secondly, the volume can be characterized as one broadly sympathetic to the veneration of the saints. Put another way, the volume rejects the positivism, materialism, and reductionism typical of so much modern and post-modern scholarship. The essays are written in the classical tradition. Within this parameter, however, the volume offers many divergent viewpoints on controversial and debatable issues such as the existence of an "Italian problem" in the Catholic Church of the United States, the relationship between "folk" and "official" religiosity, the extent and nature of contemporary Italian-American assimilation into secular culture, the symbolic significance in today's society of either embracing or rejecting a public attachment to the saints, whether an acceptance of the concept of sainthood constitutes a broadening or contracting of the horizons in human consciousness, the role of multiculturalism *vis-a-vis* an authentic sense of *Italianità*, and the current receptivity toward the tradition of the veneration of saints on the part of the contemporary Catholic Church in the United States, the Italian-American family and community, and the outside non-Catholic and non-Italian world.

The volume, thirdly, is also notable in that its making has involved the joint cooperation of two organizations, the Center for Italian Studies of S.U.N.Y. Stony Brook directed by Dr. Mario B. Mignone and the Nassau Community College Center for Italian-American Studies, the latter founded by President Sean A. Fanelli and directed by Dr. Salvatore J. LaGumina with the assistance of Dr. Joseph A. Varacalli. (The volume constitutes the *second* major project of the NCC Center for Italian Studies; the first is *Italian American History and Culture: An Encyclopedia*.) Finally of note is that all of the volume's authors are members of either the American Italian Historical Association or the Society of Catholic Social Scientists;

many belong to both groups. The volume has built upon scholarly panels presented at Nassau Community College-S.U.N.Y. (1996), Franciscan University (1996 and 1997), and the 31st Annual Conference of the American Italian Historical Association, to be held at New York City in November of 1998.

The book is divided into five sections. The first chapter includes an essay that presents to the reader some of the reasons why a scholarly investigation of the saints is important. It also contains a descriptive essay introducing the reader to some of the saints and devotional practices that have been central in the Italian-American heritage. The next section contains four essays that together provide an historical overview. Deferring to a local focus of special (but certainly not sole) interest to both the Center for Italian Studies and the Center for Italian-American Studies, Section Three analyzes the role of the saints in the Italian-American feasts and parishes of Long Island, New York.

Analytical reflections from distinctly historical, theological, psychological, and philosophical perspectives constitute the fourth section. The conclusion contains an essay placing the many swirling controversies regarding the veneration of the saints within a discussion of the various meanings of contemporary multiculturalism. The volume ends with two chapters, one outlining proposed future research in the form of a systematic social-psychological inquiry and the other consisting of an expansive bibliographical essay suggesting further readings in the area of the saints in the lives of Italian-Americans. The co-editors would like to thank Patricia Forte, Lillian E. Varacalli and Melina J. Iacovone for their assistance in the typing of the manuscript and for other services of an administrative nature. Finally, the co-editors dedicate this volume to all those saints who have been central in the lives of Italian-Americans.

JOSEPH A. VARACALLI
SALVATORE PRIMEGGIA
SALVATORE J. LAGUMINA
DONALD J. D'ELIA
CO-EDITORS

Part I

Investigating the Saints

CHAPTER 1

AS THE SAINTS (APPARENTLY) GO MARCHING OUT:
WHY STUDY THEM?

Why should the subject of the saints in the lives of Italian-Americans be a topic worthy of serious academic study, especially given recent empirical evidence that they are progressively moving to the margins of the contemporary portrait of Italian Americana?[1] There are at least seven important reasons to affirm the importance of such a scholarly investigation.

First of all, the saints were, perhaps still are, and might once again become, an important part of the Italian (especially southern Italian) and Italian American Catholic heritage. Following the *verstehen* approach of the classical sociologist, Max Weber, one of the key tasks in any social scientific investigation is to uncover what it is that provides *meaning* to the community/ individuals being studied.[2] To study the saints, then, centrally addresses the meaning question for the issue of Italian-American community and identity.

The saints were either worshiped, pagan style, manipulated in magic-like fashion, or venerated, in authentic Catholic devotion, through many different social contexts: in pre-modern Italian villages and, on the American scene, both inside and outside of the walls of the parish, including the home, the feast, and through other neighborhood venues. Additionally, scapulars of Our Lady of Mount Carmel with St. Simon Stock adorn the neck of many contemporary Italian Americans—sometimes along with such superstitious symbols as *il corno* (twisted horn), worn to ward off *il malocchio* (the evil eye). Any useful study of the saints, then, must both encompass and relate what Meredith McGuire refers to as "official" institutional religion and "nonofficial" popular religion.[3] That the various community contexts were partially given form and articulation by the saints obviously implies—in the main, at least—some very real consequences for the dialectically related issue of identity.[4]

3

The saints have threaded and, in some cases, mutually supported aspects of both official Catholic and folk religiosity. Indeed, the establishment of national and *defacto* Italian ethnic parishes in the United States started a process that not only encouraged the maintenance of old world religious beliefs but their development within an authentic Catholic framework. Ironically, however, and as argued by Nicholas John Russo among others, the hibernization of Italian American Catholics—strong between the 1930s-1960s in American society—may have slightly de-emphasized the southern Italian attraction to the saints substituting instead a concern for other (e.g., sacramental and doctrinal) components of the official Catholic world view.[5] The *widespread* abandonment of the saints on the part of Italian Americans and other Catholic ethnic groups would have to await the impact of the distorted interpretation of the theology of the Second Vatican Council and post-conciliar thought in the era from the mid-1960s to the present.

It should also be obvious that the meaning issue addressed by social scientifically studying the saints does not necessarily presuppose belief in the concept of sainthood on the part of the investigator. As the early American sociologist of the "Chicago school," W. I. Thomas, put it so well, "if something is defined as real, it is real in its consequences."[6] Simply put, the social scientific bottom line is that the researcher must understand both that the saints are a central part of *la via vecchia* (the old way) and that there are definite social and social-psychological consequences for Italian-Americans in holding a belief in saints. All things being held equal, however, a personal belief in the reality of saints should aid the researcher in the task of empathizing with the subjects under investigation and appreciating the experiential reality and impact of the saints.

Even assuming that the saints are, indeed, less meaningful to the contemporary modern Italian-American, two other important issues arise. First of all, the future might very well bring with it a resurgence of belief in the saints. Secondly, there is the immediate issue of what now serves as the functional replacement for belief in the saints. Only the most ideologically doctrinaire child of the Enlightenment could, respectively, posit a unilinear evolutionary understanding of social change that precludes, willy nilly, traditional forms of religious belief from ever returning or deny the anthropological imperative of personal/ primordial/ particularistic attachments through which our participation to the broader social world is inevitably mediated.[7] Regarding the latter, crudely put, for some Italian-American youth it may very well be possible that the rock star Madonna has replaced—at least temporarily at this point in the individual life cycle and during this specific period of American civilization—the Virgin Mother as the most central mediator to that which, following the liberal Protestant theologian, Paul Tillich, is of "ultimate concern."[8]

To study the prominent role of the saints in the lives of Italian-Americans is, secondly, to analyze simultaneously the *culture of pre-modern Italy*, especially in *Il Sud* (the South). As Primeggia and Varacalli have noted, two key traditional southern Italian values have been those of "personalism" and "familism."[9] The first encourages a religious orientation stressing the concrete and the experiential; the saints, for southern Italians, have represented palpable, immediate, warm, and accessible intercessors to a cosmos otherwise seen as too alien, distant, cold, and abstract. The southern Italian reliance on familism is similarly conducive to embracing the saints; the saints were seen by many in the southern Italian tradition as supernatural extensions of the family. In this sense, then, the "low tradition" of southern Italian thought with its emphasis on community mirrored the "high tradition" of a Catholic social thought that included in its corpus the concept of the "communion of saints." For many southern Italian peasants and immigrant Italian-Americans these "extensions," like family members, could be argued and "bargained" with as well as loved and venerated. It should come as little surprise, then, that at the center of the panoply of saints that southern Italians and Italian-Americans have been attracted to is an extended version of the Holy Family: surrounding Baby Jesus is Mary (mother), Joseph (father), and Ann (grandmother). The special attraction of the Italian-American to the Blessed Mother, relatedly, is in part a function of the matriarchal nature of southern Italian society.

Given the basic demographics of the transatlantic voyage, the baseline for the Italian-American experience *vis-à-vis* the saints was both the traditional, isolated, village existence and, relatively speaking, the more modern, open urban centers of south Italy that shaped social life prior to migration to the United States. Each village had its local Marian devotion, saint, or saints. Given the imperfect institutionalization of an official Catholic presence in such pre-modern settings, the worship of saints was oftentimes viewed as far more central to the religious and cultural celebrations and ancient way of life than were specifically Catholic practices (e.g., full participation in the sacramental system) and Catholic doctrine. Furthermore, the worship and reliance on the saints were part of a matrix of folk religiosity that fused with Catholic elements components of magic, superstition, the occult, and paganism. Regarding the latter, Richard Gambino argues that saint worship served, for many pre-modern southern Italians, as the functional replacement for formerly important Roman pagan gods or other indigenous religious beliefs. For Gambino, "as was true of ancient gods, each saint was seen as having domain over a specific area of life and often to be in competition or rivalry not only with other saints but with Satan and other demons, with witches and even on occasion with God."[10] In any event, it is clear that the southern Italian appropriation of the saints was used, in the peasant mind set qua folk religion, in a practical, world-affirming way as a vehicle to defend oneself from an otherwise hostile, poverty-ridden, and politically oppressive social order (*la miseria*). Conversely put, such a utilization underplayed the characteristic Catholic emphasis on selfless service and surrender to God as well as conformity to doctrine. The specific approach of southern Italians to the idea and practice of the saints was part of the generally recognized "Italian problem" in the Catholic Church of the turn-of-the-century United States as immortalized especially in the scholarship of Henry J. Browne. [11]

It is important to point out, in passing and following the work of Carol Field, that northern Italians also had their saints, some of them successfully being transplanted to America.[12] However, the veneration of the saints in both north Italy and among northern Italian-Americans was not as strong as the southern Italian devotion given both the impact of modern ideologies (e.g., socialism, liberalism, positivism, anarchism, etc.) and other social structural realities (e.g., urbanization, formal education, occupational attainment, etc.).[13] Finally, note should be made that not all southern Italians at the turn of the twentieth century were believers and practitioners in the concept of sainthood. Rudolph Vecoli reports that not all the Italian-American immigrants who were attracted to secular left-wing ideologies came from northern or central Italy.[14]

A third reason justifying such an inquiry is that it sheds important light on the issue of *social change* over time among Italian-American Catholics.

For one thing, the changing nature of the devotion to the saints mirrored the movement in identity from one village-oriented in southern Italy at the turn of the century to one ethnic-oriented in America during the early to mid-twentieth century. In their pre-modern settings, the typical southern Italian devotion centered around a local patron saint, in an expression of what Rudolph Vecoli has referred to as *clientelismo*.[15] In America, again following Vecoli, "as the multiple identities of the hundreds of groups of *paesani* have merged into a general Italian-American identity, so too the devotions to the multitude of local patrons have merged into the cult of a few favored saints and Madonnas."[16] While some important feasts, for instance, may have maintained their central devotion to a local saint (e.g., San Paulinus of Nola in the renowned *giglio* feast of Brooklyn)[17], the movement is clearly toward the veneration of saints with a more universal appeal.   An even more fundamental social change issue is whether or not contemporary and modern Italian-Americans still venerate the saints at all or, if so, in what manner? Rev. Nicholas J. Russo's study of the religious acculturation of three generations of Americans of Italian extraction in New York City is instructive on this issue.[18] Russo argued that the custom of having Masses, prayers, novenas, and feasts celebrated in honor of local patron saints was, as compared to Irish Catholics, very vital for the first generation Italian-American immigrant. His data indicate, for instance, that more than 55% of the Italian immigrants had at least one Mass celebrated, per year, in honor of some saint, a figure that was reduced to 25.5% and 15%, respectively, for the second and third generations.[19] Relatedly, Russo's research uncovered that more than 57% of the Italian immigrant generation routinely prayed to God through the intermediary of either the Blessed Mother or the other saints as compared to directly to God, a figure that was reduced to less than 29% and 23%, respectively, for the second and third generations.[20]

Rev. Russo's longitudinal study indicating a withering away in the belief and veneration of the saints is complemented by the contemporary study completed by David Halle on how socio-economic class affiliation is associated with the display of religious iconography in the home.[21] Among his key findings are that 1) the display of religious iconography is much less important to upper-middle class Italian-Americans than to those working-class and 2) when religious iconography is displayed, upper-middle class Italian-Americans are—*vis-à-vis* the working class—less likely to showcase it in "public" areas (e.g., living room, dining room, hall, or in front of the house) and more likely to locate it in "private areas" (e.g., the bedroom). The secularization/privatization of this religious belief and practice occurs strongest among the upper-middle class because, for Halle, this group desires both to avoid evoking images of its humbler past and offering "offense" to one's Protestant, Jewish, and secular friends and associates.[22]

A fourth reason for focusing on the saints—a supernatural and traditionally religious reality—is that it tells us much about the changing definitions of social reality operant in the broader *American culture*. Put another way, some cultures are open to the claims of transcendence, others are closed to it, and yet others allow or encourage its expression primarily in a highly "privatized" manner. As Pitirim Sorokin stated, in any modern, "sensate" culture, i.e., one stressing materialism, positivism, science, and the empirical, "the grace of saintliness has decreased in both Church and society."[23] Put another way, the general rationalization and secularization of the larger culture makes belief in any supernatural conception less plausible. Related to this is the assimilation of many highly formally educated Italian-Americans into this culture of unbelief. This assimilation brings with it the pressure to conform to external indices of "success," thus pressuring many upwardly socially mobile Italian-Americans to reject allegiances to any "old world" practice, the saints included.

Relevant also is the claim made by David Halle that "the specialities of the saints have been superceded by human specialists."[24] That is, Halle's study indicates that Italian-Americans as a group are progressively relying less and less on the saints to address their special religious, social, medical, or personal needs (e.g., St. Michael for protection from Satan, St. Rocco for plague, St. Lucy for poor eyesight, St. Blaise for throat ailments, St. Rita for hopeless causes, etc.)[25] That the relationship between the supernatural intercessions by the saints and the application of proven scientific remedies and techniques need not necessarily be viewed in a zero-sum manner by Italian-Americans or others assimilated into a sensate culture is an issue left unaddressed by Halle. [26]

A fifth reason for such an endeavor is that it provides evidence about the transformation—whether officially sanctioned or not by official Magisterial thinking—of the *Catholic Church* in the United States in the post-

Vatican II era. Many Catholic parishes over the past couple of decades have seriously "depopulated" the saints or, at least, moved them to the periphery of the church building. In some cases, the motivation for this downplaying included legitimate theological and liturgical reform, i.e., to better highlight and focus on the worship of Christ. In other cases, this rejection/attenuation is the result of an internal secularization within significant progressive sectors of the Catholic Church herself; of accepting the claim that the veneration of the saints is indicative of the acceptance of retrograde and irrational beliefs and practices. In this latter case, then, the saints have been pushed to the periphery of the Catholic Church and local parish by those individuals rejecting the devotions of the mid-twentieth century and identifying the main purpose of Catholicism to be that of pursuing this-worldly social justice causes and personal therapeutic concerns. As such, the physical migration of the saints to the periphery of the Church and parish goes hand in hand with a more important and prior social-psychological migration on the part of a good deal of Catholic clerical and lay leadership, both among intellectuals and administrators. This migration entails a movement to a more bourgeois, assimilationist, and "Americanist" mind set embarrassed by any overt display of traditional religious sentiment and piety. [27] It is one basically following the trajectory of American liberal Protestantism on through to the syncretic and highly individualized religious orientation that Ernest Troeltsch referred to as "mysticism"[28] with a possible final resting place to be found in secular humanism, pure and simple.

A fundamental question related to this observable, empirical movement arises. Is the contemporary rejection or at least the marginalization of the saints, in some sense, "inevitable" or "necessary?" Or is such an elitist display of distaste not only a quite arbitrary and historically unnecessary expression but, moreover, destructive to the core of the Catholic faith her self? Crudely put, does such a manifest distaste for the saints reflect yet another modern day expression of Gnosticism, bringing with it a shrinking of the human being's ability to comprehend a total reality consisting of both natural and supernatural planes and their intersections? Utilizing Eric Voegelin's suggestive phrase, isn't the contemporary obsolescence of the concept of sainthood part and parcel of living the "contracted existence" of modernity? [29]

Put another way, the question is "who is theologically correct: the dominant progressivist Catholic leadership in the United States or His Holiness John Paul II?" In his analysis of the "restorationist" agenda of the present pontificate, Paul Johnson notes the importance that John Paul II has placed on the role of the saints and observes that "the note he seeks to strike might be termed enlightened populism. He does not think that the great central clarities of Christianity make uncomfortable bedfellows with the pieties of the masses. Certainly, they live easily in his own breast."[30]

The key issue here, then, is "are the saints marching out of the lives of Italian-American-Catholics primarily as a consequence of internalizing the values of the broader American sensate culture and, derivatively, out of the perceived needs for upward social mobility and increased social status?" Or are the saints being pushed out because, in the main, the Catholic Church in the United States is no longer teaching and preaching about their central importance to the faith? If John Paul II's overall restorationist agenda is successful, will the saints, then, be able to recapture their turf in the parishes, homes, feasts, and, most important, in the hearts and minds of the Catholic faithful, Italian-American or otherwise?

Any resurrection of the centrality of the saints in the lives of Italian-Americans and within the Catholic Church in general would necessarily entail a reversal of the contemporary secularizing movement. If the present day emphasis on "multiculturalism" can be channeled into one authentic and "realistic," i.e., into one that truly represents the Catholic tradition on the saints in a dynamic yet orthodox manner, then it might very well afford a window of opportunity for the saints to come marching back precisely on the part of the very formally educated middle-classes who have most abandoned the tradition.[31]

A sixth social scientific reason for studying the saints is to demonstrate how a belief in saints serves to maintain, in society, *symbolic boundaries* between certain categories of people.[32] A belief and practice in the saints would, for instance, sharply distinguish believers from nonbelievers, Catholics from most-non-Catholics, traditional Catholics from progressive Catholics, "public" Catholics from "privatized" Catholics, many northern Italians from most southern Italians and Italian-Americans who have maintained *la via vecchia* from those highly assimilated into American culture. Sociologically speaking, when these boundaries are trespassed, the offending party minimally, marks himself/herself out as, in some sense, "different" and maximally, risks "offering offense" to others. The trespasses, obviously, can go either way, as in the case of the believing Catholic scholar who wears a crucifix for public display in a secular university setting or, conversely, the aspiring upper-middle class bourgeois-Italian-American who "jokes" about the religious iconography while in his working-class cousin's home. (That wearing a crucifix for public display in a secular university *should not* be viewed as a social violation is not the issue here; the issue is, more simply, that, given the presently "politically correct" nature of secular institutions of higher education, wearing a crucifix *is* so defined.)

A seventh and final justification for such a study is that it provides one way *to correct* what Pitirim Sorokin termed the "*one-sidedness of sensate social science*."[33] For Sorokin—interestingly enough writing as far back as 1950—contemporary social science has concentrated almost exclusively on the negative in social life, i.e., on various "debunking" interpretations of man, culture, and values and on pathological types of human beings and human actions.[34] Sorokin's comments, almost needless to say, have increased in their saliency given that social science has since been ideologically battered by the social activism and antinomian perspectives of the last few decades leading up to such present-day subjectivist absurdities as deconstructionism.

Sorokin offers a partial solution to this one-sidedness. "For a fuller knowledge we must concentrate on a study of positive values, personalities, relationships, and phenomena."[35] Hence, the study of the saints, with their various assorted virtues, who provide positive role models, and who point to the heavens above, is one useful way to stress the positive in a culture permeated with cynicism and despair and one promoting death. Such an age, following Sorokin again, will inevitably produce as many saintly martyrs as is necessary to keep the light of the Faith flickering against the darkness.

JOSEPH A. VARACALLI

[1] This essay was first presented as the Introduction to an academic conference, "The Saints in the Lives of Italian-Americans," organized by myself and held at Nassau Community College in Garden City, New York on April 30, 1996. Other presentations were given by Dr. Donald J. D'Elia, Dr. Richard Renoff, Dr. Salvatore Primeggia, and Dr. Salvatore J. LaGumina. Follow-up conferences under essentially the same title ensued. Dr. D'Elia organized panels at the Fourth and Fifth Conferences of the Society of Catholic Social Scientists held at Franciscan University in Steubenville, Ohio on, respectively, October 26, 1996 and October 25, 1997. Panelists included Dr. Donald D'Elia, Dr. Richard Renoff, Rev. Robert Batule, Professor Dominic Aquila, and myself. Dr. Mary Brown and I have also scheduled complementary panels on the saints in the lives of Italian-Americans at the November 1998 Conference of the American Italian Historical Association to be held in New York City. Dr. Brown's panel consists of Dr. LaGumina; Dr. Renoff; Dr. Primeggia; Rev. Lydio Tomasi, C.S., Ph.D.; and herself. My panel consists of Professor Aquila, Dr. D'Elia, Rev. Batule, Dr. John Quinn, Dr. Philip Scrofani, and myself. This volume can be viewed, then, as one logical consequence of the gradual build-up of academic interests in various aspects of the study of the saints in the lives of Italian-Americans generated by successive academic conferences.

[2] *Verstehen* is a German term which can be roughly translated as "understanding" or "empathy." For Weber, any useful sociological analysis must incorporate the subjective understandings of the individuals being studied. See the introduction to *From Max Weber: Essays in Sociology* (H. H. Gerth and C. W. Mills, Editors) (New York: Oxford University Press, 1958), p. 56.

[3] See Chapter Four of Meredith McGuire, *Religion: The Social Context* (Third Edition) (Belmont, California: Wadsworth Publishing Company), 1992.

[4] See Salvatore Primeggia and Joseph A. Varacalli, "Community and Identity in Italian-American Life," in *The Ethnic Quest for Community: Searching for Roots in the Lonely Crowd* (Editors, Michael Hughey and Arthur Vidich) (Greenwich, Connecticut: JAI Press), 1993.

[5] Rev. Nicholas John Russo, "Three Generations of Italians in New York City: Their Religious Acculturation," in *The Italian Experience in the United States* (edited by Rev. Silvano M. Tomasi and Madeline H. Engle) (New York: Center for Migration Studies, Inc.) 1977; and Joseph A. Varacalli, "Italian-American-Catholic: How Compatible? ," *Social Justice Review* (Volume 83, Numbers 5-6, May-June), 1992.

[6] W. I. Thomas and Dorothy S. Thomas, *The Child in America: Behavior Problems and Programs* (New York: Knopf, 1928), p. 572.

[7] Regarding the latter, I accept the position of those many sociologists ranging from Charles Horton Cooley to Edward Shils to Peter L. Berger who argue that primary groups inevitably mediate our participation in more abstract secondary groups. That this position is consistent with Catholic social thought is made clear in the Appendix of Andrew M. Greeley's *The Catholic Myth* (New York: Charles Scribner's Sons, 1990). Regarding this universal anthropological imperative as specifically

applied to the case of Italian-Americans, see Joseph LoPreato's *Italian-Americans* (New York: Random House, 1970).

[8] Paul Tillich, *The Courage to Be* (New Haven, Connecticut: Yale University Press, 1952).

[9] Primeggia and Varacalli, op.cit. , 1993.

[10] Richard Gambino, *Blood of My Blood: The Dilemma of the Italian-Americans* (Garden City, New York: Doubleday) 1974, p. 196.

[11] Henry J. Browne, "The 'Italian Problem' and the Catholic Church in the United States, 1880-1900," United States Catholic Historical Society, *Records and Studies* (Volume 35), New York, 1946. Also see my essay honoring and updating Browne's article after a forty-year span, "The Changing Nature of the 'Italian Problem' in the Catholic Church of the United States," *Faith and Reason* (Volume 12, Number 1, Spring), 1986.

[12] See, for instance, Carol Field, *Celebrating Italy* (New York: William Morrow, 1990).

[13] See, for instance, Paola Sensi-Isolani and Phylis Cancilla Martinelli (editors), *Struggle and Success: An Anthology of the Italian Immigrant Experience in California* (Staten Island, New York: Center for Migration Studies), 1993.

[14] See Rudolph J. Vecoli, "Primo Maggio: May Day Observances Among Italian Immigrant Workers, 1890-1920," *Labor's Heritage* (Volume 7, Spring), 1996.

[15] Rudolph J. Vecoli, "Cult and Occult in Italian-American Culture," in *Immigrants and Religion in Urban America* (Editors, Randall M. Miller and Thomas D. Marzik), (Philadelphia, Pennsylvania: Temple University Press), 1977, p. 27.

[16] Ibid., p. 39.

[17] See Salvatore Primeggia and Joseph A. Varacalli, "The Sacred and Profane Among Italian-American Catholics: The Giglio Feast," in *International Journal of Politics, Culture, and Society* (Volume 9, Number 3, Spring, 1996).

[18] Rev. Nicholas John Russo, "Three Generations of Italians in New York City: Their Religious Acculturation," op. cit., 1977.

[19] *Ibid.*, pp. 203-4.

[20] *Ibid.*, pp. 204-5.

[21] David Halle, *Inside Culture: Art and Class in the American Home* (Chicago: University of Chicago Press), 1993.

[22] Ibid., p. 174. For this general tendency in American-middle-class culture to avoid being "judgmental," see both Alan Bloom, *The Closing of the American Mind* (New York: Simon and Schuster, 1987) and John Cuddihy, *No Offense: Civil Religion and Protestant Taste* (New York: Seabury), 1978.

[23] Pitirim A. Sorokin, *Altruistic Love: A Study of American 'Good Neighbors' and Christian Saints* (Boston, Massachusetts: Beacon Press), 1950, p. 184.

[24] Halle, op.cit. , 1993, p. 189.

[25] *Ibid.*

[26] David Halle's claim is consistent with the sociological works of scholars like Talcott Parsons and Andrew Abbott on the present-day decreased reliance on priests in favor of psychiatrists, psychologists, social workers, and others in the expanding "therapy industry." Andrew M. Greeley is one Catholic theorist who argues that "gesellschaft" forms of life do not replace "gemeinschaft" forms but rather are super-imposed over the latter. Thus, for Greeley (and myself) they coexist with each other in modern American life.

[27] The basic dichotomy in American Catholic thought, i.e., "Americanizer-Anti-Americanizer," is articulated in Andrew M. Greeley's *The Catholic Experience*, (New York: Doubleday, 1967). For an outright celebration of the "Americanist" mind set, see Dennis P. McCann, *New Experiment in Democracy: The Challenge for American Catholicism* (Kansas City, Missouri: Sheed and Ward), 1987. For my critical review of McCann, consult the *Homiletic and Pastoral Review* (July 1988).

[28] Ernest Troeltsch, *The Social Teachings of the Christian Churches* (Volume I) (translated by Olive Wyon) (London: George Allen and Unwin Ltd.), 1931.

[29] See my Review Essay, "A Catholic Sociological Critique of Gustavo Gutierrez's *A Theology of Liberation*," *The Catholic Social Science Review* (Volume I, 1996) and Eric Voegelin's *From Enlightenment to Revolution* (Durham, North Carolina: Duke University Press, 1975).

[30] Paul Johnson, *Pope John Paul II and the Catholic Restoration* (New York: St. Martin's Press), 1981, p. 192.

[31] See my discussion of the possibilities for what I term "multicultural realism," "Multiculturalism, Catholicism, and American Civilization," *Homiletic and Pastoral Review* (Volume XCIV, Number 6, March 1994).

[32] For a useful sociological discussion of symbolic boundaries, see James W. Vander Zanden, *Sociology: The Core* (Fourth Edition) (New York: McGraw-Hill, 1996), pp. 103-4.

[33] Sorokin, op.cit. , 1950, p. 3.

[34] *Ibid.*, p. 4.

[35] *Ibid.*, p. 5.

CHAPTER 2

THE SAINTS IN THE LIVES OF ITALIAN-AMERICANS: SOME KEY FIGURES

One of the most Catholic of beliefs is in the Communion of the Saints. The Saints are those men, women and children who lived lives of courageous faith and virtue, and who now continue their lives of charity in heaven by interceding for the living members of the Church. The goal of their intervention, indeed of all the activities of the Church, is the Glory of God and the salvation of souls. As the Preface for Saints in the Mass states, "In the lives of your saints you offer us an example, through their intercession, assistance, and in the communion of grace, the bond of fraternal love. Comforted by their witness of faith, we can face the good fight of faith in our lives, in order to share, beyond death, the same crown of glory."[1]

Throughout the centuries this tenet has proven one of the most comforting and popular among the faithful in all lands, who invoked the heavenly intercession of their patrons for sometimes rather earthly needs. Saints were named as patrons for nations, towns, and churches, as well as for work and social unions, and spiritual organizations. Even today, the feast days of the patron saints are kept throughout the world. Many of these are more widely known because of modern literature and growing tourism during the past 25 years, which often has made the festivals more secular in tone. Two examples of this are the Feast of St. James in Compostela, Spain in July, and that of San Fermin in Pamplona, Spain in June.

Catholics in Italy are no different from Catholics in other countries, at least not in this regard. Each town—sometimes each section or quarter of a town—like each parish church, has its own patron saint. Even today, many parishes and towns continue the tradition of celebrating their patron feast day with elaborate festivities. That most publicized by the American media is the Feast of San Gennaro in Naples, on September 19th, with the liquification of the saint's blood as the interesting focal point of the festivities.

The millions of immigrants who arrived in the United States during the last and present centuries, brought their most valuable possessions with them, including their religious faith, memories, and nostalgia for the countries they had once called home. The Italians were no exception. The feast days of patron saints, or *feste*, are still part of the lives of many Italian-Americans today. While sometimes secularized, the *feste* continue to be identified as essential to the heritage of many Italian-Americans in the United States today.

Devotion to patron saints came to hold a central position in the lives of many Italian immigrants soon after arriving in the United States. Many Italian immigrants did not practice their faith, at least not in the prescribed, orthodox sense. Many had been supporters of Garibaldi, or had lived harsh lives in areas of the former Papal States, and were politically anti-clerical. Thousands more simply had not time or freedom to frequent church. Having attached themselves to labor bosses, *padroni*, in Italy, in exchange for passage to America, they found themselves exploited. This indentured servitude could last for years, offering nothing to these poor peasants other than ceaseless work and grinding poverty, until the last penny had been repaid. Roman Catholicism was, nevertheless, an inescapable part of their lives and identity. The Church eventually seized upon this, and the nostalgia for their homeland which many immigrants had, using the patron saint and the annual patron feast day as a means by which to lure their immigrant members to practice their faith, even if only occasionally each year.[2]

Special religious societies, separated by gender and age, and usually devoted to various patron saints, found their membership marching up the aisle of their local Catholic church on certain occasions, scheduled and orchestrated by their pastor. Sometimes these occasions were the only times when many members saw the inside of the church. Nevertheless, it provided the local priest the opportunity to offer the sacraments and preach the Gospel to his Italian congregation, all in the name of their patron saint. Such religious societies, often offering financial aid, or at least the cost of a Christian burial to its members, provided an identity and a sense of importance and minimal security to the impoverished Italian immigrants, who had little comfort or influence in their new home in America. The strong bond between faith and nostalgia for their hometown or province was at work in the devotion to the patron saint.

Even today, there is often a strong sense of identity and pride expressed among the children, grandchildren and great-grandchildren of Italian immigrants. Most Italian-Americans know little about Italy; fewer can speak or read Italian. Many have no greater sense of their Italian heritage than an emotional attachment to their family who arrived here. Yet, they find the opportunity to express their love for family and loyalty to an ancestral homeland in their local Italian parish, where their family may have worshiped ever since arriving in America, and where the image of the patron saint from their *paese* is lovingly enshrined.

This essay will give a brief description of those saints who have become the most popularly revered, and whose feast days have become the most favored, by Italian-Americans in the United States. The order followed is alphabetical, not according to importance in the lives of the Italian-American communities across the country. Exhaustive, this is not; it is merely an overview.

When considering such feast days, one should bear in mind that at the heart of these celebrations is a deep faith. Many Catholics today may be theologically inarticulate, clumsy in their expressions of their faith, and may engage in what might be judged "superstitions" by American society. While one would never hear criticisms or skepticism expressed in the media regarding the rituals of Native Americans, or concerning those of Oriental religions, or even a negative word about the ever-increasing interest and popularity of psychic hotlines, witchcraft and astrology, little such restraint in exercised regarding popular expressions of the Catholic faith.[3]

While those who know little about the faith or its historical roots may be swift to criticize such popular celebrations, the *feste*, nevertheless, demonstrate the overpowering faith of generations of Italian-Americans in a God who loves them, and in the Saints who have been courageous in overcoming sin and human suffering, and who offer charitable assistance to those in need by their prayers and intercession. One must further bear in mind that religious expression, especially for immigrants to this country and their offspring, is always tied up with some sense of national or cultural identity and nostalgia. These *feste* are also bound to the Italians' love and devotion to family and loyalty to neighbor. All-in-all, while these celebrations may fall short of the expectations of a secularized society, normally cynical of anything Christian, the feast days of the saints are exciting popular expressions of faith in God, love of family, and love of country. Not bad, on the whole-even if one need pierce the layers of pasta, pizza *fritta*, and brass bands to discover this.

Devotions to Our Lord [4]

Most Holy Name of Jesus
St. Paul first mentions the importance and power of the Name of Jesus in the Acts of the Apostles and in his early letters. This follows from the Judaic belief that God is so holy and omnipotent that even his name can transform and should never be spoken by sinful man. Because God took on human flesh in Christ, while the eternal Name is still powerful, it can be pronounced, as can that of any other person, but only with the utmost reverence and love. Devotion to the Holy Name, like that to the Holy Face [although this is originally an earlier, Constantinopolitan devotion], and that to the Most Precious Blood, the Sacred Wounds of Christ, etc., gained popularity during the Middle Ages. Devotion to the Holy Name was further popularized by the Jesuits, whose society is devoted to the Holy Name of Jesus.

Most Precious Blood
Because of the effect of St. Francis of Assisi upon the devotional life and popular religious imagination during the Middle Ages, devotions to every aspect of the Incarnate Lord, especially if connected with his Nativity or Passion and Death, became an object of special devotion. Devotion to the Most Precious Blood of Our Lord was one such example, whereby the faithful could immediately comprehend the depth of the suffering of the Son of God for mankind in the universal symbol of physical danger and death, the flowing of blood. This devotion also bears Eucharistic aspects, since it is the Body and Blood of the Crucified and Resurrected Christ received in communion by the faithful at Mass. This is an everyday reminder of God's immense love for us all, rich or poor.

Sacred Heart of Jesus
Another important popular devotion is to the heart of Jesus, a symbol of Divine Love for mankind. Begun in the Middle Ages, it was popularized

in France, especially by Cardinal Richelieu, and, later in the 17th century, following visions of the Sacred Heart by Saint Margaret Mary Alacoque in Paray-le-Monial, France. Devotion to the Sacred Heart, and to the Immaculate Heart of Mary, image of perfect human love in response to Divine Love, is one of the most popular of devotions in the world, even today.

Devotions to the Most Blessed Mother
Mater Dolorosa

Our Lady of Sorrows, also known as *Santa Maria Addolorata*. She is venerated as the Mother of the Dying Savior, pictured either at the foot of the Cross, or, like Michelangelo's *Pieta*, seated with the body of Her Divine Son in her lap; sometimes with her heart pierced by swords, based upon Simeon's words to Mary in the Gospel of the circumcision of Our Lord, when he prophesied, ". . . and a sword of sorrow will pierce your heart." She who suffered so greatly for the love of God and for love of us, gave great comfort to those innumerable poor of southern Italy and to those who emigrated to America, whose lot in life was filled with hardships and pain. Nearly every parish church in Italy, and nearly every Italian-American parish in the United States, has an image of Our Lady of Sorrows.

Our Lady of Loreto

In the pilgrimage town of Loreto in northern Italy, the basilica enshrines what is reputed to be the house of the Holy Family, a wooden structure, said to have been miraculously transported to Loreto from Nazareth by angels. The house was known to have existed and been revered for centuries in Nazareth; St. Louis of France is reported to have heard Mass celebrated in the tiny structure in 1253. Archaeological digs beneath the Basilica of the Annunciation in Nazareth during the past twenty years have uncovered the foundations of a house of the same dimensions as the house in Loreto, possibly carried back to Loreto during the first Crusade. The sanctuary is one of the principal shrines in Italy, and has been since 1294.

Our Lady of Lourdes

In 1858, Bernadette Soubirous, received eighteen visitations from the Blessed Mother, who identified herself to this illiterate peasant girl, saying

"I am the Immaculate Conception," employing the title which had recently been given her by Pope Pius IX in the definition of the Dogma of the Immaculate Conception. Asking for prayers and repentance for sins that the world might return to Christ, Our Lady of Lourdes requested that a shrine be erected on the spot of the apparitions. For over a century, Lourdes has been one of the most popular and well-visited shrines in the world, drawing millions of the faithful, especially the sick and invalid who come seeking a cure, each year.

Our Lady of Mount Carmel

The devotion has its origins with the Carmelites, and especially with Saint Simon Stock, who lived c. 1165-1265. An Englishman, he entered the Carmelites, was elected the superior general of the order in 1247, reorganized, reformed and expanded the order throughout England, Ireland, Scotland, France, Italy and the Holy Land. In 1237 he received a vision of Our Lady handing him a Scapular—originally a part of most religious habits—and the controversial promise that anyone wearing the brown scapular would merit eternal life. The devotion of wearing the brown scapular became immensely popular throughout Europe, and especially in Italy.

Our Lady of Pompeii

Also known as Queen of the Most Holy Rosary, one of the numerous titles of the Blessed Virgin Mary. The Feast of Our Lady of the Rosary was established soon after the Catholic victory over the Turkish fleet at the Battle of Lepanto in 1571, attributed to her intercession. The present sanctuary, outside Naples, was established through the efforts of a Neapolitan peasant, simply because he felt moved to begin a shrine to the Blessed Mother. Bartolo Longo, after hearing a voice tell him to pray the Rosary and to ask others to do so as well, decided to begin a confraternity in honor of the Blessed Virgin Mary. Deciding that his confraternity needed an image, he found one for pennies in a local junk shop. Despite having a large hole in the canvas, and of poor artistic quality, Bartolo purchased it in 1872. Through his efforts alone, he begged sufficient funds to construct a small church, and later, an orphanage for 1,000 girls, and an industrial school for orphan boys. By 1934 the shrine was attracting thousands outside Pompeii. Today, more than 1,000,000 persons each year visit the shrine, praying to the humble image of Our Lady of the Most Holy Rosary, purchased in a junk shop by a pauper from Naples. The shrine was built by the faith of an impoverished peasant, funded by the pennies of the poor, and has become the source of enormous inspiration to those poor of the world who are without hope, except in Christ.

Saints Ann and Joaquim

The parents of the Blessed Virgin Mary. The cult of St. Anne is very old, dating from the first centuries of the Church's life; that of St. Joaquim gained popularity only during the 15th century, and usually only in conjunction with the feast of his wife. The devotion to St. Joaquim was greatly enhanced in the United States by the Italian missionary priests sent by Blessed Giovanni Battista Scalabrini to minister to the Italian immigrants. In honor of Pope Leo XIII, who sponsored their missionary activities, the missionaries encouraged devotion to his patron, St. Joaquim, to whom they dedicated one of their first churches in New York City.

Saint Anthony of Padua

Born in Lisbon, Portugal, in 1195, and originally studying with the Regulars of St. Augustine near Lisbon, later in Coimbra, he was ordained a priest in 1219 or 1220. He transferred to the Franciscans the following year, taking the name Anthony, and began his life preaching the Gospel, at first among the Moors in Morocco, and then throughout Italy and Europe. His was renowned as an eloquent and forceful preacher, miracle worker, as well as a much-sought- after confessor, both talents which led to numerous conversions to the faith. He devoted himself to work among the poor, conversion of heretics and sinners, and social reforms. Exhausted by his duties, ministry and life of self-denial, Anthony died in 1231, at the age of 36 years. Renowned as the "Hammer of Heretics," "Living Ark of the Covenant," and "Wonder Worker," St. Anthony is the patron of the poor. Usually portrayed holding the Infant Jesus in his left arm, a visitor reported once seeing him carrying the Savior, so intimate was he with Our Lord. He is one of the patrons of travelers, of barren women, the poor, and is invoked by those who have lost property.

Saint Cecilia

A young girl who suffered martyrdom during an early persecution possibly in the late second century in Rome. Betrothed to a Roman patrician, she had consecrated her life to virginity, and successfully worked to convert her fiancé. Exposed by their devotion to the Catholic faith, they were both martyred. The beautiful "Acta" of her passion exists, which captivated the hearts of generations, to come. She is one of the great patronesses of the Church in Rome, named in the Roman Canon of the Mass from the earliest days.

Saint Charles Borromeo

Born in 1538, and the nephew of Pope Pius IV, Charles received a legal education and was named the cardinal secretary of state and administer of Milan at an early age. Despite these fruits of nepotism, the Church found in Charles one of her saintliest practitioners of charity and heartiest of Church reformers. He lived a life of constant penance, giving everything he owned to the poor, feeding them, nursing the sick and defending them whenever possible. He strove to implement the reforms of the Council of Trent in his archdiocese, establishing seminary education, religious education and wholesale reform of the Christian lives of both clergy and laity within his archdiocese. He died in 1584. He is the patron of seminarians.

Saint Frances Xavier Cabrini

Born in 1850, she entered the convent at eighteen. After some difficult beginnings, she established the Missionary Sisters of the Sacred Heart. Desiring to enter into missionary work in the Far East, she was convinced by Pope Leo XIII and Blessed Giovanni Battista Scalabrini to go west to the Americas and work for the salvation of the thousands of Italians immigrating to the New World. Overcoming enormous difficulties presented her by clergy and laity alike, she and her sisters established numerous religious houses, schools, orphanages, and hospitals for poor Italians in North and South America. She became an American citizen in 1909; she died in 1917. She is the patroness of immigrants.

Saint Francis of Assisi

Born in 1181, Francis was born to a pleasure-filled life in Assisi, until, in 1206, he experienced a vision of Our Lord in Spoleto. Returning from a pilgrimage to Rome in that year, Francis, unaccountably, changed his life to one of service to the poor and care of the sick. Disdaining any pleasure, he abandoned his family fortune and position, seeking only a life of prayer, solitude and penance. During the subsequent years of intense prayer, he gathered around himself followers. In a vision he sensed a call from God to shore up the Church, weakened by corruption. He founded the Franciscan Order, which received papal approbation in 1210, and, two years later, was joined by St. Clare who established a female branch of the order. Francis preached in the Holy Land and Palestine, desiring to convert the Moslems, and throughout Europe. He was devoted to the Incarnation of the Lord, developing the nativity creche at Christmas as a means of stimulating popular devotion to the reality of God's love for mankind as manifested in his taking on flesh for the salvation of the world. So keenly did he pattern his life on that of Christ that, in 1224, Francis received the stigmata-the wounds of Christ on his hands, feet and side. Francis is one of the most beloved and influential of all the saints of the Church. He is the patron of merchants and, according to one modern source, ecologists.

Blessed Giovanni Battista Scalabarini

Beatified by Pope John Paul II in October 1997, Scalabrini was, along with Mother Cabrini, the most influential and important defender of the Italian immigrants of the last century. Born in 1839, the youngest of three children, Scalabrini was ordained a priest in 1863 for the Diocese of Como, Italy. He was a seminary professor and pastor of a local church, and was named Bishop of Piacenza in 1875. During his first pastoral visit of his diocese, Scalabrini became aware of the plight of the Italian immigrant. He was a prolific, and controversial, writer concerning the immigrants' rights, and worked for legislation to stem their suffering. He founded the Italian branch of the Saint Raphael Society for the benefit of Immigrants, and formed the Missionary Society of Saint Charles Borrmeo, of both priests and laymen devoted to attending the needs of Catholic Italian immigrants in the Americas. His work and that of his missionaries provided parishes, schools and charitable institutions for the millions of Italian immigrants, in order to bolster their Catholic faith and assist them in their new homes.

St. Januarius

Purported to have been the bishop of Benevento, near Naples, Italy, he is said to have been martyred during the Diocletian persecution, around the year 305. The legend runs that Januarius went to visit deacons and laymen imprisoned in nearby Pozzuoli. Thrown to wild beasts, which refused to harm them, they were finally beheaded. His relics, especially vials of his blood, found their way to the cathedral in Naples, and for centuries have been the object of particular devotion, especially credited with having saved Naples from numerous eruptions of nearby Mount Vesuvius. Twice each year, the vial of his blood is exposed to the assembled throngs of the faithful, who come to see it miraculously liquify, and bubble. It is popularly held that on the rare occasions when the miracle does not occur, some horrible tragedy is foretold. The last two occasions coincided with the march of Napoleon into Italy, and the rise to power of Mussolini. He is, unimaginatively, said to be the patron of blood banks, at least according to some modern sources.

St. Joseph

The foster father of Jesus and husband of the Blessed Virgin Mary, Joseph is one of the most beloved of saints, despite the lack of information concerning his life. Protector and provider of the Holy Family, St. Joseph's popularity stemmed from his strong fidelity to God, love for Jesus and for his wife, Mary, despite great difficulties and self-sacrifice. The fact that he was a carpenter further enhanced his attractiveness, especially among workingmen. He is the protector of workmen, the patron of social justice and of the Universal Church, and model for fathers of families.

Saint Lucy

According to legend, she was a Sicilian, born of noble parentage in the city of Syracuse. Engaged to be married, Lucy announced her desire and intention to devote herself to God, bestow her fortune on the poor, and renounce her engagement to be married. Indignant, her suitor, so the story goes, denounced Lucy as a Christian during the persecution of the Emperor

Diocletian early in the fourth century. Resolutely professing her faith and protecting her virtue, she was finally martyred. Along with Cecilia, Lucy was remembered in the Roman Canon of the Mass soon after her martyrdom, a fact which pointed to the strength of her cult. She is the patroness of those with eye diseases.

St. Mary Magdalen

Well-known because of the Gospel narratives of Jesus' life and ministry, Mary Magdalen, a reformed notorious sinner, became one of the followers of Jesus, receiving the signal dignity of being the first to encounter the Resurrected Lord. Her enormous popularity stems from very human life. Despite her weakness and sin, she responded to the grace and mercy of God, devoting herself entirely to Our Lord. For many, Mary Magdalen is an exemplar of hope for everyone who, despite personal weaknesses, can find salvation and peace through God's mercy and grace.

St. Michael the Archangel

One of the seven Archangels, along with Raphael and Gabriel. It was Michael, whose name means "Strength of God," who led the celestial armies into battle against Satan, according the Book of the Apocalypse. The popularity of the devotion to St. Michael is an early one, with a festival of great solemnity having been celebrated during the end of September since at least the sixth century. It was Pope Saint Gregory the Great who led a procession around Rome in the sixth century, pleading for an end to the plague which was destroying the population. Prayers were answered, according to legend, when St. Michael the Archangel appeared atop Hadrian's Tomb on the Tiber River, evermore known as the *Castel Sant' Angelo*. By then there existed an already famous church of St. Michael on Monte Gargano, and, in the sixth century, a newer one in Rome on the Salarian Way. He is the patron of policemen, paratroopers, and mariners.

Saints Peter and Paul

Peter, the Prince of the Apostles, and Paul, Apostle to the Gentiles, are held in unique reverence by the Church and her faithful. It is Peter, the Rock, as his name implies, upon whom Christ established His Church, giving to him the keys of the kingdom of heaven with which to forgive sins. He is the first of the Apostles, a ministry which continues through his successors, the popes. St. Paul, also personally called by Christ, set forth on years of missionary journeys to preach the crucified and resurrected Lord. His was a mission to the non-Jewish world, offering the life of grace and salvation to everyone who would acknowledge Jesus as Lord. Both were martyred in Rome during the persecution of the Emperor Nero in the year 64, and both are celebrated as the Founders of the Church of Rome.

St. Raphael

Another of the seven Archangels, Raphael is known as "God has healed." Thus it was that he attended to and healed aged and blind Tobias, guided and preserved him, brought him together with Sara, daughter of Raguel, along with various other activities, especially associated with healing in the Old and New Testaments. He is the patron of nurses and physicians.

St. Rita of Cascia

Born in 1381 in Roccaporena in the central Apennines, was a woman of extraordinary piety and love for prayer. Against her own wishes to enter the convent, she consented to wed in order to obey her parents. Her husband was brutal, violent and unfaithful; Rita remained faithful and patient for eighteen years. She bore two sons who followed their father's dissolute example. Following the unexpected death of her husband and sons, she entered the convent. She became exemplary in her virtues of obedience to authority, penance and prayers offered for others, and her extraordinary charity toward her sisters and those considered beyond hope. The ruling passion of her life was fervent love for God, and an especial devotion to the Passion of Our Lord. Afflicted later in life by wasting diseases, she bore her pain heroically, offering all for the salvation of the poorest and neediest soul. She died in 1457. Since at least the seventeenth century St. Rita has been popular as the saint of the impossible and the advocate of desperate cases.

St. Rocco

According to one story of his life, Rocco was born to the governor of Montpellier. After the death of his parents, he journeyed to Rome on pilgrimage. Italy at the time was stricken with plague, which urged Rocco to stop in many cities to minister to the poor and dying. Near Piacenza he, himself, was stricken. According to the story, not wanting to burden anyone, he crept away into the local forest, where he was attended to by a dog. The dog's master discovered him and brought him to his home to convalesce. After continued travel, constant prayer and attendance upon the sick and dying, Rocco, much changed physically and spiritually, returned to Montpellier. Unrecognized, he was arrested, as were any itinerant travelers during the times of plagues. He died in prison, recognized only after his death in 1378. Almost immediately Rocco was venerated as the patron against plague and infectious diseases, and a popular patron of invalids.

St. Sebastian

St. Sebastian were born of Milanese parents in Narbonne in today's France, possibly in the third century. A Christian from birth, he decided to enter the army at Rome, about the year 283, in order to be of service to the confessors and martyrs during the time of persecution. Despite his Christian faith, which brought about the conversion of many, Sebastian was made captain of a company of the Praetorian Guard. Betrayed to the Emperor Diocletian for his faith, Sebastian was shot with arrows and left for dead. The widow of St. Castulus, another martyr, discovered him still alive, and nursed him to health. Instead of fleeing after his recovery, Sebastian accosted the Emperor, upbraiding him for the cruelties to the Christians paid out by his regime. Sebastian was seized and beaten to death, buried in a catacomb on the Appian Way, now bearing his name. His name is to be found in the Roman Canon, and his cult grew swiftly, especially among soldiers, and particularly against plague. He is the patron of soldiers, archers and athletes.

St. Therese of the Little Flower

Born to middle class family in Lisieux, France in 1873, she became a professed Carmelite nun in 1890. During the next, and final, seven years of her life she pursued a life of piety and holiness. Determined that her mission in the Church was one of charity, even behind the cloister wall, she devoted herself to the well-being of her sisters, offering her personal sufferings from tuberculosis for the salvation of the world. The author of one of the most influential and well-read spiritual diaries, "The Autobiography of a Soul" has touched the lives of millions. Devotion to her spread immediately after her death. She was named a Doctor of the Church in October 1997. She is the patroness of the missions.

St. Vitus

Along with Saints Modestus and Crescentia, Saint Vitus was venerated from a very early date, believed to have been martyred with these latter two sometime in the late third century in the Roman province of Lucania, in southern Italy. They may have been natives of Sicily, but nothing other than legends and fantastic tales about them have come down to us. The legend has it that Vitus, born to pagan parents, converted to Christianity as a boy. He performed many miracles and cures, came to the attention of the author-ities, and was forced to flee when persecutions began. An angel guided the boy's boat to Lucania, where he, his tutor Modestus and attendant Crescentia, preached the Gospel. They then traveled to Rome, where St. Vitus cured the son of the Emperor Diocletian. After a variety of revolting torments, the saints were set free by the miraculous intervention of an an-gel, who sent them back to Lucania where they died later, exhausted by their sufferings. St. Vitus has been invoked to cure epileptics or those suf-fering from a nervous condition known as "St. Vitus's Dance." He also became the patron of dancers and actors, and was invoked against the bites of vipers, mad dogs, and wild beasts, against oversleeping, and storms. In the town of Regalbuto in Sicily, St. Vitus is invoked to help cure people with mental or emotional sufferings.

Other Devotions
All Souls

The Holy Souls are those of the faithful departed. The Church has always prayed for her dead. A specific feast day was observed first in Cluniac monasteries throughout Europe, beginning about 998. The faithful departed are those who have died free from grave sin, but who are in Purgatory, being cleansed of the effects of sins whose guilt has been remitted through the Sacrament of Confession. The prayers of the faithful in the Church, especially on November 2nd, All Souls' Day, are offered for the purification of these souls and their freedom from the punishment due to sin. The day, and devotion, are particularly popular in Latin countries.

The great feast days of the Church have always been celebrated with much splendor—hence the name, "feast day." Easter, Pentecost, and Christmas were the earliest special celebrations in the early centuries of the Church's life. Following the centuries of persecution by the Roman Empire and the development of the cult of the saints and martyrs, more and more days of special celebration and significance appeared on the calendars of local churches and dioceses. The anniversary of the martyrdom of a revered bishop, laywoman or man of outstanding virtue and courage for the faith began to be celebrated with more and more festivity as the "birthday" of the martyr into heaven. With the development of monastic piety, the normal calendar of fast and abstinence would be enlivened by the occasional day of extraordinary religious significance.

By the Middle Ages and Renaissance, patron feast days grew in number and became linked to national or civic pride and identity. Local parish communities, local religious societies, as well as cities, towns and nations, celebrated the feast of their patron saint or favorite event in salvation history. Even countries and individual cities began their individual calendar new year on the feast day of the patron celebration. France, for example, began its New Year on Easter, the date for which changed yearly. Italy, which until 1870 was composed of small independent city-states and realms, did the same. For example, March 25th, the feast of the Annunciation, was the patron feast for the cities of Pisa and Ferrara, and marked the beginning of their calendar year; December 25th, Christmas, served the same purpose in the Cities of Arezzo, Bologna, Como, Florence, Genoa, Milan, Naples, and Rome; January 1st, the feast of the Circumcision of the Lord, was the patron feast and New Year's day in Benevento. In much of pre-World War II Europe, when a strong bond still existed between individual states and the Catholic faith, especially in agricultural societies, such celebrations abounded.

In this country, with the arrival of the immigrants from around the globe, arrived the patron festivals with them. For the Italian immigrants, especially from southern Italy, the purpose of the *festa* was religious, but it served many other needs. It reminded the immigrants of their longed for homeland, and, more importantly, their home village or city. Never fully united, other than on paper, Italy at the turn of the century was non-existent, at least in the reality of most Italians. Individual cities, towns, provinces, and *paesi* were, to the vast majority of Italians, the only "Italy" they knew, and their loyalties were to the area in which they were born and in which their families lived, worked and died for generations.

The annual *feste* continue to be celebrated in most American cities wherever a Little Italy was once the center of the life of the local Italian colony. The elements of each are the same, differing only in elaborateness and size. Some statue or artistic representation of the saint is usually at the heart of the celebration. Beginning in the local parish church, and conducted by members of the local religious society, the image, adorned with flowers and, usually ribbons for the pinning of dollar bills, is borne through the streets, accompanied by brass bands, first communion children, altar servers and clergy, members of the local religious societies in their distinctive garb, devotees, occasionally barefoot, sometimes praying, sometimes chatting with neighbors and family members. There is always an enormous quantity of Italian food, usually offering the local specialties from a specific region of Italy, but also everywhere offering the staple foods of pizza, pasta, pizza *fritta*, sausage and peppers, grinders, wines, beers and Italian pastries.

Occasionally there are aspects of the observance unique to the individual feast. For example, the Parish of Our Lady of Mount Carmel celebrates its annual patron feast day on July 16th. Among the thousands in attendance, hundreds of Italian-American young men shoulder the *Giglio*, an immensely heavy tower, originally constructed of wood, but today of metal, at least 100 feet in height, atop of which is a statue of St. Paulinus of Nola, a bishop and early theologian who died in southern Italy in 431. The tower and statue are borne aloft by the devotees on their shoulders. At certain points, the procession stops, and all dance, with the *Giglio* bobbing up and down, to the accompaniment of the band. This unique ritual sometimes employs secular tunes, such as "New York, New York," adding another dimension to the entire spectacle.

Another of the largest *feste* in the United States is that of San Gennaro (*Januarius*) celebrated every September in New York's "Little Italy." Thousands of people come to sample the Italian fare, and to pay homage to the saint, whose decorated image, covered in dollar bills, is enshrined amid the festivities and innumerable food concessions.

MONSIGNOR STEPHEN M. DI GIOVANNI

---

1. Conferenza Episcopale Italiana, *Messale Romano* (Vatican: Libreria Editrice Vaticana, 1983) p. 363.

2. Cf. Di Giovanni, S., *Michael Augustine Corrigan and the Italian Immigrants* (Our Sunday Visitor, 1994).

3. For a fine presentation of the importance of studying the Saints, please refer to the essay by Joseph A. Varacalli, Ph.D., "As the Saints (Apparently) Go Marching Out: Why Study Them?," Chapter 1 of this volume.

4. The titles and patron saints chosen are those most popular in Italian parishes created by the early years of this century throughout the United States. For more detailed information, one should refer to the excellent archives of the Center for Migration Studies on Staten Island, N.Y. This archive houses the largest collection of information on all details and aspects of early Italian national parishes in the country. Their staff is extraordinarily knowledgeable and helpful.

Part II

Historical Overview

CHAPTER 3

ITALIAN-AMERICANS AND THEIR SAINTS: HISTORICAL CONSIDERATIONS

Relationships between Italian-Americans and their saints *has* a history; that is the first point of this article. It is not the saga of timeless traditions, but the dynamic story of how religious and social rituals adapt, persevere and survive in a changing world. Like any historical development, this relationship has changed over time, shaped by forces in Catholicism, in Italian history and in the history of the United States. This presentation identifies some of these forces and points out areas in which further research is needed.

For some scholars, the relationship between Italian-Americans and their saints predates Christianity. At least since Sir James George Frazer's publication of *The Golden Bough* in 1906, scholars have traced many continuities between pagan and Christian rites, between ancient deities and modern saints.[1] One recent scholar who has studied these connections is Lucia Chiavola Birnbaum. She has compiled data on numerous sites along the Tyrrhenian and Adriatic seacoasts of the Italian peninsula and on the island of Sicily. At each of these sites has been found evidence of a prehistoric civilization that revered a dark female goddess. Such cultures were receptive to Catholicism's introduction of veneration of the Blessed Virgin Mary. Their communities maintained statues modeled after dark-skinned, full-figured Mediterranean women, the "black Madonnas" of Birnbaum's title.[2]

Birnbaum drew a continuous line between ancient goddesses and modern Marian devotion. However, the introduction of Christianity provided a host of new holy heroes. Early Christians in Italy, Greece, the Middle East and North Africa were instrumental in identifying saints not only for their own communities but for the universal Church. These Mediterranean Christians also developed some of the conventions of veneration of the saints still in use. As Kenneth L. Woodward explains in *Making Saints,*

35

the earliest saints were martyrs killed for their faith. When martyrs died, surviving Christians retrieved their remains for burial. These early Christians transferred their worship services from private homes to martyrs' tombs, and the remains of saints are still placed in each altar used in Catholic worship. Early Christians began the custom of observing the anniversaries of saints' dates of death, a practice which contributed to the development of the modern calendar of saints' feast days. The early Christians were also the first to report miraculous events taking place in proximity to martyrs' remains, and to begin the custom of using the remains, or relics, as aids to prayer, and to pray to the deceased to intercede with God. Finally, it was the early Christians who first interpreted answered prayers and miracles as proof that those to whom they prayed were indeed in heaven with God.[3]

In short, the earliest canonizations, or additions to the list of those considered saints, were processes in which the laity actively participated. It was these faithful who perpetuated the memory of Saint Agatha, a native of Catania, a province in Sicily, who was martyred during the Decian persecution of 249-251. Christians in Syracuse, also on Sicily, preserved the story of Saint Lucy, martyred in the Diocletian persecution of 297-305. The devout in Pozzuoli, province of Benevento, recalled the story of the martyrdom of Saint Januarius, or San Gennaro, also in the Diocletian persecution. Christians in Milan remembered Saint Sebastian, another victim of the Diocletian persecution. The Lucanian province in southern Italy preserved the memory of the martyrdom of Saint Vitus, also in the Diocletian persecution. It was from the evidence of popular devotion that scholars such as Saint Jerome compiled the martyrologies modern scholars used to check popular tradition against the historical record.[4]

Even during the period when Christianity was a persecuted cult, it was possible to be a saint without being a martyr. Ascetics practiced a living martyrdom, denying themselves comforts, conveniences and even necessities. By avoiding worldly distraction and temptation, ascetics hoped to focus more fully on God. Sometimes, though, asceticism led to martyrdom, as when a woman who had consecrated her virginity to God found herself denounced to the authorities by a rejected suitor. In other cases asceticism led to the kind of popular veneration given martyrs, as the faithful came to hear someone like Simeon the Stylite preach. The faithful honored deceased ascetics as they did martyrs, considered their tombs holy sites, marked the anniversaries of their deaths, used their relics as prayer objects and counted the miracles obtained through their intercession. The faithful were encouraged in their veneration by bishops and preachers, who incorporated stories of ascetics into sermons as examples for Christians to emulate. One ascetic who became important for Italian and Italian-American history was Saint Paulinus of Nola. In 389, Paulinus and his wife, Therasea, adopted an ascetical lifestyle and began to distribute their belongings among the poor. Paulinus was ordained a priest in 394, and consecrated bishop of Nola, in the province of Avellino, in 409. He served in that position for 22 years, devoting himself to building and restoring churches and to promoting the cults of the saints, particularly his compatriot Saint Felix of Nola. Upon his death in 431, his flock concluded San Paolo was worthy of canonization, too.

Several forces combined to formalize the canonization process. Ironically, one force was popular piety. Devotees who wanted more than local honors for their saints asked the papacy to lend its authority to the popularization of their holy heroes. For their part, successive popes saw the canonization of saints as congruent with their responsibilities for maintaining unity among Christians and for perpetuating authentic Christian teaching. In 1170, Pope Alexander III decreed that no one could be venerated publicly, not even locally, without papal approbation. The Council of Trent wrote Catholic teaching about the saints into its documents. In 1588, Pope Sixtus V made the Congregation of Rites the department of the Vatican's administration, or Curia, responsible for certifying the authenticity of relics and for drawing up documents for the papacy to use in determining canonization. Under Pope Urban VIII (1623-1644), the Vatican developed a two-step process that remained in place until well after the Second Vatican Council. In the first step, officials studied the proposed saints' earthly lives for signs of heroic virtue, scrutinized their writings for orthodoxy and gathered evidence that miracles were worked through their intercession. If all went well, the individual was *beatified*, a term which meant that person could be venerated publicly by those who wished to do so. After additional evidence of miracles, the individual could be canonized, or recognized as a saint. At this point, veneration became incumbent upon the universal Church, and the individual was assigned a feastday.

In reality, it was the faithful who remained the first to identify individuals as saints, and whose veneration led to Vatican investigations for beatification and canonization. Sometimes, the Vatican followed the faithful quickly. Saint Anthony of Padua died at Arcella, near Padua, June 13, 1231; Pope Gregory IX canonized him May 30, 1232. In other cases, the papacy moved more slowly. Saint Roch, or San Rocco, died at Angera, Lombardy, in 1378 or 1379. Popular devotion to him spread quickly after his intercession was credited with stopping a plague at Ferrara in January of 1439. The Vatican approved his cult almost 200 years later, in 1629. Saint Rita of Cascia died at an Augustinian convent in Cascia, Umbria, in 1447. By 1456, her cult was so popular that her remains had to be transferred to a sarcophagus suitable for public veneration. Not until 1626 did the papacy beatify her, and not until 1900 was she canonized.

It was also the faithful who took the lead in identifying sites as Marian shrines. In 1001, a hunter and a peasant saw a vision of a woman in an oak tree at Cervano, Foggia. The apparition announced that she was the Mother of God and asked that a church be built at the site. This is the origin of devotion to Santa Maria Incoronata. In 1291, the faithful in Loreto, fifteen miles south of Ancona in the Marches, began to worship at a house they claimed belonged to the Blessed Mother and which angels had transported from Palestine, from which Muslim troops had recently expelled Christian crusaders, to their town. Historian Jaroslav Pelikan has noticed that in the High Middle Ages, the cult of the Mater Dolorosa, Our Lady of Sorrows, and the doctrine of Mary as Mediatrix, grew up together and reinforced each other; people venerated the sorrowful Mother and thought of her as being so close to her Son that she could ask him any favor on behalf of her devotees.[5] Although Father Stafford Poole, C.P., has recently shown that the story is more complex, the cult of Our Lady of Guadalupe traces its origins to December 9, 1531, when Blessed Juan Diego (Cuatitlatoatzin) described how the Blessed Mother had appeared to him and left her image in his cloak.[6] The laity also developed an enhanced role for the Madonna in the story of Christ's Passion and Death. In Trapani, Sicily, and in the place to which the Trapanese migrated, in Brooklyn, the Good Friday procession began with a scene in which Jesus took leave of His mother. The story of the Resurrection culminated in a joyous reunion of mother and Son.[7]

During the same time that the canonization of saints developed this two-step process of popular recognition followed by a verification from ecclesiastical authorities, the ritual ways of expressing devotion were also developing. The scholar and documentary film maker Barbara Corrado Pope has outlined the process. In what Westerners call the Dark Ages, the era between about 400 and 1000, Christian liturgy, especially as practiced in southern Italy, followed practices developed under Byzantine ecclesiastical leadership. Ritual gestures were designed to indicate the worship due a highly exalted divinity and to point toward the soul's final goal of eternal life in heaven. Increasingly, the liturgy added elements of drama. However, the dramatic additions had disadvantages. Extra dramatic rituals made the service too unwieldy. Drama was also open to manifold interpretations, some of them unorthodox. By the thirteenth century, when what scholars call the High Middle Ages were already underway, drama became detached from the liturgy and from ecclesiastical authorities. It became an opportunity for lay expression of faith.[8]

To call a devotion "popular" is not to call it "spontaneous," divorced from all structure and organization. Pious practice was governed by lay leadership and by tradition. The first important tradition to consider here is that of saintly patronage. In addition to being saints, the saints discussed in this article are *patron* saints, that is, they are especially identified with particular locales and causes. Saints become patrons in various ways. In modern times, the papacy identifies a saint as a patron, as Pope Pius XII named Saint Frances Xavier Cabrini patroness of immigrants and as Pope John Paul II named Saint Francis of Assisi patron of ecologists. Some saints seem to have become patrons by a process of free association. For example, one of the tortures Saint Agatha supposedly suffered prior to her martyrdom was the amputation of her breasts. In memory of that, she is often depicted holding two breasts on a dish. Lying on their plate, the breasts look like small round loaves of bread, or like beehives, and it is not surprising Saint Agatha is patroness of bakers and beekeepers. In other cases, the connection between the saints and their objects of patronage is more straightforward: saints became patrons of the towns or regions where they lived or died.

Lay societies developed around patron saints. These societies were multipurpose. A society devoted to the saint of a particular trade, craft or profession could also function as a guild, regulating that particular business, setting standards for judging apprentices and experts and developing consensus on wages and prices. A society could also function as a mutual benefit society, a kind of insurance program whereby the payment of dues guaranteed sick or death benefits. What is important here is that these societies maintained their patrons' cults.[9]

The work of maintaining the cult was divided by sex and by status within Catholicism.[10] (Perhaps there were also divisions of labor by age or by social class; this is a subject which requires more research in the source materials at the various sites in Italy.) Community men were the most obvious public leaders. They organized the events celebrating the annual patronal feastday. In broad outline, the schedule called for preliminary devotional exercises, such as the thirteen Tuesdays leading up the feast of Saint Anthony of Padua.[11] On the day itself there was a Mass, an outdoor ritual, a town fair with opportunities for charity, commerce and recreation, and evening entertainment. The normative outdoor ritual consisted of carrying the saint's statue in procession, but the specifics depended on the saint. For example, the feastday of Saint Joseph on March 19 had no statue. Instead, a tiny group representing the Holy Family of Joseph, Mary and Jesus, went through town seeking shelter, a kind of re-enactment of the Flight into Egypt. Conversely, the June 22 feast of San Paolino of Nola was an elaborate dramatization of a traditional story in which the saint offered himself as a substitute for a widow's only son, captured by North African pirates who had raided Nola and taken its young men to sell as slaves. So impressed were the kidnappers by the saint's courage and compassion that they released him, the youth for whom the saint had offered his life, and all the victims of their raid on Nola. When San Paolino and his companions returned home from their ordeal, the townspeople turned out to welcome them with lilies. The reunion was, and is, acted out annually. One group of men carry a replica of the ship, sailing it through the streets as San Paolino sailed toward home. This group is met by a much larger procession consisting of groups of men representing the townsfolk and their lilies, or *gigli*, which are symbolized by tall, totem-pole-like wooden carvings. Groups of men design the *gigli* and carry them on platforms, pausing to "dance" with their burden, raising and lowering it and performing maneuvers with it, captivating the crowd and building up suspense until the two processions meet.[12]

The clergy had a different role than the laymen. They connected popular piety to Catholic tradition. The clergy carried out their duties in two ways. First, they presided over paraliturgical and liturgical events associated with the feast. The liturgy is the official worship of the Catholic Church; paraliturgy is a useful word from the 1960s that refers to the devotions, pious practices and rituals that are not official obligations and are not sacraments but are still widespread religious rites, elements of individual and community prayer life. Prior to the feastday, priests scheduled novenas (nine consecutive days of prayer), triduums (three consecutive days) and other preliminary devotional exercises. (American experience suggests a pastor might use an upcoming feast to increase participation in confession and communion, but research is needed to test that thesis in Italy.[13]) During the feast itself, the clergy offered mass. At the devotions or the mass, the clergy carried out their second responsibility. They gave panegyrics, sermons focusing on the honored saint. Such panegyrics were ways to convey Catholic teaching. The saint was upheld as a model of Christian virtue. Account of miracles further reinforced the idea that the saint was a person enjoying God's favor, and provided an example of Catholic doctrine about prayer and the work of God in the world.[14]

In some instances, women represented the community in public rituals. When the small group representing the Holy Family came knocking at the door on the feast of Saint Joseph, women invited the guests to a table spread with elaborate foods especially prepared for the occasion. The women's most common role, however, was as links between individual families and the community feast. Women made up the majority in the pews for the preliminary paraliturgies. During the feast itself, they either petitioned the saint for aid to the family or offered prayers of gratitude for past favors received. The ways the women presented their prayers contributed to the drama of the feast, for their prayers were not silent or even verbal, but acted out. Those seeking healing purchased small wax sculptures of the body parts to be healed and either carried them in procession or laid them at the foot of the statue of the patron saint. Those grateful for past favors pinned money to the clothing on the saint's statue as it went by, or followed the statue barefoot to show their humility before their patron.

Women also linked the family to the larger cult of the saints beyond the hometown patron. Besides local patrons there were other saints who could be prayed to for intervention in specific cases. Saint Ann, for example was the traditional patroness of women in childbirth (a position currently occupied by Saint Gerard Majella). Although men could and sometimes did participate in these cults, women were the major practitioners, seeking out saints who could help with specific problems, saying the prayers, participating in devotional exercises and purchasing religious medals, holy cards, scapulars and home-size statues.

One element which seems to require further research is change over time. Research already done raises some questions. Barbara Corrado Pope has noted that southern Italian Good Friday processions followed a particular line of development: first, dramatic elements were added to the liturgy, then the liturgy was moved to the street. How much did the feastday celebrations of saints borrow from the liturgy, and how much did the liturgy borrow from the rituals associated with honoring the saints? Immigrants from Ricigliano, south of Naples, preserved the story of how in 1908 the women of the town defied rainstorms, flood and the laymen, clergy and government officials who—for reasons of weather and politics—wanted to cancel the annual procession, and brought the statue of Santa Maria Incoronata from a mountain chapel to the town church.[15] Were there other controversies over incorporating patriotic imagery during the nineteenth century, as Church and state clashed over unification? Such research would contribute to an understanding of how succeeding generations of faithful made inherited traditions their own.

It is clear that devotion did change over time, incorporating new elements over the years. One exceptionally full description of feastday activities in the early twentieth century shows how at least one Sicilian community mixed various elements together in its feastday celebration. In 1908 or 1909, Joseph McSorley, an Irish-American Paulist priest, visited Catania and saw the feast of Saint Agatha. He wrote a travelogue which the Paulists published in their monthly magazine, *Catholic World*, in 1909. Although Saint Agatha's feastday is February, feastday activities began January 29. At 5:30 p.m. that day, and again on January 30 and 31, the cathedral held a solemn triduum. The more festive activities began the afternoon of February 1, with band music, a horse race and a balloon launch. February 2 featured charitable activities. A lottery awarded three prizes of marriage dowries for poor girls and three other prizes of cash for families whose sons had been conscripted into the army. Then there was another late afternoon of music, horse-racing and balloons. The activities of February 3 focused on prayer. Those wishing to petition Saint Agatha and those wishing to thank her prepared elaborate portable candelabra. At 1:00 p.m., a procession of candelabra went from Saint Agatha's church to the cathedral. The procession ended by 2:30, in time for a concert. After dinner, there was a combination parade and concert, with the area's young people walking in procession and singing. The evening ended in fireworks. The next day, the relics of Saint Agatha were carried out of her church for a procession, and there was an evening concert. The feastday itself was celebrated with a pontifical Mass offered by a cardinal, and there was a final evening of concerts and fireworks.[16]

There is one element of change over time, and distance, that is fairly well documented. Ever since the evangelist recorded Jesus' advice to "Go to your room, close your door, and pray to your Father in secret," there has been a vein in the Christian tradition that ran counter to dramatization and display.[17] Perhaps this less demonstrative style was already evolving when the early Christians of the Italian peninsula were proclaiming new saints through community acts of veneration. By the late Middle Ages, there was a spectrum of attitudes toward public displays of faith. At one end was the *devotio moderna* exemplified by the *Imitatio Christi* of Thomas a Kempis, which stressed interior spirituality and the individual's call to a life patterned after Christ's. At the other end of the spectrum were the Italians, particularly those of the *Mezzogiorno* and of Sicily, with their life-like statues and their relics, their processions and re-enactments of the lives and legends of the saints, and their extravagant and flamboyant local cults.

The quieter end of their spectrum was present in the United States before the era of mass migration. The few English Catholics in the colonies were heirs to the *devotio moderna*. James M. O'Toole has analyzed a set of sermons preached in New York City in 1808-1809, and commented on their christocentric and sacramental focus, and their lack of references to Marian piety or to the saints.[18] Early American Catholic expressions of faith were also shaped by recent historic events. Catholics were a numerical minority in the English-speaking colonies that became the first thirteen United States, and they faced various forms of persecution and discrimination. Some states retained the discriminatory legislation of the colonial period in the constitutions and laws they wrote after the signing of the Declaration of Independence. There was much prejudice against Catholics, and a widespread opinion that their loyalty to the papacy precluded their becoming good Americans. Also, the cult of the saints was connected to one doctrine which set Catholics apart from most other American Christians, the belief that intercession was efficacious. Given this situation, American Catholics concentrated on pointing out that their religion did not inhibit their patriotism, and that their faith was in many ways not all that different from that of the rest of American Christendom. Historians have not identified any change in the situation of American Catholics that resulted from the addition of Franco-American Catholics through the Louisiana Purchase or the addition of Hispanic Catholics through the Mexican-American War; these people were too far away from the main population center, and no one then thought to incorporate many cultures into a new American culture. The arrival of the Irish immigrants expanded the range of American Catholic pious practice only a little. Historians have demonstrated how the persecution and discrimination the Irish Catholics faced in their own country seriously damaged their ability to maintain their faith or to hand it on to their children, and forced them into undemonstrative ways of practicing that faith. In the United States, the Irish could afford more display, more highly visible churches in more prominent parts of town and more Saint Patrick's Day parades. However, they did not have much of a tradition to draw on. German immigrants had greater freedom to express their faith in their home country and had a tradition of public displays (for example Corpus Christi processions), but they had neither the Italians' variety of devotions nor their way of combining Church-sanctioned devotion with popular religiosity and with secular activities.[19]

The first recorded feastday celebrations of Italian patron saints in United States cities date from the early 1880s. The best documented example is the feast of Our Lady of Mount Carmel in East Harlem, New York. In 1881, migrants from Pollo, in the province of Salerno, organized a mutual benefit society. On July 16, 1882, the society sponsored its first feast-

day. It was a simple affair. The society did not have a Mass at a neighborhood church, or even a priest to preach a panegyric. (The nearest Catholic
parish was Saint Paul's on East 117th Street, and it had no Italian clergy.)
There was an outdoor celebration, though the "outdoors" was a building
courtyard rather than the piazza and the streets of the home town. There
was no procession, because there was nowhere to go and no large picture
or statue to carry, just a holy card with an image of Our Lady of Mount
Carmel on it, around which the laity gathered for a rosary and a recitation
of the Magnificat. The entertainment consisted of a community meal.[20]

Over the twenty years between the 1880s and the turn of the nineteenth century, more Italians migrated, the populations of Little Italies
increased, and communities could support more complex celebrations.
Photojournalist Jacob A. Riis and Theodore Roosevelt, then New York
City's Police Commissioner, attended the feast of San Donato on October
22 of 1895 or 1896. They had not planned on going, but their attention was
caught by a brass band leading a procession near the Sixth Precinct police
station on Elizabeth Street between Canal Street and Bayard Street. Riis
and Roosevelt followed the procession to an Elizabeth Street saloon. The
band, and some of the men following it, entered the saloon. The rest of the
procession, with Riis and Roosevelt, went down an alley between buildings
to a rear courtyard. They found an outdoor celebration was already in progress. In the courtyard was a temporary altar on which stood a statue of
Saint Donatus of Fiesole, or San Donato, a ninth-century Irish priest and
bishop of Fiesole canonized in 876. Before the statue was a table full of
flickering candles and before that was a space for people to kneel, pray,
make their offering and light candles. Tenants whose apartments overlooked the courtyard had draped sheets on their fire escapes to make balconies, where they sat watching the procession disperse and waiting for the
afternoon entertainment to begin. Riis and Roosevelt went back to the
saloon to talk to the proprietor, and then returned to the courtyard to join
the fun. Roosevelt even bought a raffle ticket, though he was relieved when
the prize, a live sheep, went to another player, an elderly widow.[21]

Riis's article was suffused with affectionate, amused respect for peo-
ple who worked so hard to rise above their dehumanizing surroundings.
Other writers concentrated on the spectacular show the Italians provided.
One writer described how the Sicilians of East 11th Street celebrated the

Triumph of the Cross, a September feast, in 1903.[22] They decorated their block with seven rows of red, white and green electric lights, the colors of the House of Savoy and patriotic colors of Italy. In the center of the block they erected a crucifixion scene, apparently complete with Jesus, the thieves on the right and left, and the Blessed Mother and Saint John the Evangelist at the foot of the cross. Above the Crucifixion went some kind of representation of the Resurrection. During the day, people out in the street stopped by this scene and dropped offerings on a collection plate. In the evening there was a procession with a brass band and children, the girls in white dresses, the boys in Sunday suits. Two smaller children, dressed as angels and strapped into harnesses, swung out over the crowd on a rope strung between buildings, dropping flowers and reciting prayers. Fireworks completed the evening.

Italian feastdays may have inspired amusement and delight in some onlookers; others regarded them with consternation. An article written by the Reverend Bernard J. Lynch and published in *Catholic World* in 1888 offers an example. Bernard Lynch was the brother of Thomas Lynch, a priest of the Archdiocese of New York and pastor of the Church of the Transfiguration, a parish on Mott Street on the Lower East Side. At that time, Transfiguration had a dwindling population of Irish-American parishioners, a large number of non-Catholic Chinese neighbors and a growing population of Italian Catholic immigrants. Father Bernard Lynch complained that the Neapolitans of Mulberry Street, a block away from Transfiguration, had "the luxuries of religion without its substantials," that is, they had the cult of the saints, a panoply of devotions and a vast folklore of tales of the miraculous, but they did not attend Mass, receive the sacraments, respect the clergy, support the Church, send their children to parochial school or realize they should have been doing any of these things. Father Thomas Lynch was attempting to reorient Neapolitan religious priorities though an "annex congregation." The Italians met in Transfiguration's basement chapel, where they were ministered to by Italian-speaking clergy. These priests offered Mass, preached, administered the sacraments, conducted liturgies besides the sacraments (for example, vespers), and presided over paraliturgical devotions acceptable to American Catholics, such as First Fridays, Holy Hours and recitations of the Rosary.[23] From such beginnings came the later development of Italian national parishes.

Most parishes were, and are, organized territorially, with geographic borders and a requirement that the Catholics within those borders attend and support the parish for their area. Beginning with German migration to the United States a system of parishes with linguistic borders evolved in which Catholics attended parishes staffed by clergy who spoke their language. In the case of the Italians, this became a formal system of "national" parishes.

Many journalists echoed Father Bernard Lynch's charges. Contemporaries referred repeatedly to an "Italian problem."[24] The sentiments were so widespread that historians can get suspicious when they are not readily apparent. For example, in 1903, *Catholic World* published a brief description of "May Customs in Italy" by Grace V. Christmas.[25] On one level, the piece read as a pleasant travelogue of quaint and pious religious mores. The article, though, repeatedly linked contemporary Italian practices and those of the pagan world, pointing out that May was still not considered a good month for weddings, a holdover from pagan days, when marriages were scheduled for June, the month dedicated to the goddess Juno. It connected the practice of scattering petals before the Blessed Sacrament in procession to ancient celebrations of the goddess Flora. It seems strange that a Catholic publication would treat Catholic devotions as holdovers from pagan practice—except that this was the common stereotype of Italians.

Even other Italian clergy regarded their compatriots' cult of the saints as unsound. Giacomo Gambera, who was born in Brescia and who worked among Italian communities in New Orleans, Pittsburgh, Boston, Chicago and New York, complained:[26]

> First of all in a city in which you have a mixture of nonbelievers and those of other faiths, this parading of statues exposed religion to irreverence and derision. . . . In the second place, the promoters of these external feasts were generally not trustworthy individuals, they were not exemplary, they were not practicing Catholics and they were suspected of pure speculation. In fact, without any authorization, they used to solicit offerings from their fellow townsmen in the name of the feast of the parish. Then, when the parade was over, they would strip the statues of the offerings made and not render an account to anyone; at the most, they would give an account to their societies as they wished.

In 1946, Father Henry Browne included "racial antipathies" on the part of Irish-American Catholics toward the Italians as one of several factors contributing to the Italian problem.[27] One can see evidence of such ethnocentrism in Father Lynch's writing. However, there is another charge against the Italians that needs to be explored briefly here. Father Browne had other causes of the Italian problem: "political-religious conceptions brought from Italy, inadequate churches, Protestant proselytizing, immigrant priests of poor quality, and over and above all this a woefully uninstructed people. . . ." Other priests also focused on the Italians' supposed lack of knowledge of their faith. Francesco Zaboglio, who worked among Italian immigrants in the United States in the late 1880s and early 1890s, observed:[28]

> All over the United States, wherever there are Italians, all the bishops and priests (Italian and non-Italian alike) are greatly surprised at the incredible, phenomenal religious ignorance of the Italians who come to America, especially the Italians from the old Kingdom of Naples. The clergy ask in wonder: 'What in God's name are the priests and bishops of that region doing?' I am not judging anybody—I am just relating facts.

Father Bernard Lynch complained that sacraments performed for the Italians "would be invalidly administered for want of knowledge on the part of the recipients."[29] In 1969, historian Rudolph J. Vecoli published an important article on "Prelates and Peasants: Italian Immigrants and the Catholic Church," in which he explored the Italian problem from the Italians' point of view.[30] In his article, Professor Vecoli explained why the Italians, southern Italians particularly, were so ill-informed: The Catholic hierarchy in Italy identified with the great landowners and other elites. They did not extend proper pastoral care to the poorer members of the faith and, for their part, the poor had little incentive to seek them out. Professor Vecoli explained the sources of Italian ignorance; he did not refute the charges.

Historian Robert A. Orsi approached the issue of Italian knowledge of the faith from another angle. Professor Orsi used the cult of Our Lady of Mount Carmel in East Harlem as a case study. He examined devotional practice as a complex dramatization of what the Italians understood of their faith. He concluded:[31]

And so the street theologians proclaimed: that divine and human were in a relationship of mutual responsibility and reciprocity; that the divine needed the human as the human needed the divine; that Christ's redeeming blood established an intimacy between heaven and the domus [home]; that the power of the divine was awesome, not always comprehensible from the perspective of the human and to be approached with love and fear; that the divine was bound to behave with *rispetto* (respect) towards the human; that living and dead, holy and human existed together in the communion of saints; that what God proposed men and women must respect, though they were also free to entreat the divine for help and support; that reality was communal, not individual, and destiny was shared; that suffering could become triumph.

Except for the intimation of equality between human and divine, none of these statements is all that unorthodox, and the equation of humanity and divinity is not some uniquely *Mezzogiorno* unorthodoxy. Also, a case could be made that the Italian veneration of the saints had some counterpart in the actions of a host of Italians who lived about the time of the nineteenth-century migration out of Italy and who were themselves saints.

Saint Giuseppe Benedetto Cottolengo, for example, was born near Bra, in the province of Turin, May 3, 1786. He was ordained in 1811 and spent the first sixteen years of his priesthood as a pastor. In 1827, inspired by the example of Saint Vincent de Paul, he turned to the care of the sick poor. He developed what he called the *Piccola Casa della Divina Providenza,* the Little House of the Divine Providence, which actually grew to a big medical complex treating the mentally ill, the physically handicapped, the blind and the deaf, as well as housing orphans. He was instrumental in founding an institute of women religious, the Sisters of Saint Vincent de Paul. He died at Chieri, also in Turin, April 30, 1842, and was canonized May 19, 1934. Saint Vincent Pallotti was born in Rome April 21, 1795, and died there January 22, 1850. He founded institutes of male and female religious to minister to the poor and working-class people who might otherwise be lost to the faith; today these institutes are known as the Society of the Catholic Apostolate, or Pallottines, and the Pallottine Sisters of Charity. Saint John Bosco was born at Becchi, near Turin, August 16, 1815, and died in Turin January 31, 1888. He was ordained in 1841 and that same year discovered his particular calling, working with boys who suffered from poverty, difficult family situations, and poor education, who were at risk for delinquency and criminality. In 1850, he began to gather other priests whom he trained for this work, the origins of the Salesians. Don Bosco's priestly mentor, Giuseppe Cafasso, and one of his early students, Domenico Savio, have also been canonized.

Nineteenth-century Italian women also became saints. Benedetta Rossello was born in Albisola Marina, Liguria, on May 27, 1811. The same year that Giuseppe Cottolengo decided to follow Saint Vincent de Paul, she became a member of the Third Order of Saint Francis, following Franciscan spirituality while remaining at home and involved in her regular work. In 1837, she and three companions, Pauline Barla and sisters Angela and Domenica Pescio, organized a community dedicated to the care of abandoned girls in the Diocese of Savoy. In 1839, Rosello pronounced her vows and took the name Maria Giuseppe. The next year she was elected superior general of her institute, and continued in that post until her death December 7, 1880; Maria Giuseppe Rossello was canonized in 1949. Paolina Francesca Maria Di Rosa was born at Brescia November 6, 1813, and died there December 15, 1855. At first, she seemed intended for the life of a dutiful daughter. In 1830, after completing her education with Visitandines, she returned home to manage her widowed father's household. However, events drew her into the larger world. In 1836, she and a companion, Gabriella Bornati, tended victims of a cholera epidemic. In 1840, she organized a religious institute which grew into the Handmaids of Charity; it was in this community that she took the name Maria Crucifissa. She spent the next fifteen years tending the victims of Italy's drive to become a modern nation-state:other religious institutes harassed by anticlerical and antireligious forces, and civilians and soldiers wounded in battle. She was canonized in 1954. One might also mention Saint Maria Mazzarello (1837-1881, canonized 1938), foundress of the Daughters of Mary, Help of Christians, or Salesian Sisters, yet another of those in Don Bosco's circle who became saints themselves. Perhaps the best known of these female saints was Frances Xavier Cabrini, who was born in Sant' Angelo Lodigiano in the province of Lombardy July 15, 1850, and who died in Chicago December 22, 1917. She founded the Missionaries of the Sacred Heart of Jesus, which provided a variety of forms of care for Italian immigrants in North and South America: running orphanages, schools, and hospitals, and sending sisters to visit immigrants in their home and to minister to those imprisoned.

To these acknowledged saints, one might add the name of Giovanni Battista Scalabrini, who was recently approved for beatification and who lacks only evidence of a miracle to qualify for canonization. He was born in 1837 in Fino Mornasco and in 1876 was consecrated Bishop of Piacenza, in which capacity he served until his death in 1905. During his episcopate, he distinguished himself by his thoughtful approach to the problem of Church-state relations, his holistic methods of pastoral care of his diocese, which included attention to the sacraments, to religious education and to social action, and by his work on behalf of immigrants, those people between nations so easily marginalized in the age of the nation-state. He organized lay societies, communities of sisters and a community of clergy, the Society of Saint Charles-Scalabrinians.

There are other sorts of nineteenth-century Italian saints, such as the mystic Saint Gemma Galgani, who died in 1903 and the martyr Maria Goretti, who died in 1902 of stab wounds incurred defending herself against attempted rape. However, what is important about the aforementioned saints is how their lives cast another light on popular Italian devotion. During the nineteenth century, the government of Italy was evolving in the direction of a classic liberal state. It was minimizing its influence in a whole range of human activities, separating church from state, following laissez-faire economic policies and permitting its citizens relative freedom of migration. With this increase in human freedom came an increase in human vulnerability, a lack of protection from exploitation and misfortune. Into this breach stepped the nineteenth-century Italian heroes of charity, founding religious institutes, developing institutions for the needy and living lives which proclaimed first that God cared for each and every human person; second that this care encompassed the entire human being, physical as well as spiritual; and third, that as befitted a Church in which human beings are baptized into the divine life, God works through individuals, inspiring them to acts of charity. That was what the Italian faithful "preached" through their veneration of the saints. The biggest difference was that Frances Cabrini was on earth and one could watch her found a hospital, while Saint Anthony of Padua was in heaven and his activity consisted of intercession leading to miracles.

To return to the history of the development of the relationship between Italians and their saints, those who, like Father Lynch or Father Gambera, criticized Italian veneration of the saints overlooked, at least for the length of time it took them to voice their observations, how the veneration of the saints functioned as a kind of hook for catching the Italians and assimilating them to a more American spirituality. Before outreach programs to bring the Italians to parishes began, the Italians recreated the mutual benefit societies that maintained the cult of the saints in Italy. It was these societies and their devotions that the clergy built on as they gathered congregations.[32]

Some Italians refused to have their cults so used. At the time Jacob A. Riis and Theodore Roosevelt dropped in on San Donato's feastday, there was one church, the Scalabrinians' Saint Joachim's, a little southeast of their neighborhood, another, the Franciscans' Most Precious Blood, northwest, and a third, the Jesuits' Our Lady of Loreto, on Elizabeth Street itself. Nevertheless, the saloonkeeper stored San Donato's statue in his loft between feastdays, as Riis explained,[33]

> lest the priest get hold of him and get a corner on him, as it were. Once he got him into his possession, he would not let the people have him except upon payment of a fee that would grow with years. But the saint belonged to the people, not to the Church. He was their home patron, and they were not going to give him up. In the saloon they had him safe.

Other Italians were more willing to work with the clergy. In August of 1891, Jesuit Nicholas Russo completed the process of remodeling a double tenement into the church of Our Lady of Loreto. He scheduled opening day for August 16, the feast of San Rocco, and invited the local San Rocco Society to participate, which it did with grand style. "Toward eleven o'clock about fifty men in full regalia, preceded by two policemen and cheered on by hundreds of people on the side-walks, accompanied and followed by many children, made their solemn entrance into my new Basilica . . . . Opening day was pronounced a success, but I could not help but worry about the next week."[34]

Other pastors forged more lasting connections between saint and parish. In East Harlem, migrants from Pollo wanted to continue and expand upon their traditions, which meant getting a statue of Our Lady of Mount

Carmel and a church to house it. The archdiocesan hierarchy—the arch-bishop was John Cardinal McCluskey, but he was ailing and his coadjutor, Michael Augustine Corrigan, did much of the work—wanted the Italians to support parishes as other Catholics did. Accordingly, Archbishop Corri-gan recruited the Pallottines to provide Italian-speaking clergy and in 1884 authorized two new parishes in East Harlem: Holy Rosary for the Eng-lish-speaking and Our Lady of Mount Carmel, which served the Eng-lish-speaking in the main church and the Italians in a basement chapel. The Pallottines sent as the first pastor Father Emiliano Kirner, a Swiss German who had previously served Italian immigrants to England. By the time Father Kirner arrived, the immigrants from Pollo had purchased a statue replicating the one in their home town. Father Kirner purchased the statue from the mutual benefit society, and, although he gave it no greater dignity than the basement chapel, the devotees decided this was better than what their society alone could provide, and they followed their statue to the church.[35]

Another church dedicated to Our Lady of Mount Carmel, this time in Melrose Park, just outside Chicago, exemplifies another route from lay devotion to parish church. In this case, the devotion was deeply personal. Emilio De Stefano had come from Potenza to Melrose Park in 1873. There he became a local merchant and community leader who channeled many of his compatriots from the old town to the new, and there he fell deathly ill. When he recovered from his life-threatening illness his wife, Emmanuella, vowed to establish the observance of Our Lady of Mount Carmel's feastday in Melrose Park as a token of her gratitude. She arranged for the importa-tion of a statue and in 1894 had the first feastday celebration. Unlike the devotees in East Harlem, she had access to Italian-speaking clergy, and she got Father Tomaso Moreschini, O.S.M., of the Servite parish of Our Lady of the Assumption, to say Mass. Mrs. De Stefano also purchased a small wooden chapel to house her statue. Archbishop James E. Quigley of Chi-cago thought that the devotees that came to pray at the chapel and to cele-brate the feastday could be molded into parishioners, and he assigned a secular priest, Anthony Petrillo, to gather a congregation.[36]

The transition from devotee to parishioner was seldom smooth. In the case of Our Lady of Mount Carmel in Melrose Park, one step in that transi-tion was to transfer the deed to the chapel from lay trustees to the corporation which held property for the Archdiocese of Chicago, of which the archbishop was the sole trustee. The lay trustees did not want to transfer the property. By 1903, when this happened, Mrs. De Stefano had moved in town to Chicago. She wanted her project to grow into a parish church, and she went back out to Melrose Park to convince the trustees to transfer the chapel to the archdiocese or, failing that, to reclaim her statue. Alerted to the possibility that Mrs. De Stefano might try to move the statue, trustees and devotees gathered at the chapel to keep the statue there, by force if necessary. A confrontation between Mrs. De Stefano and her former colleagues in devotion was avoided only when a thunderstorm sent everyone scrambling for cover. This gave Mrs. De Stefano another opportunity to persuade the trustees to yield, and she succeeded. However, the problems were not over. In 1905, Father Petrillo left and Archbishop Quigley had no Italian-speaking priests to replace him. He asked the Missionaries of Saint Charles-Scalabrinians, to provide clergy, and they sent a Trentino, Beniamino Franch. It took years for Father Franch to be accepted by his parishioners.[37]

Even in states in which the law gave the laity more authority in parochial affairs, mutual benefit societies did not always fit neatly into parochial structures. Events at Saint Joachim's in New York City provide a case in point. Saint Joachim's was established in 1888, again under Archbishop Corrigan. Its clergy were from the Society of Saint Charles-Scalabrinians. Saint Joachim's first pastor, Felix Morelli, attempted to gather parishioners and to stabilize finances through contracts with the numerous mutual benefit societies in his Lower East Side neighborhood. The mutual benefit societies contributed financially to the parish. In return, Saint Joachim's housed their patronal statues, provided clergy to offer Mass and to preach panegyrics on feastdays, and also provided clergy for society members' funerals. Father Morelli left no record of any problems with his system, but difficulties arose under a successor, Father Paolo Poggi. The San Rocco Society divided, with a portion of the members wanting to maintain the status quo and another portion wanting to break the contract with Saint Joachim and make another agreement elsewhere. The anti-Saint Joachim faction removed the statue from the church and stored it at a local funeral parlor, pending negotiations. This action sent the pro-Saint Joachim to court seeking relief, and they obtained a court order to keep the statue at the church until a final decision was rendered. Announcement of the court order brought the women of Saint Joachim's into the streets, where they formed a procession that stormed the funeral parlor, retrieved the statue, and reinstalled it in its niche at the church. This in turn led to more newspaper publicity about the Italians and their simple, passionate devotional style.[38]

Dependent as they were on the cults of the saints for congregations and contributions, pastors also tried to distance the parish from the mutual benefit society, to make it clear that the parish was not just a vehicle for perpetuating and extending veneration of a particular patron. Often, this distancing was reflected in names. After the fight between the pro- and anti-Saint Joachim factions of the San Rocco Society, Saint Joachim's got a new pastor, Vincenzo Jannuzzi. Father Jannuzzi made peace with the San Rocco Society by encouraging it to set up its own chapel. From that chapel, Father Jannuzzi developed a new parish. When it came time to choose a patron after whom to name the new parish, the honor went to Saint Joseph, who, among other titles, is the patron of the Universal Church.[39] Historians of Holy Spirit in Providence, Rhode Island, carefully explained that the name was chosen to avoid giving preference to any of the patrons of parishioners' home towns. (The continued determination of some devotees to get a church for their saint was a factor in the erection of Saint Ann's parish a few years later.)[40] Perhaps the most interesting compromise was struck by the Scalabrinians, who named several of the parishes they staffed in honor of Our Lady of the Rosary of Pompei. Although devotion to the Rosary was medieval, the situating of that devotion at Pompei was a late nineteenth-century innovation. The shrine at Pompei was the creation of a pious layman, Bartolo Longo, who designed it around a painting of the Blessed Mother, Infant Jesus on her lap, giving the Rosary to Saint Dominic and Saint Catherine of Siena, the founder of the Dominicans and the best-known Dominican nun, the Dominicans being known for their promulgation of the recitation of the Rosary. Thus the Scalabrinians honored a universal Italian favorite, the Madonna, without having to choose from among many hometown patronesses.

Once they had gathered the faithful, clergy tried to encourage frequent reception of the sacraments, to build parish plants, to educate youth and to develop parish programs. Instead of being the focal point of the community, the veneration of the saints became one strand in the web of Italian-American Catholic life. One can fix the dates for this stage of Italian-American history. It began after World War I, when the war and then legislative changes in the United States and in Italy ended mass migration. It ended after World War II, when the postwar economy led to an Italian-American exodus from city to suburb. There is not as much research on this period in Italian-American devotion to the saints as there is for other periods, and what material there is points to no one conclusion. Rather, it seems that a variety of patterns of devotion to the saints continued.

At least one organization perpetuated the lay, male leadership that had dominated prior to the establishment of Italian national parishes. In 1926, New York City's San Gennaro Society held its first feast. The men of the society carried the bust of their patron saint, which they usually kept in their Mulberry Street headquarters, in procession. One participant also remembered a small street fair, a block long, featuring barbecued chickens.[41] Several factors contributed to the development of the San Gennaro feast thereafter. First, it had good potential as a tourist attraction. The feast was, and is, September 19, after summer vacations but still in the warm part of the year in New York, when it is possible to go to an affair held outdoors. The Italians' reputation as peasant-like people who practiced near-pagan rites and indulged their taste for the simple pleasures of food, fireworks and band music, however patronizing, was also nonthreatening and attractive to tourists. Second, holding a street fair in New York City became more complicated as the twentieth century progressed, and the San Gennaro Society furnished a group of men who could do the work of obtaining permits, waivers, licenses, and vendors.[42] By 1956, when a *New Yorker* reporter visited the San Gennaro Society, the street fair element had grown exponentially, and there were blocks of vendors selling Italian food and trinkets, plus pioneer non-Italian vendors selling other ethnic food and souvenirs. The Franciscans at Most Precious Blood on Baxter Street offered the feastday Mass, as they had for many years, then went about their usual work, oblivious to the secular celebration in front of their friary.[43]

The other trend, of using a parish church as a focal point of a feastday celebration, also continued. In the mid-1920s, migrants from San Fratello, near Messina in Sicily, brought their devotion to Saint Benedict the Moor, the emancipated son of converted African slaves and a member of a Franciscan community in their town, to their new home on East 107the Street in East Harlem. They celebrated Saint Benedict's feastday with a procession that ended at Saint Ann's on East 110the Street. In some cases the feast continued as part of the parish calendar. In Saint Benedict's case the feastday celebration continued until the mid-1940s. The statue, though, remained at the church, available for individuals to approach for private devotions.[44]

Documents permit the reconstruction of a third pattern, in which the parish church swallowed the devotion to the saint. In 1892 or 1893, women from San Stefano, a commune near Genoa, brought their veneration of Our Lady of Guadalupe to the parish of Our Lady of Pompei in Greenwich Village. During the first quarter of the twentieth century, the feastday was an annual event. Unlike the other feasts, it took place entirely within the church building. It was also unlike other events in that it was a women's affair; during the Mass in honor of Our Lady of Guadalupe, there were even female ushers. However, women left the parish, and when death and socioeconomic mobility claimed a critical mass, the annual feastday celebration disappeared, the only evidence that it was ever celebrated being preserved in the parish announcements books and in the correspondence between the pastor and a devotee in Stamford, Connecticut, who every August for over 30 years sent in her annual contribution.[45]

In some ways, Italian veneration of the saints remained conservative. Other devotions did change to accommodate new developments. For example, the Claretians who tended the shrine to Saint Jude at the Church of Our Lady of Guadalupe in Chicago found ways to attract devotion to their saint among people who did not live anywhere nearby. Instead of a "sacred space," devotees observed a "sacred time," a sequence of events in which they encountered difficulties, prayed to Saint Jude, received the benefits of the saint's intercession and offered prayers of gratitude for it.[46] Italian devotions did not make a similar transition from sacred space to sacred time. Instead, Italians practiced different styles of devotion in different cases, maintaining traditions for Italian saints and the Madonna, and attending perpetual novenas or wearing Miraculous Medals as called for by newer devotions.

Between World War II and the economic crises and ethnic revivals of the 1970s, several new factors intervened to shape the cult of the saints in

Italian-American communities. The first was the war itself. World War II was a difficult period for Italian-Americans. It tested their loyalties both to Italy and to the United States, and it caused years of intense, anxious concern for home towns and relatives left therein, as well as for family and friends in the armed forces. The end of the war was an occasion for great relief and even more solemn feastday celebrations. The feast of Our Lady of Mount Carmel in East Harlem seldom featured a procession with the statue of the Madonna, but in the euphoria following V-E Day and V-J Day it seemed appropriate to hoist the heavy statue and platform onto the shoulders of men happy to carry it.[47] Similarly, the dancing of the *giglio* in honor of San Paolino in Brooklyn had languished just before World War II, but was revived in 1949.[48] Immigrants from Ricigliano relocated to Chicago celebrated by holding a bigger-than-usual feastday and by collecting money to restore the church housing the statue of Santa Maria Incoronata in their home town.[49]

In some cases,the burst of gratitude that followed the end of World War II was a last hurrah for community feastday celebrations before the movement to the suburbs reduced the congregations of Italian-American parishes. However, that same suburban shift stimulated feastday celebrations in other ways. For example, Saint Anthony of Padua, in a part of Greenwich Village that later became known as SoHo, had never held an outdoor feastday celebration for its patron saint. Yet, there were several factors favoring such a celebration. Saint Anthony of Padua's June 13 feastday falls during good weather for an outdoor affair in New York. There is a traditional devotion leading to the feastday, the thirteen Tuesdays of Saint Anthony, around which a street fair could be organized. Father Arthur Lattanzi, Saint Anthony's pastor from 1950 to 1964, realized that former parishioners tended to return to the parish for the thirteen Tuesdays devotion and the feastday, and reasoned that providing a large festival with street-fair games and food vendors might give returning parishioners more opportunities to support the parish. Thus the feast of Saint Anthony of Padua joined the feast of San Gennaro on the calendar of New York City events.[50]

Events within Catholicism further influenced the practice of the cult of the saints. The first session of the Second Vatican Council convened October 11, 1962, and lasted until December 8 of that year. The second session met from September 29 to December 4, 1963, and the third from September 14 to November 21, 1964. Given the changes in liturgical practice and devotional life that followed the Second Vatican Council, there was some fear that the cult of the saints was being devalued. The increasing pace in beatifications and canonizations has not changed that fear, because the saints recognized during the tenure of the first post-conciliar pontiff to hold the position for an appreciable length of time, John Paul II, indicated that even if the cult of the saints was not being devalued, it was still being valued differently. Under John Paul II, the Church recognized saints from a variety of geographical locations and cultures, mostly persons whose achievements included the founding of religious communities and attention to charity. Together, the saints are a kind of composite portrait of the People of God. This is different from key elements of Italian-American veneration of the saints. Historically, there was an intense two-way relation between the saint on the one hand and the Italians of a specific geographic community and those who migrated from it on the other. The saints didn't represent their people to outsiders, but bonded with them in a community that did not have that much interest in what the outside world thought of the relationship.

Another enduring factor shaping the cult of the saints was the increase in interest in white ethnicity in the early 1970s. The phenomenon of ethnic revivalism also had factors that shaped it and through it the cult of the saints. At the time, white ethnicity was perceived in relation to the black power, gay rights and feminist movements, all of which had developed just before, in the middle and late 1960s, and all of which encouraged identification with a group that shared some one personal characteristic. White ethnicity supposedly both emulated these groups and reacted against them, using the common characteristic of Italian background to build a community dedicated to conservative family and community values. Such an explanation, though, does not preclude the possibility that white ethnicity gained added strength from other sources. In immigration history there is an aphorism named in honor of the pioneer immigration historian Marcus Hansen. Hansen's Law states, to the effect, that the grandparent wishes to forget the grandchild wishes to remember.[51] The 1970s was the decade in which the third generation of Italian-Americans, the grandchildren of migrants, reached maturity. Even if there had been no civil, gay or women's

rights movements to challenge traditional values and neighborhood cohe-
siveness, the white ethnic revival might still have occurred. Support for
this comes from the revival of the feast of Our Lady of Mount Carmel in
White Plains, New York, and the inauguration of a feast in honor of Our
Lady of the Rosary of Pompei at Greenwich Village in New York City. In
those cases, Italians were not just reacting to contemporary concerns about
challenges to their community, they were reaching back into their history
and developing a way to share it with others.[52]

World War II, then, provided a kind of electric shock to restore the
heartbeat of the cult of the saints. New financial realities and what Michael
Novak termed "the rise of the unmeltable ethnic" served as pacemakers,
establishing a steady beat, a calendar of celebrations which different parishes sponsored for their neighborhoods. However, even pacemakers need
checking and adjustment, and that seems to be what has happened by the
1990s. New forces reshaped the cult of the saints for the next generation.
What were these new forces, and how did Italian veneration of the saints
fit into them?

The first new force that must be mentioned is Pope John Paul II's
renewal of the processes of beatification and canonization. On January 25,
1983, the Holy Father issued an apostolic constitution, *Divinus perfectionis
magister*. The identification of saints still begins with the local church.
After a person's reputation for holiness has persisted for some time past
that person's death (the exact length is not specified), the local ordinary
may begin the process of investigating that person. If this first search turns
up no counter-indications of holiness, the case is forwarded to the Congregation for the Causes of Saints at the Vatican. There, a postulator is
assigned to the case; that person is responsible for determining if the timing
of the case is opportune, for gathering the evidence, and for keeping track
of the expenses of research. The postulator assigns a relator to write a
positio, a special kind of biography, one which emphasizes the issues the
Vatican looks at when determining sainthood, particularly holiness in life,
orthodoxy in writing, and evidence of miracles. Consultors read the fin-
ished *positio* and pass judgement as to whether the person is among the
beatified. Once beatified, the norm is to wait for additional evidence of
miracles before making the case for canonization, but the pope may decide
to proceed with beatification or canonization even without miracles. In

some ways, the saints likely to be recognized under the new procedures might be different from those traditionally recognized by the Italians; the Italian holy heroes are known at least partly for miracles performed through their intercession, the new saintly heroes will be known for their good deeds on earth. Inasmuch as both sets of saints are honored for their charity—modern saints for their benevolent lives, Italian saints for the miracles that benefitted ordinary people—the difference may not be that significant.

Another recent force is the scholarly attention paid to veneration of the saints. For researchers, veneration of the saints is like a prism. When a scholarly light is shone through it, a spectrum of color—the immense variety of motives behind any human action—is revealed. Devotees of Italian saints are especially good prisms. Most adventurously, Lucia Chiavola Birnbaum has studied the hyperdulia accorded the Blessed Mother in several shrines in Italy as the articulation of beliefs held by women and by members of the working class, ages old and long repressed, regarding the characteristics of a truly just society. Another possible direction for future research can be found in the work of Salvatore Primeggia and Joseph A. Varacalli, who used participant-observer methods and interviews to study what participation in the feast of San Paolino of Nola meant to devotees in Williamsburg, Brooklyn. Robert Orsi has considered prayer to Saint Jude as one of many strategies women used to cope with difficulties and challenges in life, and I will admit to having borrowed that technique for studying how Italian immigrant women used prayer, as well as other techniques, for coping with the problems they faced during migration and resettlement.[53] How much effect does scholarship have? It trickles down. People do read books, even scholarly articles now and then, especially if it is something that interests them. Certainly, the material is available for future church leaders to find in their colleges, universities and seminaries. The final result may simply be to make church leaders and laity more conscious of how the veneration of the saints "works," in terms of individual and communal spiritual development.

A third force is the perpetual interest in spiritual life. One lesson to be learned from the almost exaggerated variety of the American religious experience is that no one kind of spiritual life works for everyone; some people are drawn to the awesome intellectual approach of Jonathan Edwards, others to the moral profundity of Martin Luther King, others to the practical charity of the Catholic Worker movement, still others to the aesthetic experience of listening to American spirituals. That individuals have to develop a spiritual life meaningful to them is nothing new. Perhaps the Italian-American experience with saints still has something to offer.

MARY ELIZABETH BROWN

---

[1] Sir James George Frazer, *The Golden Bough: A Study in Magic and Religion*, third edition, revised and enlarged, 12 volumes (London: MacMillan, 1925-1930). Frazer published the first edition of *The Golden Bough* in 1906.

[2] Lucia Chiavola Birnbaum, *Black Madonnas: Feminism, Religion, and Politics in Italy* (Boston: Northeastern University Press, 1993.)

[3] Kenneth L. Woodward, *Making Saints: How the Catholic Church Determines Who Becomes A Saint, Who Doesn't, and Why* (New York: Simon and Shuster, 1990), chapter 2.

[4] The Bollandists, a group of men who are both Jesuits and scholars of sainthood have since 1643 periodically issued studies of the lives of the saints, titled *Acta sanctorum,* that sort out fact from legend. The *New Catholic Encyclopedia*, 17 volumes (New York: McGraw-Hill, 1967) contains entries on most saints. Reference works in English of no more than one volume include Donald Attwater, *The Penguin Dictionary of Saints,* second edition (Middlesex [England] Penguin, 1983), John Coulson, *The Saints: A Concise Biographical Dictionary* (London: Burns and Oates, 1958), John J. Delaney and James Edward Tobin, *Dictionary of Catholic Biography* (Garden City, New York: Doubleday, 1961) and David Hugh Farmer, *The Oxford Dictionary of Saints* (Oxford: Clarendon Press, 1978). Unless otherwise noted, the biographical information in this essay comes form cross-checking *New Catholic Encyclopedia* with Attwater and Farmer.

[5] Jaroslav Pelikan, *Mary Through the Centuries: Her Place in the History of Culture* (New Haven: Yale University Press, 1996), 125-136.

[6] Stafford Poole, *Our Lady of Guadalupe: The Origins and Sources of a Mexican National Symbol, 1531-1797* (Tucson: University of Arizona Press, 1995.) There are exceptions to the generalization of lay leadership in Marian

hyperdulia. In 1251, Saint Simon Stock, then superior general of the Carmelites, began to promote the wearing of a scapular (two small squares of cloth joined by two strings so that one square hangs down the wearer's chest and the other down the back) based on a version of Our Lady of Mount Carmel. In 1467, Augustinian priests discovered a portrait of Our Lady of Good Counsel newly imprinted on the wall of the shrine they had staffed since 1367.

[7] Barbara Corrado Pope, "The Origins of Southern Italian Good Friday Processions," in Paola A. Sensi Isolani and Anthony Julian Tamburri, eds., *Italian Americans Celebrate Life: The Arts and Popular Culture: Selected Essays from the Twenty-Second Annual Conference of the American Italian Historical Association . . . 1989* (New York: American Italian Historical Association, 1990).

[8] Corrado Pope, 163-167.

[9] For information on mutual benefit societies, see John W. Briggs, *An Italian Passage: Immigrants to Three American Cities, 1890-1930* (New Haven: Yale University Press, 1978) and Ernesto Milani, "Mutual Aid Societies Among Italian Immigrants in the United States of America, 1865-1977" (Ph.D., Istituto Universitario Lingue Moderni, 1977). Despite the American-sounding titles, both contain information on Italy.

[10] For information on religious practices in Italy, see Leonard Covello, *The Social Background of the Italo-American Schoolchild: A Study of the Southern Italian Family Mores and Their Effect on the School Situation in Italy and America* (Leiden: E. J. Brill, 1967), Silvano M. Tomasi, *Piety and Power: The Role of the Italian Parishes in the New York Metropolitan Area, 1880-1930* (New York Center for Migration Studies, 1975), chapter 2, Rudolph Vecoli, "Cult and Occult in Italian-American Culture: The Persistence of a Religious Heritage," in R. M. Miller and T. D. Marzik, *Immigrants and Religion in Urban America* (Philadelphia: Temple University Press, 1977) and Phyllis Williams, *Southern Italian Folkways in Europe and America* (New Haven: Yale Institute of Human Relations, 1938).

[11] Saint Anthony of Padua died on a Tuesday, and the number thirteen was derived from the date of his death, June 13.

[12] I. Sheldon Posen, Joseph Sciorra, and Martha Cooper, "Brooklyn's Dancing Tower," *Natural History* XCII (June 1983), 30, and Salvatore Primeggia and Joseph A. Varacalli, "The Sacred and Profane Among Italian American Catholics: The Giglio Feast," *International Journal of Politics, Culture and Society* IX:3 (Spring 1996), 424-425. The ritual meeting of two processions appears in other settings. Some *Mezzogiorno* Good Friday processions focus on the Blessed Mother's search for her Son, who has been betrayed and is being walked to His death on Calvary. At Ricigliano, the popular patroness, Santa Maria Incoronata, meets the official town patron, Saint Christopher. Scholars of spirituality might

comment on the importance of the pilgrimage motif underlying a drama in which one procession goes to meet another, and psychologists might comment on the acting-out of a fear of abandonment and a dream of reconciliation, but there is also a practical dimension. Two processions increases the number of participants. They also increase the amount of space utilized, which in turn increases the area which can accommodate spectators. They add to the complexity of the event, and thus to its holding power over the audience.

[13] Primeggia and Varacalli, 437.

[14] Admittedly, the evidence regarding sermons comes from clergy on the American side of the Atlantic, from Luigi Toma and Giacomo Gambera. Panegyrics from both are preserved at the Center for Migration Studies, collections #043 and #069, respectively.

[15] Michael Rubino, *Ave Maria! History of the Devotin to Our Blessed Mother Under the Title of Maria SS. Incoronata di Ricigliano* (Chicago: Santa Maria Incoronata, 1979), 6-7.

[16] Joseph McSorley, C.S.P., "In Sicily," *Catholic World* LXXXVIII (1909), 652-659, 810-819.

[17] Matthew 6:6.

[18] James M. O'Toole, "From Advent to Easter: Catholic Preaching in New York City, 1808-1809," *Church History* LXIII:3 (September 1994), 365-377.

[19] Jay P. Dolan, *The Immigrant Church: New York's Irish and German Catholics, 1815-1865* (Baltimore: The Johns Hopkins University Press, 1975), chapters 3 and 4.

[20] Orsi, "The Madonna of 115th Street: Faith and Community in Italian Harlem" (Ph.D., Yale University 1983), 95. This has been published as Robert A. Orsi, *The Madonna of 115th Street: Faith and Community in East Harlem, 1880-1950* (New Haven: Yale University Press, 1982). The dissertation version is the more richly detailed.

[21] Jacob A. Riis, "Feastdays in Little Italy," *The Century Magazine* LVIII (1899), 491-499.

[22] "Italian Festivals in New York," *Chautauquan* XXIV (1901), 228-229. The date given in the article is September 23; the calendar places the feast on September 14.

[23] Bernard J. Lynch, "The Italians in New York," *Catholic World* XLVI (April 1888), 67-73. Since it is not clear when Father Bernard Lynch researched his article, it is not clear who ministered to the Italians in Transfiguration's basement. Up until 1887, Franciscans from Saint Anthony of Padua took pastoral care of the Italians. In 1887, Father Marcellino Moroni came from Italy as a pioneer in a new method of pastoral ministry advocated by Bishop Giovanni Battista Scalabrini of the Diocese of Piacenza in the extreme north of the province of

Emilia-Romagna. If it was Father Moroni, then one can get the priest's own view of what Father Bernard considered a beneficial arrangement for the Italians. Father Moroni did not consider it beneficial at all, reporting to Bishop Scalabrini that he had to negotiate with Father Lynch every time he wanted to use the basement for devotions or catechism. In turn, the Reverend Stephen Michael Di Giovanni has uncovered some evidence as to how the Italians in the basement evaluated Father Maroni. He disdained his southern Italian parishioners and worked more closely with men whose background was in northern Italy and whose occupations—neighborhood shopkeepers and professionals—made them prominent in Little Italy. See Stephen Michael DiGiovanni, "Michael Augustine Corrigan and the Italian Immigrants: The Relationship Between the Church and the Italians in the Archdiocese of New York, 1885-1902" (Ph.D., Pontificia Univrsitas Gregoriana [Rome], 1983), 287-289. This dissertation has been published as Stephen Michael DiGiovanni, *Archbishop Corrigan and the Italian Immigrants* (Huntington, Indiana: Our Sunday Visitor, 1994), but the dissertation version is the more richly detailed.

[24] Silvano M. Tomasi and Edward C. Stibili, *Italian Americans and Religion: An Annotated Bibliography*, second edition (New York: Center for Migration Studies, 1992) lists many Progressive Era articles on Italian religious practices.

[25] Grace V. Christmas, May Customs in Italy, *Catholic World* LXXVII (1903), 155-158.

[26] Giacomo Gambera, *A Migrant Missionary Story: The Autobiography of Giacomo Gambera* (New York: Center for Migration Studies, 1994), 157.

[27] Henry J. Browne, The 'Italian Problem' and the Catholic Church in the United States, 1880-1900, United States Catholic Historical Society *Records and Studies* XXV (1946), 53.

[28] Francesco Zaboglio to Giovanni Battista Scalabrini, Boston, August 5, 1889, quoted in Mario Francesconi, C.S., *The Scalabrini Fathers in North America, 1888-1895*, volume II, trans. Joseph Zappulla (New York: Center for Migration Studies, 1983), 150-151.

[29] Lynch, 69.

[30] Rudolph J. Vecoli, Prelates and Peasants: The Italian Immigrants and the Catholic Church, *Journal of Social History* II (1969), 217-268.

[31] Orsi, 405-406.

[32] Some societies had other bases for membership. In 1903, migrants from Santa Ninfa, relocated to Williamsburg and to Bushwick in Brooklyn, organized two Santa Ninfa societies, one for unskilled workers and another for artisans. The two economically based societies were after reorganized into one geographically based society open to all men who could trace their origins to Santa Ninfa. Even

then, the society retained an interest in economic issues. It had a speaker's bureau chaired by a socialist, Giovanni Sala, who invited other political leftists to give talks. Despite its religious-sounding name, the Santa Ninfa Society had neither patron saint nor feast day. See Anthony F. Lazzaro, The Santa Ninfa Society, unpublished paper on file at the Center for Migration Studies, Staten Island, New York.

[33] Riis, Feast Days in Little Italy, 495.

[34] Nicholas J. Russo, The Origin and Progress of Our Italian Mission in New York, *Woodstock Letters XXV* (1896), 137.

[35] Orsi, 95-100.

[36] For information on Emilio De Stefano, see Rudolph J. Vecoli, The Formation of Chicago's 'Little Italies,' *Journal of American Ethnic History* 11:2 (Spring 1983), 17. For Emmanuella De Stefano and Our Lady of Mount Carmel in Melrose Park, see *Eightieth Anniversary of Our Lady of Mount Carmel Church, Melrose Park, Illinois* (Chicago: C.D. Stampley, 1975.)

[37] Carbon of speech dated 1980, Society of Saint Charles-Scalabrinians, Provence of Saint John the Baptist archives, Box 20, Fr. B. Franch folder.

[38] *New York Evening Post,* July 19, 1906.

[39] *Saint Joseph Church Fiftieth Anniversary, 1925-1975, New York City, New York* (New York: Park Publishing Company, 1977.)

[40] Robert J. Hayman, *Catholicism in Rhode Island and the Diocese of Providence: 1886-1921*, 2 vols. (Providence: The Diocese of Providence, 1995), 11:174-175.

[41] *The New York Times*, September 16, 1977, C26, column 1.

[42] The increasing complexity of street fairs has also led to the possibility of corruption in organizing the San Gennaro feast of using bribes to obtain government favors and extorting kickbacks from vendors wishing to set up stalls for the festival. Mayor Rudolph Giuliani investigated the San Gennaro Society with an eye to weeding out such corruption.

[43] Festa, *New Yorker XXXIII* (October 5, 1957), 34-36.

[44] Anthony D'Angelo, Italian Harlem's Saint Benedict the Moor, in Mary Jo Bona and Anthony Julan Tamburri, eds., *Through the Looking Glass: Italian and Italian/American Images in the Media* (Staten Island: American Italian Historical Association, 1996), 235-240. The Italians and Saint Benedict also crossed paths at Our Lady of Pompei in Greenwich Village. When the Scalabrinians and trustees at Pompei were looking for a new church, their previous one having been damaged in a gas explosion, the Archdiocese of New York steered them toward a church owned by the parish of Saint Benedict the Moor, the first African-American congregation in New York, which was hoping to sell the property to buy new land nearer the growing black neighborhood in the West 50s. The

transfer was effected, Saint Benedict moved to West 53rd Street, and Pompei moved to Saint Benedict's previous church, located on Bleecker Street. In the 1990s, long after Pompei had moved to a new church and right after Saint Benedict was suppressed, Pompei received statues of the Blessed Mother and Saint John the Evangelist that Saint Benedict had taken from the Bleecker Street Church to the West 53rd Street one, and installed them in Pompei's second Bleecker Street church.

[45] The letters are in the Our Lady of Pompei collection, #037, at the Center for Migration Studies. Letters include those dated August 19, 1916, in Box 2, folder 18, August 10, 1920, Box 3, folder 25, August 18, 1921, Box 3, folder 26, August 18, 1922, Box 4, folder 28, and August 17, 1923, Box 4, folder 30.

[46] Robert Orsi, The Center Out There, In Here, And Everywhere Else: The Nature of Pilgrimage to the Shrine of Saint Jude, 1929-1965, *Journal of Social History* XXV:2 (Winter 1991), 213-232.

[47] Orsi, 301-303, 93.

[48] Primeggia and Varacalli, 425.

[49] Rubino, 4.

[50] *Saint Anthony of Padua Church, New York City* (South Hackensack, New Jersey: Custombook, 1967), unpaginated. The perception that Harlem is an undesirable place to visit has kept Our Lady of Mount Carmel from joining the calendar of city fairs. However, it has become a popular feast for migrants from the Caribbean. And, with every square inch of Manhattan being exploited for tourist revenue and with double-decker tour buses traveling as far north as 125th Street, the heart of Harlem, it is reasonable to expect tourist interest in Mount Carmel to increase.

[51] Marcus L. Hansen, *The Problem of the Third Generation Immigrant* (Rock Island, Illinois: Augustana Historical Society, 1938), 9-10.

[52] Denise M. Di Carlo, The History of the Italian *Festa* in New York City: 1880s to the Present (Ph.D., New York University, 1990.)

[53] Robert A. Orsi, *Thank You, Saint Jude: Women's Devotion to the Patron Saint of Hopeless Causes* (New Haven:Yale University Press, 1996) and 'Have You Ever Prayed to Saint Jude?': Reflections on Field Work in Catholic Chicago, in Robert Bruce Mullin and Russell E. Richey, eds., *Reimagining Denominationalism: Interpretive Essays* (New York: Oxford, 1994), 134-161; Mary Elizabeth Brown, Italian Immigrant Clergy and an Exception to the Rule: The Reverend Antonio Demo, Our Lady of Pompei, Greenwich Village, 1899-1933, *Church History* XLII:1 (March 1993), 41-59.

CHAPTER 4

THE SOCIAL CONTEXTS OF RELIGIOUS DEVOTION: HOW SAINT WORSHIP EXPRESSES POPULAR RELIGIOSITY

To understand fully the special place saints hold in the lives of contemporary Italian-Americans, it is necessary to take a socio-historical look at former ways of life in Italy and examine the roles of saints in eras past. The relationship today's Italian-Americans have to their saints has evolved from centuries-old beliefs, dating back to pre-Christian times. It is possible to trace how the surviving folk-religion components of Italian-American faith were passed down (with multiple adaptations) through the generations, from the Old World to the New World.

In ancient times, the most common venue for paying homage to the various gods was the festival. Those considered sacred were accorded their rightful honor of a festival, which all residents were obliged to celebrate.[1] As Christianity began to spread, many established customs, including festivals, were incorporated into the new religion.[2] Pagan worship of gods, idols, and holy relics, as well as beliefs about how the forces of good and evil were manifested—or could be thwarted— were all part of the prevailing world view. Drawing from pagan and Moslem beliefs and practices, the early Christian church consisted of,

> A whole panoply of saints [who] were pressed into service to fulfill the functions of the gods they supplanted. As was true of ancient gods, each saint was seen as having domain over a specific area of life and often to be in competition or rivalry not only with other saints but with Satan and other demons, with witches and even on occasion with God.[3]

Through the ages, Italians, most especially the southern Italian *contadini* (peasants), blended cult with occult and still, in counter distinction to the perception of others, considered themselves to be *cristiani*. (Christians). Living in a land constantly challenged by earthquakes, floods, volcanoes, and plagues, the downtrodden peasants were open to any and all extant sources of power to offset adversity. Many of their superstitious ways encompassed magical elements, which gave practitioners a perceived sense of some control over their environment. Never did they see any inconsistency in the pairing of religion with superstition. Rather, the overlay of magical beliefs and Catholicism made sense to these people who, for so long, were "battered" by physical and social forces.[4]

The Rise of Saint Worship

The peasant's existence of southern Italy was harsh, brutal and often threatening, and given these difficulties, people sought coping assistance in numerous spheres, including witchcraft, sorcery, superstition and formal religion. At times, the black arts were seen as more powerful than the resources of the Catholic Church; and southern Italians, especially, believed that when formal religion failed to help them, magic words, spells, and potions were viable and valuable substitutes. At the very least, they felt these practices could be utilized in conjunction with formal religious rites to provide a formidable protective shield against the sinister forces of nature and evils of Satan. Thus, the southern Italian peasants' religion became a comprehensive belief system of combined folklore with doctrinal tenets.

These new Christians, who continued to give credence to *streghe* (witches) and *maghi* (sorcerers), had no trouble adopting saints as festival-worthy personages who held an exalted status in the religious, communal, and personal lives of the people. Members of the southern Italian peasant class felt vulnerable and subject to violent and mysterious forces (natural phenomena not understandable to them); the unexpected and the unknown .[5] The Italian peasant, who believed a multitude of disasters could befall him and his loved ones at any given moment, embraced the Christian vision of heavenly reward through otherworldly salvation. Prior to arrival in Paradise however, while peasant families were enduring earthly travails, they sought the protection, assistance, and guidance of saints, to whom they assigned supernatural powers.

It is no wonder that saints became focal points of southern Italian devotions. The prevailing *miseria* (misery) and hardships of peasant life, required constant vigilance against evil, and help was crucial if one was to achieve even the most meager of successes. Saints were credited with the ability to improve selected aspects of their believers' lots, by fending off problems, maladies, and misfortunes. Given their folkloric heritage, and in pragmatic terms of everyday situations, the cult of the saints made more sense to the peasants than a far-off, bureaucratic, and often perceived as alien-to-southerners, Catholic Church.

Southern Italian peasants believed saints had the power to heal, as well as to protect from calamities yet to occur.[6] The role of the saint was to act as intercessor and petition God on behalf of the people. Because the peasant saw himself in a lowly position (reinforced by his economic status and the perceptions of those around him), he thought any direct communication with God was not possible. "God, like the king, was a lofty, distant figure who would hardly have time to listen to the peasant's complaint about his dry cow, but the local saint, as a friend of God, could serve as an intermediary."[7]

Just as pre-Christians called upon a host of specialized gods, the southern Italians compiled a formidable directory of saints, each of whom operated in his or her unique miracle-working arena. There was a saint to field every possible catastrophe. According to Gambino:

> San Vito protected against the bites of animals, especially rabid dogs, and Santa Barbara shielded her supplicants against the devastation of lightening. Even gamblers had their patron saint: San Pantaleone. In addition, each region, town, family, and even individual had special saints, a custom that dated back to Roman household gods or lares. Each saint had his day in the calendar on which he was to be specially celebrated, worshiped, or placated. For example, Neapolitans thought that the husband of a pregnant woman risked harm to his wife and unborn child if he worked on St. Aniello's Day.[8]

Gambino is consistent with Vecoli's [9] appraisal that, "The saints of Southern Italy were legion: San Rocco, Santa Lucia, San Michele, San Gennaro, la Madonna del Carmine and many others, some whose names 'will not be found in any hagiology.'" Popular saints in Italy, whether formally recognized by the Catholic Church or not, had in common the ability to perform miracles; they were "wonder-working" saints.[10] Those suffering from general women's ailments prayed to Santa Rita, but more specifically, Santa Agata was the one to call upon to relieve inflammations of the breast. San Cologero cured hernias, while Sant' Onofrio healed burns and Santa Apollonia calmed toothaches. Individual specialization was based on stories that demonstrated a saint's particular power. "Thus, San Biagio cures sore throats because he cured a boy choking on a fish bone; Santa Agata cures diseases of the breasts because her own breasts were cut off while she was being martyred; San Sebastiano cures wounds because his body was riddled with arrows; and so on." [11]

It should be noted that the specific specializations of saints varied, from region to region, throughout Italy. Still, to a national underclass such as the peasants, miracles were deemed necessary survival tools, and the saints who provided miracles were objects of the peoples' outright devotion and worship. Prayer alone was not always enough. "Rather they regarded the saints as supernatural beings who could be enlisted in their cause by the performance of certain acts." [12] These enlistment acts were a form of self-styled negotiation, which had to be delineated and communicated to the saint before any assistance could be expected. For example, there would be promises of daily mass attendance for a specified period of time. Acts of charity, sacrifice, and abstinence were popular bargaining chips, as well as novenas, votive candles—and most importantly— continued devotion and public tribute to the saint by the petitioner.

Historically, and even to this day, the religious rituals followed by southern Italians are markedly distinct from the religious practices in northern Italy or the rest of Europe. [13] Besides worshiping statues and sacred relics, and vesting saints with specific powers, the southern Italians created a hierarchy for God, the Madonna, and the saints:

> Christ is more powerful than God the Father, Mary is more powerful than Christ; ...But more powerful than God the Father, Christ, and the Madonna together is the one saint that—from as far back as the distant centuries of the Middle Ages— the inhabitants of a given place have selected as their patron. The patron saint is a veritable *deus loci*, the god of the place, to whom the peasant turns in times of despair [14]

God was viewed as the most distant, the priest peripheral, while the Patron Saint, the Madonna and the forces of nature became the more tangible, approachable entities for the southern Italian.

Certain occupations were assigned patrons—most notably, San Giuseppe (St. Joseph) became the Patron Saint of carpentry. Gower [15] recounts that in Palermo, for example, San Cosimo was the patron of bricklayers, while San Damiano watched over barbers. San Crispino was the patron of shoemakers and San Paolino was the patron of gardeners; while on the dark side of the subsistence coin, San Panteleone was the patron of lottery players and San Gerlando was the patron of thieves. However, more often, Patron Saints were delegated to watch over geographical areas— a village, town, city, province, or country, and Italian Catholics chose these patrons based on legends relating to the history of a particular locale. San Gennaro of Naples and Santa Rosalia of Sicily are two examples, but in fact, it was quite common for communities, especially larger cities, to recognize more than one Patron Saint. Co-patrons, it was widely held, increased the likelihood of protection and therefore could see their devotees through a wider range of difficulties.

The city of Naples has many Patron Saints, but San Gennaro is considered the most important when it comes to the general well-being of the populace. The supernatural sign of continued guardianship is the miracle of liquefaction of San Gennaro's blood relic, three times a year, in May, September, and December. City dwellers interpret failure of the blood to liquify as a portend of danger and possible disaster for Naples.[16] San Gennaro's, however, is but one of many liquifying blood relics in Campania. From 1389, the first year San Gennaro's blood liquefied to 1864, the year of San Lorenzo's blood liquefaction, there were 15 other saints in the region that had this miracle attributed to them on a regular basis, throughout this time period.

The Cult of the Saints

Italians account for more saints (38% of the total) than any other national group.[17] "This greater propensity of Italian Catholics to create saints is one of the most distinctive features of the cult of the saints in Italy ..."[18] While they have always made a distinction between the *santo edificante* (the exemplary saint) favored by church authorities, and the *santo miracolante* (the saint with miraculous powers) held in high esteem by the public, [19] the cult of the saints includes portions of accepted church rituals, as well as many local, village, regional, familial, and personalized variations of devotions. The Church criteria for defining saintliness are: doctrinal purity, heroic virtue, and some evidence of miraculous intercession after death. For the Italian public, however, sainthood is all about miracles, such as making dead flowers bloom or dried blood flow, curing illness, changing the weather to nurture a crop, or stopping a natural disaster from destroying a village.[20]

In the past (as in the present), the southern Italian perception of saints was, by and large, reality-based and defined in everyday terms. Furthermore, the peasants' oral tradition, their source of lore and legend, liberally laced information with creative annotation and personal conjecture. Much like Roman mythology, through the medium of storytelling, human qualities and earthly motivations were attached to the saints, which enabled believers to understand and relate to the divinities on more solid ground. St. Francis of Assisi, for example, is beloved by Italians and Italian-Americans alike, having had particular appeal to the peasant class, as he was said to have forgone a life of luxury and wealth to become a humble follower of God and dedicate his life to charity and serving the poor. Tales of St. Francis' love of animals and nature added a pastoral dimension to his being, with which an agrarian person could identify easily. These kinds of associations lead to a general attitude of respectful familiarity toward the saints.

Always the pragmatist, the southern Italian peasant never expected something for nothing, in neither his worldly dealings, nor his otherworldly dealings. Hence, the southerner instituted a custom of making all manner of up-front bargains with saints or the Madonna. There was an ever-growing, continually enhanced catalog of prescribed acts of self-denial, self-deprivation, or self-humiliation (of intensities that corresponded to the gravity of the problem at hand, or the extremes to which individuals were willing to go) to elicit saintly assistance. Beyond pre-miracle agreements, struck prior to a saint's intercession; as the custom became a tradition—passed on and embellished through the ages—some believers began making conditional promises. That is, upon the granting of their requests, they would perform additional sacrificial acts, *after the fact.*

An offshoot of bargaining and perceived familiarity with the objects of their devotion, was a popular belief held by southern Italians that they could embarrass or coerce saints into doing their bidding. This humanizing notion is illustrated vividly in the story that, "during the volcanic eruption when a stream of hot lava headed toward Naples, residents of the city placed statues of the city's patron, San Gennaro, directly in the path of the threatening flow, shouting to the saint, 'Save our city or perish!'"[21] Although this "perform, or else" attitude was not endorsed by the Catholic Church, there are countless stories of saints' statues being pelted with mud, drowned in the sea, thrown in the garbage, or relegated, in shame, to closets or cellars. To Italians, "a saint had failed to protect people he was supposed to protect and was being punished in order to insure that this did not happen again."[22] Often, if the dishonored saint finally lived up to expectations, or it was felt he or she had been sufficiently chided, the statue would be returned from exile. One scholar sees the practice of humiliating saints or presenting them with ultimatums as one of the most distinguishing features of the religion of the *Mezzogiorno* .[23]

A further elaboration on the cult-prescribed saint psyche, distinctive to Italian Catholicism, was the idea of a saint's or the Madonna's capacity to hurt as well as help. Many believed their godlike protectors could turn into sources of danger, if devotees were careless in maintaining the cult. Stories spread of saints and even the Madonna directing all manner of afflictions at people, or at least, allowing misfortune to befall. To this day, one of the most popular saints throughout Italy, "Sant' Antonio *Abate*, the protector of animals, like San Donato is both loved and feared—loved for the protection he can bring and feared for the harm he can send."[24] Believers agree, the only remedy for saint-sent maladies is renewed or deepened devotion. This two-sided attribution keeps followers from taking a saint's benevolence for granted. Unless properly honored, he or she can and will demonstrate saintly displeasure, in most unpleasant ways.

An integral component of Italian (and Italian-American) devotion to any saint or the Madonna is the procession. Carrying a statue or painting of the saint through the streets of a village or city remains a core activity for believers, because it reestablishes the relationship between saint and protected space. As stated previously, it is imperative to Italians that their saints be accessible, and this is the underlying reason why so many celebrations dedicated to saints begin in the church, then move out onto the streets. This two-part process makes veneration both institutional and popular. The church is the acknowledged repository of sacred images and relics, but at procession time, the objects of devotion are brought into their followers' mundane environment. There is usually, "a society, named for the saint, [that] looked after the business part of the occasion and furnished bearers, music, and fireworks"[25] and during the procession, many parishioners (especially those giving thanks, or petitioning, for certain favors) present offerings, including money and jewelry for the saint. The procession enmeshes the sacred with the profane, as it ensures that each home it passes will be blessed with the protection of the saint.

Another cult practice, more common in Italy than in any other Catholic country, is the use of the *ex voto* .[26] An *ex voto* is an object that is brought to the church—most often into its sanctuary—which is symbolic of a vow made to a saint or the Madonna.[27] While virtually anything can serve as an *ex voto* (e.g., clothing, jewelry, weapons, living animals, or orthopedic devices), the most common articles are models of body parts, such as a heart, made from pressed metal, candle wax or painted on a tablet.[28] *Ex voto* items such as these are public displays of thanksgiving to a saint or the Madonna for having cured a particular illness or injury, represented by the graven organ or limb. More generic items are also employed to acknowledge an affirmative response to a devotee's plea. Exhibition, " . . . can be done by affixing the *ex voto* to an interior wall of the church; it might be displayed in a special room adjacent to the main body of the church." [29]

Popular southern Italian devotion to the saints has always contained an element of ritualistic masochism as an accepted accompaniment to pious dedication. Tongue dragging and self-flagellation are examples which require petitioners to crawl or walk barefoot, from the entrance of the church to the altar, licking the floor or striking themselves the entire way and causing bleeding. The pain, sacrifice, and mortification is offered up in part as an acknowledgment of the suffering or martyrdom associated with almost every saint's legend. However, for some petitioners, it may also have a cathartic effect, relieving them from guilt or anxiety while, at the same time, demonstrating the depth of their sincerity and devotion. Although not displayed as dramatically by second-generation Italian-Americans, many immigrants and their children continued these humbling practices as offerings to the saints who sustained them in Italy.

Adoration of the Madonna

The Virgin Mary has long been a key recipient of devotion in Latin Catholic countries, primarily Italy and Spain. The Mary cult remains quite formidable throughout Italy, as evidenced by the extraordinary number of religious rituals that revolve around the Madonna, [30] but this is especially true in southern Italy, where she is seen as one of the principal religious forces in the lives of the people. Among the feasts that honor the Blessed Mother are: Madonna dell' Arco , Madonna dell' Assunta, Madonna delle Galline, Madonna dei Bagni, Madonna Avvocata, Madonna della Pace, Madonna del Carmine, Madonna Addolorata, the Madonna of Piedigrotta and the Madonna of Monte Vergine.

Southern Italy's strong attachment to the Madonna is related by and large to the matriarchal character of its peasant society. Historically, and to this day, southern Italian mothers have played focal familial and social roles, so popular veneration of the Madonna, the mother of Christ, was a normal and natural outcome. For those already primed with a pre-Christian background of goddess worship, it was no great leap to assign exaggerated maternal qualities—nurturer, teacher, wise counsel—and more, to this most exalted mother. For peasant women in particular, Mary, who had experienced ultimate spiritual glory and earthly tragedy, was seen as the one who could best understand a mortal mother's hopes, fears, and concerns for her family and surroundings. In the eyes of many, Mary was the strongest advocate for petitioners, for she alone could plead their cases directly to her son, the God-made-man Christ.

In her many manifestations, the Madonna is always conferred a two-part title. "The first part is usually Madonna, Maria Santissima, Nostra Signora, Santa Maria, Maria Vergine, or Madre, while the second part associates the Madonna with some location, object, or attribute"[31] For example, two quite common titles are *Madonna delle Grazie* and *Madonna dei Miracoli,* which refer to her capacities to grant favors and perform miracles. She is most often called Madonna (an archaic term of address, most closely related to the English term Milady) or Maria Santissima (*Santissima* being a superlative form of *Santa*). Of course, there is only one mother of Christ, but for Italians, the Madonna has many identities or titles, which differ based on her numerous abilities and her special relations with people in various locales. Hence, there are distinctive devotions that call upon her specific titles and attributes.

While there are many similarities between the cult of the saints and the cult of the Madonna in Italy, the one crucial distinction is apparition. An apparition is defined as a face-to-face encounter between a human and supernatural being. While apparitions of Christ and certain saints have been recorded, the overwhelming number involve the Virgin Mary; and over the centuries, Italian Catholics have been more prone to these Marion apparitions than any other national group.[32] In fact, the multitude of Marian sanctuaries, which have been constructed throughout Italy at purported apparition sites, attest to the scale and scope of this country's Mary cult. Moreover, this sanctuary phenomenon makes a noteworthy statement about the southern Italians' relationship to the Madonna. Simply put, "they see her as a goddess who craves veneration." [33]

In Italy, both the cult of the saints and the Mary cult remain more popular than the cult of Jesus Christ. In part, this is the result of a sustained belief that the saints and the Madonna are more accessible and receptive to human needs. His transitory humanity notwithstanding, Italians relate only marginally to Jesus Christ. With the exception of Christ child adoration (more often than not on the lap of his mother) and Crucifixion commemoration (also featuring the grieving Madonna), Jesus of Nazareth is generally seen as too abstract a figure to correlate with everyday existence.

The Italian Feste

Perhaps the best-known of southern Italian traditions relating to saints are feast days *(feste),* on which the people come together for a shared celebration and commemoration of their village, city, or regional patrons— in religious, communal, and personal contexts. On the feast day, a saint or the Madonna is honored through all manners of rituals, as family, friends, and *paesani* forgo mundane activities to demonstrate their individual and group devotion. Though it is considered a religious function, the epitome of the *festa* is its merging of the sacred and the secular. Even the Italian men, whose male socialization fosters resistance to more formalized aspects of Catholicism, are happy to immerse themselves in feast-related activities and express devotion to a saint in the process. Year after year, at various intervals during the year, the *feste* serve as periodic divergences from the work-a-day norm and have become crucial elements of the traditional southern Italian way of life.

The feasts, many of which have been celebrated for centuries, vary in breadth and scope from subtle, candle-lit processions, to spectacular, week-long events. On these occasions, southern Italians are motivated to take unusual action, even go to extremes, to demonstrate adoration of their protectors. Various rituals, including frenzied dancing, feats of physical strength and endurance, chanting in trances, and processions that involve sacrificial acts often go on for days.[34] Throughout the *Mezzogiorno*, especially, a number of *feste* have developed into flamboyant vehicles for paying homage to the saints. In Viterbo (Province of Lazio, not too far from Rome), for example, 62 men carry a large, tower-like structure through the streets in honor of Santa Rosa, while in Nola (Province of Avellino, a short distance from Naples), crews of 100 men each shoulder eight towers and a boat across the town, for several days and nights, in a tribute to San Paolino that has been reproduced every year since 434 A.D.

In an Easter Procession that has been reenacted for over 400 years,[35] the townsmen of Trapani carry 19 holy statues, called *i misteri* (the mysteries) and one of the Madonna on a 24-hour journey that begins at 3:00 p.m. on Good Friday. Black-clad women follow their beloved Mother of Sorrows solemnly, for they are all in mourning and in search of her Son. A general disposition of sympathy and grief for the Madonna's and all mothers' losses builds, as the procession follows an intricate route throughout Old and New Trapani. The faithful pin notes of condolence or supplication to the statue's robe, until the cortege comes full circle to the church. Finally, when the statues are replaced in the sanctuary, the participants weep unashamedly in a mass catharsis.

In Sciacca, Sicily another tribute to the Madonna has been replayed for hundreds of years.[36] Here, the men carry a two-ton marble statue of the Madonna del Soccorso to signify their love and devotion. This ceremony is both an offering of Thanksgiving and an appeal for the Madonna's continued favor and protection. To intensify their display of sincerity and exhibit their willingness to do penance, the men of Sciacca walk barefoot as they carry the statue throughout this fishing town. At certain points, they are compelled to run synchronously uphill to maintain momentum, causing lacerations of the shoulders and feet. For the participants, however, their exertion and the resulting injuries, attest to the depth of their dedication.

Indeed, much of the pageantry associated with contemporary Italian feasts features an interrelationship between physical pain and emotional devotion. Deliberately choreographed rigors, such as complicated march cadences, short clipped steps, exaggerated swaying, and waltz-like movements are offered as ritualistic expressions of penance, thanksgiving, or consecration. *I portatori,* those who carry massive statues or monuments to Patron Saints and the Madonna for prolonged periods, endure discomfort as a symbol of their abiding faith. Moreover, they look forward to these rites, passing on their enthusiasm through the generations. Therefore, beyond the religious implications, these acts of shared perseverance reinforce familial and communal bonds, as they reaffirm a collective commitment to upholding tradition.

Italian-American Religious Practices

The majority of Italians who arrived in America during mass migration, beginning in the 1880s, were *contadini* (the peasants) from the *Mezzogiorno* (Southern Italy), who clung to many of the codes and values that had sustained them in the old country. Among the old ways which arrived with the new Americans was their combined religio-folkloric belief system. "Their folk religion was a syncretic melding of ancient pagan beliefs, magical practices, and Christian liturgy."[37] In a strange and often incomprehensible new world, Italian immigrants turned to those security and defense mechanisms that had served them so well in their homeland or *paese.* When they encountered an Irish-American-dominated Catholic Church, which did not, or would not, understand their unique religious practices, the newcomers were all the more convinced that the best way to survive was to hold onto the convoluted belief structure that had protected them against misfortune in Italy.

Vecoli[38] and others have commented on the Catholic Church's so-called "Italian Problem." In part, the clash of cultures resulted from an innate anti-clericalism which the Italian immigrants transposed to the United States. However, the discord was exacerbated by priests who saw the Italians' refusal to follow purely doctrinal components of the Church as a basic flaw in the religiosity of these newcomers. Members of the Italian immigrant generation, who infused their Catholicism with pagan superstition, were, therefore, seen as "outsiders" to the faith, because much of their religious belief tied into spells, potions, witches, amulets, and the evil eye. "The Italians brought with them to America a religion which did not so much embrace Catholic Christianity as encompass it. Surrounding a core of Catholicism was a folklore of the ages . . ."[39]

Things started to look up, when national parishes began to flourish from the 1900s onward. By the end of World War II, national (or ethnic) parishes had mushroomed in number to between 500 and 600 throughout the country. These national parishes allowed Italian priests to administer the socioreligious needs of Italian-Americans, easing the mandate that immigrants follow the formal dictates set by their Irish coreligionists. "In short, particularly for the first generation immigrants, the national parish provided the opportunity to practice their peculiar religion much as always they had in Italy." [40] Renewed freedom to synthesize Catholicism, magic, superstition, and folklore afforded the newcomers a much needed sense of validation. In fact, the ethnic parish was the venue where, "the immigrants most successfully transplanted their religion, that aspect of their old way of life which had been institutionally sustained in the old country." [41]

The advent of national parishes rekindled another Italian socio-religious paradigm: the spirit of *campanilismo* (defining one's community boundaries as within the sound of the village church bell). Beyond enrichment of their religious experience in America, the ethnic parish provided Italian immigrants with a social and community structure— and in many cases, a source of identity. Those living in urban Catholic America came to define themselves, and delineate their neighborhoods, in terms of parish service boundaries. Coincidentally, the same *campanilismo* that facilitated their adjustment to new surroundings, also caused transplanted Italians to maintain strong emotional bonds to their distant *paese,* as village bells went on resonating in nostalgic minds and hearts. Accordingly, ethnic parish members were like-minded when it came to continuing their traditions of honoring Patron Saints and the Madonna; and now, the parishioners had the support of Italian and Italian-American priests, who understood and encouraged devotion to the saints and feast day celebrations

An outgrowth of this cooperative effort to preserve tradition was the creation of societies—which grew proportionately, in number and membership, with increased migration—named after Patron Saints of Italian villages. Some of these societies were connected with ethnic parishes, while others operated outside the auspices of the Church, but both orders were largely responsible for sustaining the cult of the saints and the Mary cult in the new world. One of the societies' major charges was producing (or importing) exact replicas of statues, structures and icons used to honor Patron

Saints and the Madonna back in Italy. Even today, one can often "determine the regional composition of an Italian parish by the saints and Madonnas ... venerated there ... At times ... a half-dozen images of different Madonnas about the altar, each, the object of devotion of a particular group of *paesani.* " [42] Ultimately, the societies became the primary vehicles for the continued celebration of saints' feast days in America. The feasts, neighborhood parishes, and the societies were, in turn, kept alive by descendants of the southern Italian immigrants, and thus, ties to family, to community, and to Italy remained strong through the generations.

Vatican II and the Veneration of the Saints

In 1972, when the Vatican Council dictated removal of saint statuary from the main altars of churches, Italian-Americans were not pleased. As these parishioners saw it, the dictate was an indication that the Catholic Church was becoming "Protestantized." In response, many churches with strong Italian-American presence designated certain areas, or even created separate sanctuaries, in which the statues could remain the objects of candle-lit intentions and direct prayer. In the Shrine Church of St. Anthony, in New York City's Greenwich Village (once a largely Italian-American neighborhood), for example, saints' statues line the side aisles of the church, fronted by kneelers and banks of votive candles.

Even prior to Vatican II, the predominantly Italian-American parish of the Shrine Church of Our Lady of Mount Carmel in Williamsburg, Brooklyn, featured a spacious chapel containing no less than 35 statues of saints and Madonnas who hold special meaning for parish members. Among those represented are Our Lady of Fatima, St. Ann, San Donato, San Sebastian, St. Joseph, St. Theresa, Mother Cabrini (America's first saint), and San Cono. The chapel is continuously filled (before, during, and after masses) with prayerful parishioners and visitors, who feel this shrine area for the saints counterbalances the comparatively bare altar. In many such chapels across the country, devotees come to meditate, to touch the hand or foot of a statue with reverence, to light candles, and feel connected to the saints that they continue to revere, honor, and respect.

Private Devotions

Beyond the church setting, Italian-Americans also carry their devotion to the saints over into the home, invoking protection for their families and living space. One scholar[43] believes that the display of religious objects, figures, pictures and reproductions of famous religious paintings serves to emphasize the sacredness of the *domus*. As Vecoli observes:

> Within their homes, the immigrants (and their descendants) also clung tenaciously to their sacred, ancestral traditions. Religious images adorned the walls; votive lamps burned before shrines to the saints and Madonnas. Saints' days were observed with special foods and prayers and few homes lacked a *presepio* (manger scene) at Christmas.[44]

On this subject, in an excellent study and analysis of working-class and upper-middle-class Catholics in urban and suburban communities, Halle[45] uncovered major differences between these groups in their distinctive settings. As representative working-class urban and suburban settings, Halle studied Greenpoint, Brooklyn and Medford, Long Island respectively. Halle's designated upper middle-class urban and suburban models were New York City's Manhattan Borough, and Manhasset, Long Island respectively. Halle found that working-class Catholics (including Italian-Americans) in Greenpoint and Medford were more likely to display religious images than those living in Manhattan and Manhasset. Thus, urban or suburban settings notwithstanding, the study indicates that religious iconography holds more significance to working-class Italian-American Catholics than those of the upper middle-class.

According to Halle, in the Greenpoint and Medford communities, not only were there more religious images to be found, but they tended to on display more prominently and publicly:

> Every Greenpoint home with Catholic iconography has at least one item in a public area—living room, dining room, hall, or garden—as do 68% of the Medford houses with Catholic iconography. In Manhasset, by contrast, only 23% of the households with Catholic religious items displayed any publicly; religious items here are usually confined to the private areas, mostly the bedrooms.[46]

The lack of public displays in upper middle-class Catholic communities reportedly lay in the residents' belief that such actions would be an affront to non-Catholic neighbors and a sign of lower-class, ethnicity. In contrast, working-class Greenpoint and Medford Catholics did not consider the public display of religious statues, paintings, votive candles, and shrines in the home or exterior mini-grottos socially inappropriate or unacceptable. Rather, they considered them to be symbols of their love and devotion to particular saints or the Madonna—testimonies to their faith.

Even taking into account the crucial differences between urban and suburban working and upper-middle-class Catholics (including the numbers of Italian-Americans living in the study areas), it is important to note that the custom of private devotions to saints in the home lives on. In Goffman's[47] terms, the practice is sustained, either "front stage" or "back-stage," decades after it was transposed to this country by the immigrants.

The Evil Eye

A throwback to pre-Christian beliefs in witchcraft and sorcery was the southern Italian notion that everyday people have the power to bring misfortune down on one another through the means of a certain look. In the minds of the peasants, a fearful stranger or envious neighbor could, even unwittingly, cast "the evil eye" on an unprepared victim, causing the subject to experience bad luck, disfigurement, or bodily harm. In reference to the Italian immigrants arriving in America, Vecoli[48] adds, "Nor had the ocean crossing diminished their dread of *malocchio* (the evil eye). Amulets were worn and rituals performed to ward off the evil spirits."

Reflecting their immigrant roots (and incidentally, current fashion trends), today's Italian-Americans still wear various amulets and good-luck charms conspicuously, with renewed ethnic pride. First and second-generation Italian-Americans, however, made more prevalent and focused use of such protective items, as Gambino tells us:

> My fellows at P.S. 142 had a typical assortment of pagan and Christian amulets hanging side by side or in little sacks from necklaces worn under their clothing or attached to their undershirts with safety pins. In addition to those already mentioned, I saw pictures of saints, little fish (the ancient Christian symbol for Christ), and tiny scissors and daggers to cut or impale powers of evil . . . In the generation preceding mine some Italian-American children were sent to school wearing teeth-like cloves of garlic under their garments.[49]

Gambino [50] goes on to share his grandmother's need to elicit as much protection from the evil eye as was humanly possible. "The red horns over her door were supplemented by an array of pictures and statues of Madonnas and saints liberally distributed throughout her home. In fact each room had what was in effect a little shrine set up around a favorite picture which was lit by religious candles and adorned with the dried palms from masses of the last several Easters."

While many of the past symbols have been discarded, the *corno* (a twisted horn)—cast in materials ranging from red plastic to 24-karat gold—is still a popular image among Italian-Americans. Although there are some who might eschew the *corno* in favor of the scapular, the cross, or the religious medal, much like their overly cautious forebears, it is neither unusual nor unacceptable for contemporary Italian-Americans to wear a combination of secular and religious items on their persons.

The Italian-American Feste

By far, the most dynamic manifestation of ongoing Italian-American devotion to the saints is the feast. Originally designed to replicate *feste* commemorated in Italy, these annual events continue to take place tenaciously, despite the erosive nature of assimilation and the dissolution of *campanilismo* in many Italian-American communities. Today's feasts have been modified for more broad-based appeal, reaching beyond neighborhood participation, to include and involve general Italian-American attendance and often attracting members of other ethnic groups.[51] Many of these celebrations now honor well-known saints who hold significance for all Italian-Americans rather than locale-specific Patron Saints. "As the multiple identities of the hundreds of groups of *paesani* have merged into a general Italian-American identity, so too the devotions to the multitude of local patrons have merged into the cult of a few favored saints and Madonnas." [52] Some of these generalized feasts, especially in suburban settings, have diminished, or severed completely, their connection to the Catholic Church, and in the process, have reinvented and revitalized a cult of the saints in suburban Italian-American enclaves.

While the immigrant generation dealt with a chilly reception from the American Catholic Church at-large, participation in traditional feasts honoring Patron Saints and the Madonna not only met their religious needs, but helped forge a unique Italian-American identity for the newcomers. Each feast celebration was a high-energy, shared affirmation of religious devotion and community bonds and ethnic pride. "The *festa* was the most authentic expression of South Italian culture transplanted to the New World. No effort or expense was spared . . . to recreate the feast in every detail." [53] To this day, Italian-American feast organizers and participants do their utmost to remain true to the celebratory customs introduced to this country by their immigrant forebears, who were attempting to capture the essence and recreate the substance of the Old World *festas*. Installing lighted arches that span the street in front of the church or shrine, for example, is one such long-standing *festa* tradition. These feasts, with the depth of planning and scope of preparation they entailed, were the much-anticipated high points of peoples' parish, neighborhood, and personal calendars. Indeed, the religious life and social interaction of Italian-American communities climaxed annually at feast celebrations.

Throughout the feast days and nights, "the streets of the Italian quarter took on the aspect of a village fair: streets and houses were decorated with banners, flags, and lanterns, while streets were lined with shrines and booths. Delicacies to titillate the Southern Italian palate were dispensed from sidewalk stands, as were religious objects and amulets . . . Everything was contrived to create the illusion of being once more in the Old Country."[54] Processions throughout the neighborhood, attendance at daily novenas and masses, as well as public displays of personal sacrifice marked the religious component of the feast. Just as in the old country, street bands accompanied the processions, and devotees pinned money to the vestments of the saint statues, while "women fingering rosary beads or carrying candles marched barefoot in the parade behind the politicians, businessmen, and musicians." [55]. As if to highlight the religious and secular intermingling of the occasion, "the procession paraded the streets of Little Italy, which were decked out with sidewalk altars, food stands, [and] vendors of sacred and profane objects." [56] Year after year, these celebrations pulled together the disparate elements of Italian-American life, offering a sensational mixture of sights, sounds, aromas, flavors, and a remarkable spirituality which came to enrich the American experience.

Today, with certain exemptions, most Italian-American feasts are celebrated during the week closest to the saint's feast day on the Catholic calendar. They are held either on church grounds or at a large community area (such as a park, a parking lot, or a number of closed-off streets). Some booths sell the typical feast foods, including *calzoni*, sausage-and-pepper heroes, rice balls, sweet breads, and *zeppole*, while others peddle trinkets and amulets, and still others offer games of chance. There is usually an area set off with a stage on which traditional entertainment fare is presented, including singers vocalizing classic Italian standbys and comics performing humorous bits and skits that address Italian-American issues and in-jokes. Changing times and the quest for a more profitable, general audience appeal are evidenced by the presence of multi-ethnic food vendors, clothing and jewelry stands, non-Italian pop entertainers and rock groups. With these concessions, Italian-Americans are able to continue celebrating their identity and honoring their saints, in deference to the United States' melting-pot society in which they enjoy a unique niche.

A number of present-day feasts still honor specific Patron Saints or Madonnas and adhere to ages-old traditions. For example, in Jessup, Pennsylvania the Italian-American population participates in a conjoined celebration of the feast days of San Ubaldo (Patron Saint of Gubbio), Saint George, and Saint Anthony in a spectacular ritual, which includes a race between teams representing the three saints. "On Saturday evening, each team lifts a quarter-ton platform bearing the statue of its saint onto their shoulders for a two-mile run through the city streets . . . The race reaches its conclusion at the community athletic field where the teams finish their run with three laps around the track." [57] Helping to keep this and other such handed-down observances alive and intact are contemporary Italian-Americans who return regularly (both physically and emotionally) to the "old neighborhood" parishes and who have rediscovered their *Italianità.*

An extraordinary illustration of enduring tradition (with which the author is intimately involved) is the *Giglio* Feast honoring San Paolino and the Madonna del Carmine, held in the Williamsburg neighborhood of Brooklyn, New York. Originally introduced to this community by immigrants from Nola, the feast is reproduced annually at the Shrine Church of Our Lady of Mt. Carmel and is highlighted by the "dancing" of a sixty-five-foot, four-ton tower. This structure called a *giglio* (lily) is a symbol of the story of San Paolino, who offered himself into slavery in place of a widow's only son, and who, after regaining his freedom, was met by rejoicing town folks tossing lilies into the harbor to welcome his returning ship. Decorating the steel-framed *giglio* tower are papier-mâché angels, saints, flowers, and a map of Italy. On top is a statue of San Paolino. Beneath, 112 men, known as lifters, are dedicated to the carrying, or "dancing," of the *giglio,* while a second crew of lifters does the same, bearing a huge boat representative of the vessel which brought San Paolino home to Nola in 434 A.D.

The focal points of feast activities are *Giglio* Sunday and its reprise, Old Timers' Day.[58] After a jubilant high mass, celebrators spill out into the streets, and the dancing of the *Giglio* and boat commences. After the pastor blesses the structure and the lifters, and offers the invocation to Our Lady of Mt. Carmel and San Paolino, the men take their places under 28 support poles. They begin on bent knees to position their shoulders, then stand simultaneously to elevate the *giglio* in what is called a "lift." Responding to the commands of their *capos* (leaders) throughout the day, the structure is moved from 20 to 40 yards at a time, during two to four-minute lifts. The pageantry reaches its dramatic apex when the *giglio* and boat meet in front of the church and, "the front ranks of each structure clasp hands in the symbolic re-enactment of the historic return of San Paolino to Nola."[59]

For 111 years, this feast has drawn out peoples' devotion and dedication for various reasons. For some participants, it is a way to honor the Patron Saint and the Madonna through penance; for others, the sacrifice of the lift is offered in behalf of deceased relatives; while others see their involvement as a link to their roots in Italy and a tribute to their Italian-American way of life. Whatever their motivations, the organizers, participants, and spectators resolutely foster the continuance of Old World-style religious devotion in this New World ethnic community. Indeed, the Italian-Americans of Williamsburg take pride in the fact that they honor San Paolino and the Madonna del Carmine in very much the same manner their *paesani* (past and present) in Nola have; and as their forebears prescribed in the late 1880s. In fact, the feast rituals practiced in Williamsburg uphold earlier forms of the tradition more so than the ongoing *festa* in Nola, which has been modernized and commercialized in many respects. More importantly, however, as is easily read on the faces of exuberant participants, ranging from toddlers to elders, neither version of the celebration show any signs of fading in interest or popularity among current and upcoming generations.

The Immigrant Influence Through the Generations

In the years following mass migration, while deeply immersed in the assimilation process, the tradition-oriented, second generation nevertheless upheld certain of their forebears' religious convictions. Among them, the element of sacrifice, as a demonstration of *rispetto* (respect), remained a crucial component of their devotions. For Italian-Americans, displays of respect, through sacrificial acts, for saints and the Madonna—just as for one's spouse, family members, and friends—means you love them. As Orsi [60] puts it, it "was as though people were saying to her: this is what we are willing to do for you. They offered their sacrifices as gestures of grati-tude for the Madonna's care and as an expression of a deep and abiding faith . . . " Walking barefoot in a procession, for example, as an act of sacri-fice, penance or humiliation was not uncommon. A dramatic illustration, which continued into the 1970s, was the annual pilgrimage of women who had moved from New York City's Italian Harlem to the outer boroughs. Every year, they could be seen walking barefooted across the Triborough Bridge to attend the feast of Our Lady of Mount Carmel at their former church on East 115th Street. Reports of more extreme sacrificial displays also exist from earlier eras; of devotees crawling on their bellies (dragging their tongues along the floor, in some cases) down church aisles.

The third and subsequent generations of Italian-Americans tended to be more selective about which practices they chose to sustain. One surviv-ing tradition is the Name Day (celebrated in households on the feast day of the saint after whom an Italian-American family member is named). Chil-dren learn the stories of their namesakes and about the miracles associated with their patrons, still believing in personal protectors who will hear and act upon special intentions. In ethnic neighborhoods, Name Day greeting cards (in English or Italian) can be purchased for celebrants. Another per-petuated devotion, and time-honored tradition, is the St. Joseph's Altar, celebrated in New Orleans and other large cities with sizable Sicilian-American populations. St. Joseph Day parades, which combine festive pageantry with sedate processions, are held annually. Throughout the streets the men carry St. Joseph's statue, surrounded by mountains of

baked goods, which will ultimately be distributed among charitable organizations. [61] In smaller Italian-American communities, St. Joseph "tables" are
set in central locations to honor the saint and to make collected food available for the poor.

It is widely held that the general population in both the Old and New
Worlds has experienced a gradual decline in devotion to the saints, because
specific powers once attributed to them has been superseded by mod-
ern-day medicine and technology. While earlier in this century, Italians and
Italian-Americans often turned to specialized saints to assist in the healing
of the sick, the current generation is more likely to call on the skills and
expertise of the medical profession.[62] However, there are still many who,
in varying degrees—like their pragmatic ancestors—will not discount any
available option. Their collective consciousness sees no harm in taking the
extra precaution of praying to the saints to help them or their loved ones
avoid or overcome physical injury or malady. It is a simple matter of additional insurance to ask that a saint guide the hand of a surgeon through a
successful operation, bring about a complete recovery, or arrest whatever
illness may have befallen an individual.

In contrast, devotion by Italian-Americans to the Madonna appears to
be as strong as ever among the third and fourth generations. In East Harlem,
New York, a distinct Mariology arose in the 1950s and 1960s, in which,
"the women in the community believed that Mary had suffered the pains of
childbirth, that she had menstruated, and that she worried constantly about
her child. They felt that she could understand and help them because she
had their most private experiences . . . " [63] Throughout Italian-American
parishes today, formal and cult adoration of the Madonna continues to
flourish. For these Italian-Americans the honoring of the specific Madonna
(e.g., Our Lady of Mt. Carmel, Our Lady Assumed into Heaven, or the
Immaculate Conception), remains a relevant remnant of the faith handed
down by the immigrants.

Even as they sought a new way of life in the United States, many of
the immigrants' Old-World ideas were transposed and maintained, including folk-religious beliefs drawn from the southern Italian experience. While
saint and Madonna worship have innumerable variations of expression
around the world, what is significant here is that, into the present era,
Italian-American Catholics continue to keep alive, and find relevant, so

many of the devotional practices put forth by their immigrant forebears. The actions and attitudes of contemporary Italian Americans attest to the strength of a powerful value system which has been passed down through the generations in the United States and, before that, in Italy. Beyond the religious ramifications, the principles and activities surrounding the core of devotion to the saints and the Madonna have been fundamental avenues for preserving the traditions that delineate and define Italian-Americana.

SALVATORE PRIMEGGIA

[1] Numa Denis Fustel de Coulanges, *The Ancient City*, (Garden City, New York: Doubleday and Company, Inc., 1956), 158.

[2] Richard Gambino, *Blood of My Blood: The Dilemma of The Italian Americans*, (Garden City, New York: Doubleday and Company, Inc. 1974), 196.

[3] Gambino, 196.

[4] Meridth B. McGuire, *Religion: The Social Context*, (Belmont, California: Wadsworth Publishers, 1992), 105.

[5] Michael P. Carroll, *Madonnas That Maim: Popular Catholicism in Italy Since the Fifteenth Century*, (Baltimore: The Johns Hopkins University Press, 1992), 138-139.

[6] Carroll, 37.

[7] Rudolph J. Vecoli, "Cult and Occult in Italian-American Culture: The Persistence of a Religious Heritage," in *Immigrants and Religion in Urban America* edited by Randall M. Miller and Thomas D. Marzik (Philadelphia: Temple University Press, 1977), 28.

[8] Gambino, 197.

[9] Vecoli, 28.

[10] Carroll. 33.

[11] Carroll, 43

[12] Vecoli, 28.

[13] Denise Mangieri DiCarlo, *The History of The Italian Festa in New York City: 1880's To the Present*, Ph.D. Dissertation, New York University, New York City, 1990, 24.

[14] Carroll, 15-16.

[15] Charlotte Day Gower, *The Supernatural Patron in Sicilian Life*, Ph.D. Dissertation, University of Chicago, Chicago 1928.

[16] Carroll, 118.

[17] Donald Weinstein and Randolph Bell, *Saints and Society,* (Chicago: University of Chicago Press, 1982).

[18] Carroll, 33.

[19] Carroll, 35

[20] Weinstein and Bell, 142-143.

[21] Gambino. 208.

[22] Carroll, 122.

[23] Emilio Sereni, *Il capitalismo nella compagne (1860-1900),* (Torino: Giulio Einaudi, 1947/1968), 196.

[24] Carroll, 76.

[25] Phylis H. Williams, *Southern Italian Folkways in Europe and America,* (New York: Russell and Russell, 1938/1969), 138.

[26] Mary Lee Nolan and Sidney Nolan, *Christian Pilgrimages in Modern Western Europe,* (Chapel Hill: University of North Carolina Press, 1989) 352.

[27] Carroll, 82.

[28] Annabella Rossi, *Le feste de poveri,* (Bari: Editori Laterza, 1969), 167-168.

[29] Carroll, 83.

[30] Carol Field, *Celebrating Italy,* (New York: William Morrow, Company, Inc., 1990).

[31] Carroll, 27.

[32] Carroll, 52.

[33] Carroll, 54.

[34] Gambino, 207.

[35] Susan Caperna Lloyd, "Processione: A Sicilian Easter," (University of California Extension Center for Media and Individual Learning, Berkeley, California, 1989).

[36] Beth Harrington, Producer and Director, "The Moveable Feast," (University of California Extension Center for Media and Individual Learning, Berkeley, California, 1992).

[37] Vecoli, 26.

[38] Rudolph J. Vecoli (b), "Prelates and Peasants: Italian Immigrants and The Catholic Church," *Journal of Social History,* (1969) volume 2, no.3, 217-268.

[39] Paul W. McBride, *The Solitary Christians: Italian Americans and Their Church,* (Great Britain: Gordon and Breach Science Publishers Ltd., 1981), 339.

[40] McBride, 345.

[41] Silvano M. Tomasi, "The Ethnic Church and the Integration of Italian Immigrants in The United States," in *The Italian Experience in The United States,* edited by Silvano Tomasi and Madeline H. Engel (New York: Center for Migration Studies, Inc., 1977), 25-47.

[42] McBride, 30.

[43] Robert Orsi, *The Madonna of 115th Street: Faith and Community in Italian Harlem, 1880-1950,* (New Haven: Yale University Press, 1985), 105.

[44] Vecoli (b), 233.

[45] David Halle, *Inside Culture: Art and Class in The American Home,* (Chicago:

University of Chicago Press, 1993), 173.

[46] Halle, 179.

[47] Erving Goffman, *The Presentation of Self in Everyday Life*, (Garden City, New York: Doubleday Company, Inc., 1959).

[48] Vecoli (b), 233.

[49] Gambino, 200.

[50] Gambino, 201.

[51] Frances M. Malpezzi and William M. Clements, *Italian American Folklore*, (Little Rock, Arkansas: August House Publishers, Inc., 1992), 100.

[52] Vecoli, 39.

[53] Vecoli (b), 232.

[54] Vecoli (b), 232.

[55] DiCarlo, 3.

[56] Vecoli, 31.

[57] Malpezzi and Clements, 105.

[58] Salvatore Primeggia and Joseph A. Varacalli, "The Sacred and The Profane Among Italian-American Catholics: The Giglio Feast," *International Journal of Politics, Culture and Society,* (1996) volume 9, no. 3; 423-449.

[59] Primeggia and Varacalli, 428.

[60] Orsi, 223-224.

[61] Malpezzi and Clements, 99.

[62] Halle, 189.

[63] Orsi, 227.

CHAPTER 5

SAINTS OVER SACRAMENTS?:
ITALIAN AND ITALIAN-AMERICAN
SPIRITUAL TRADITIONS

Saints play a central role in Catholic teaching. For the faithful, they serve as models of holiness and as intercessors with Christ.[1] Among the roughly 10,000 canonized saints there are Roman martyrs, desert fathers, holy virgins, pious popes and even devout boys and girls.[2] Countries and many towns have their special patrons as do most professions and trades. And there are saints that the laity have traditionally turned to for help in matters small and large: to find lost objects, Saint Anthony of Padua; for healing of throat ailments, St. Blaise; for troubled pregnancies, St. Gerard Majella; and for seemingly hopeless causes, St. Jude the Apostle.

No people in America have outdone the Italians in expressing devotion and love for the saints. In Italian neighborhoods elaborate celebrations known as *festas* would be held each year to honor the Virgin Mary or a favorite saint. Over the course of several days, special Masses would be offered, processions would take place and fireworks would be set off. Everyone in the neighborhood would surely take part in the *festa.*

The Italian-Americans' attachment to saints and *festas* was troubling to most Catholic leaders in America. In the 1880s, when large numbers of southern Italians began arriving in the United States, assimilation-minded Catholic prelates—most of whom were Irish—decried the Italians' rituals as pagan and superstitious. For decades, relations between the Irish-dominated clergy and the Italian laity were often tense. Even today, long after the conflict ended, scholars continue to argue about the merits of the "Irish" and "Italian" positions on saints and *festas.*[3]

The Saints in History

As Kenneth Woodward has noted, "The lives of the saints constitute an important—some theologians would say the most important—medium for transmitting the Christian faith.[4] The heroism of the martyrs, the wisdom of the doctors, the purity of the virgins and the faith of the confessors can inspire and instruct the laity. The example of the saints often resonates more profoundly with believers than catechisms or other Church documents.

At the same time, Church leaders have from the beginning recognized dangers associated with the veneration of saints. As early as the second century, questions were raised about whether the faithful might not confuse the saints with Christ. Some Church Fathers worried that the laity were becoming obsessed with obtaining relics from saints and making frequent trips to their tombs. They feared that believers were not simply venerating the saints but were offering them the worship that the Church believes is due to Christ alone.[5]

In the middle ages, Catholic leaders generally defended the veneration of the saints, seeing it as an edifying practice. Saints' feast days were recognized on the church calendar and more than three dozen saints' names were regularly recited in the Roman Canon of the Mass. Along with the Virgin Mary, the Roman Canon honors the apostles, several popes and about twenty Roman martyrs.[6] In 609 Pope Boniface IV re-christened the Pantheon—Rome's great pagan temple—as a church of the Virgin Mary and all saints. At the Second Council of Nicaea in 787, bishops rejected the arguments of iconoclasts in the Byzantine Empire who had condemned the veneration of images and prayer to the saints. The bishops declared that icons of Jesus, Mary and the saints were worthy of veneration (dulia) but not worship (latria). They also decreed that every altar must have a stone inside it containing saints' relics.[7]

Controversy over the saints flared up again during the sixteenth century. Martin Luther, who as a young man had been deeply devoted to the saints,[8] from 1517 on viewed their veneration as one of the Catholic Church's many false teachings. He had concluded that people would be saved by faith and faith alone; sinners could not rely on their good works to justify themselves before God. Nor could they count on the intercession of the saints for assistance.

When the Council of Trent convened in 1545, the bishops took up all of the issues Luther and other Protestant leaders had raised, including the question of saints. On doctrinal matters, the bishops firmly reasserted Catholic teaching, but on practical subjects they were willing to admit that abuses were widespread and needed to be eradicated.[9] With the saints, the

Council fathers defended their invocation, but then added that all superstitious practices involving the Virgin Mary and the saints must cease.[10]

The Council of Trent thus made clear Catholic teaching on the saints. Praying to the saints and venerating their images and relics were commendable activities but were not to supplant the worship of Christ. And while it was acceptable to seek help and healing through saints' intercessions, the laity were not to engage in any magical practices involving the saints.

St. Francis de Sales, the Counter Reformation bishop and spiritual guide, took this view in *The Introduction to the Devout Life*:

> Let us join our hearts to these heavenly spirits and blessed souls. Just as young nightingales learn to sing in company with the old, so also by our holy associations with the saints let us learn the best way to pray and sing God's praise.[11]

In this and other passages, St. Francis stressed that the saints are subordinate to God and are to be seen principally as role models rather than as wonder workers.

While Trent's teachings were unmistakable, Catholic practices in the decades following did not necessarily reflect the decrees of the Council. In some states Trent's reforms were never implemented. Although close to Rome, southern Italy is one part of the world where "Trent never arrived."[12]

Catholicism in Naples and Sicily

When Italian immigrants started reaching America's shores in the 1880s, Church leaders were shocked to learn that hardly any of them were regular churchgoers. Few seemed interested in providing financial support for their parishes or in sending their children to parochial schools. Bishops were soon openly commiserating about their "Italian problem."

The problem was surely rooted in the immigrants' homeland. But who was to blame for their lack of knowledge of the faith? Why were so many people steeped in pagan practices—like using horns to ward off the "evil eye?"[13]

A popular explanation is one that was offered by Rudolph Vecoli, a left-leaning historian, in 1968. In an article published in the *Journal of Social History*, Vecoli claimed that southern Italians were deeply anticlerical and thus had little interest in attending Masses and other priest-run services. Instead, the peasantry expressed its spirituality on its own terms.[14]

Vecoli blamed the clergy for the anticlericalism that allegedly pervaded the South. He claimed that the priests allied themselves with the landowning class and showed little sympathy for poor tenant farmers. Other writers have made a related claim: the clergy shared the views of the reactionary landlords and did all that it could to thwart the nationalist aspirations of the Italian people.[15] As the *Risorgimento*—the campaign for Italian unification—gained momentum in the 1840s and 1850s, Church leaders from Pope Pius IX on down condemned the movement.

With the bishops and priests holding such benighted views, it was no wonder that the people of Naples and Sicily would become alienated from the institutional Church. These claims seem reasonable and have been accepted by many scholars.[16] They are in fact largely inaccurate, however. If anything, southern Italians were clericalists not anticlericals. When King Ferdinand IV of the Two Sicilies was deposed in 1799 by radical republicans sympathetic to the French Revolution, the people of Naples rushed to join Cardinal Fabrizio Ruffo's Army of the Holy Faith which ousted the revolutionaries and restored the king.[17]

In the nineteenth century, three men from northern Italy—Giuseppe Mazzini, Giuseppe Garibaldi and Camillo Cavour—played key roles in the *Risorgimento*. Mazzini was the political visionary, Garibaldi was the soldier and Cavour was the shrewd diplomat. By 1870, the nationalists had completed their quest: the King of Piedmont, Victor Emmanuel II, had become King of Italy.[18] In that year, the King entered Rome and took possession of the Pope's residence, while Pius IX retreated across the Tiber and declared himself a "prisoner of the Vatican."[19]

Often overlooked in all the pious accounts of the *Risorgimento* is that Italian unification was essentially a bid by northern Italians for control over the rest of Italy. In general, southern Italians were indifferent at best to the campaigns launched by Cavour and Garibaldi. Indeed, in the 1860s when Victor Emmanuel had wrested control of southern Italy from the Bourbon king, the people rose up again in defense of the Bourbons.[20] Thus to suggest that southern Italians were angry at the Pope and other Church leaders for not backing unification is simply untrue.

To determine the reasons for southern Italians' low level of church attendance and syncretic belief system, one must look elsewhere. Patrick Carroll, a religious historian, links their folk Catholicism to the Church's inability to implement Trent's teachings there. If Trent's decrees had taken effect in Naples and Sicily, Carroll thinks that their beliefs and practices would have been very different.

Perhaps the most significant reform decrees of the Council were that bishops were required to reside in their dioceses and that candidates for the priesthood had to be formally trained in seminaries.[21] In southern Italy even the most zealous of bishops had to contend with formidable obstacles. Aside from the city of Naples, most of the south was impoverished and disease-ridden. For most bishops the idea of building seminaries was simply out of the question. There were no funds available. Indeed, for many bishops even their basic responsibility of visiting all of their parishes on a regular basis was not always feasible given the rough terrain.[22]

Carroll also contends that a unique parish structure existed in the rural south which worked against Tridentine reforms. Most churches were *chiese ricettizie*. Literally translated as "received churches," they were jointly run by a group of priests who all had been born in that community. To be received as a parish priest, a man had to be from the village. Priests associated with these churches lived with their parents or siblings—or in some cases their wives—and did not wear any distinctive clerical dress. This system was deeply rooted in southern Italy. Even in the late 1700s—more than two centuries after Trent—most parishes and some cathedrals were set up this way.[23]

Carroll presents a very different portrait of southern Italian religious life than Vecoli. He does not depict the peasants as angry Socialist anti-clericals. Instead he argues that there was little to differentiate the priests from the peasants. Priests dressed like the peasants, lived with them and sometimes engaged in farming with them. Since they were not seminary trained, priests had little more education than anyone else in the community. Consequently, they were not in a position to condemn age-old practices or to promote orthodox beliefs among their parishioners.

Coming to America

Starting around 1880, southern Italians—most of them male—began to set off for the New World. A series of crop failures combined with heavy taxes imposed by the northern-oriented government in Rome forced them out. When arriving in America, the immigrants were not welcomed by anyone. Most were unskilled, illiterate and unable to speak English. Sadly, some unscrupulous Italians who had arrived earlier in America often greeted the newcomers at the docks and promised to find them jobs and housing. These *padrones* usually took advantage of their compatriots by demanding that they be paid a large percentage of their wages in return for their help.[24]

The immigrants were not exactly embraced by Catholic Church leaders in America, either. At this time, the Church was dominated by Irish bishops, who were for the most part Americanists. These churchmen were enamored with all things American and were determined to prove that Catholics could assimilate into America's democratic and Protestant-dominated culture. The last thing these prelates wanted was an influx of Sicilians and Neapolitans and other Italians who were unable to speak English.

By the early 1880s, the Archbishop of New York, Michael Corrigan, had become very concerned about the spiritual welfare of the Italians under his jurisdiction. He calculated that out of the 50,000 Italians living in New York only twelve hundred were attending Mass on Sundays. Furthermore, of the twelve Italian priests in the archdiocese, ten were wanted in Italy on one charge or another.[25]

Corrigan and several other bishops wanted the "Italian problem" addressed by the American hierarchy at the Third Plenary Council which was to be held in Baltimore in 1884. Officials at the Vatican discouraged him and so the issue was not formally considered. Before the decade ended, though, the American bishops received word twice from Italian prelates. First in 1887, Bishop Giovanni Scalabrini of Piacenza recognized that more priests had to be provided to minister to the Italians in America. Consequently he set up a college to train priests for the mission in America. Soon Scalabrini priests were working in Italian parishes in the northeastern states.[26]

In 1888, Pope Leo XIII sent a letter to the American bishops pleading the cause of the Italian immigrants. The Pope acknowledged that there was "everywhere with this people a decay of Christian morality and a growth of wickedness."[27] He attributed these problems to the lack of Italian-speaking priests in America. He hoped that Bishop Scalabrini's college would help fill the void and he asked the bishops to encourage Italian-American families to send their sons to the school.

While the Pope was sanguine that the immigrants would become practicing Catholics if the right priests were provided to them, many American churchmen were not so optimistic. Father Bernard Lynch, writing in the *Catholic World*, an influential Americanist journal, claimed to be shocked by the Italians he had encountered in New York:

> The Italians in the jurisdiction of Transfiguration parish . . . come to America the worst off in religious equipment of, perhaps, any foreign Catholics whatever. There are thousands of Italians in this city who do not know the Apostles' Creed. Multitudes of men and women of this people do not know the elementary truths of religion, such as the Trinity, the Incarnation, and the Redemption . . . [T]he old Neapolitan States are daily sending to all quarters of this hemisphere grown men and women who are not well enough instructed to receive the sacraments . . .

> What, then, has been their religious life at home? Some peculiar kind of spiritual condition fed on the luxuries of religion without its substantials. "Devotions," pilgrimages, shrines, miraculous pictures and images, indulgences, they have been accustomed to, together with, in all too many cases, an almost total ignorance of the great truths which can alone make such aids of religion profitable. [28]

Lynch's only hope for the Italians lay with annex congregations where Italian-speaking priests would serve the Italians in a parish's basement chapel. He reasoned that since Italians would not contribute to their parishes, they couldn't be given their own churches. He claimed that the Italians didn't mind this arrangement: "The persons among them who object to the basement are not numerous, the Italians as a body are not humiliated by humiliation."[29]

The Festa

Most Church leaders, though, even the most ardent Americanists, recognized that the annex congregations were not a suitable solution to the "Italian problem." The Italians would have to be allowed to have their own parishes. As more and more national parishes were established, more and more *feste* were held.

Robert Orsi provides a detailed description of the *festa* associated with Our Lady of Mount Carmel Church in the East Harlem neighborhood of New York City. Near the church, "vendors of religious articles set up booths along the sidewalks . . . filled with wax replicas of internal human organs and with models of human limbs and heads. Someone who had been healed—or hoped to be healed—by the Madonna of headaches or arthritis would carry wax models of the afflicted limbs or head . . . in the big procession."[30]

Some of the marchers walked barefoot and all carried candles—some of which were enormous and might weigh as much as sixty pounds. When the crowd reached the church, "penitents crawled up the steps on their hands and knees, some of them dragging their tongues along the stone."[31] After a solemn high Mass, the crowd would again be on the streets marching in a parade with their statue of the Madonna aloft. The marchers were accompanied by bands and fireworks which lit up the sky. As the statue wound its way through the neighborhood, onlookers would pin money onto it in hopes that the Virgin Mary would answer their prayers or to thank her for prayers answered.

Orsi claims that the Irish clergy in New York from the Archbishops on down were never enthusiastic about the *festas*. One Italian priest from the neighborhood who Orsi interviewed said that the Irish "didn't accept it at all . . . We were always looked upon as though we were doing something wrong."[32] Still, Church authorities made no effort to clamp down on any of the festivities for fear of driving the Italians out of the Church.[33]

The America Debate

By the early part of the twentieth century the "Italian problem" which had seemed so pressing in the 1880s had eased somewhat. The Americanist churchmen who had been so intent on shedding all foreign appearances from the Church had been chastened. In 1899 Pope Leo XIII issued *Testem Benevolentiae*, an encyclical that criticized certain aspects of Americanism. The Americanists had been quarreling for the most part with German Catholics, who were determined to maintain their own national parishes and German language parochial schools.[34] Nevertheless, the Pope's intervention redounded to the benefit of the Italians. Resistance to Italian national parishes dissipated. By the end of World War I there were more than 500 Italian national parishes, many of which were staffed by Italian priests.[35]

Still an article published on Italians in *America* in 1914 created a furor and demonstrated that there remained serious disagreements in the Church on the subject. The trouble was sparked by an article written by an Italian Jesuit, Joseph Sorrentino. Father Sorrentino claimed that the majority of the

Italian people were "good, practical Catholics." As proof he cited not only Mass attendance but also their "love for the Madonna . . . a love that knows no bounds and makes them hope to obtain all heavenly favors through her."[36]

Sorrentino's claim provoked several responses from readers, including one from Herbert Hadley, who wondered how it could be that when all those pious Italians reach America, "99 per cent of them stay away from Mass."[37] And as for the Italian people's Marian devotion, Hadley was not at all impressed:

> Piety does not consist in processions or carrying lighted candles, in prostrations before a statue of the Madonna, in processions in honor of the patron saints of villages, but true piety consists in the daily fulfillment of the religious duties exacted of us by God Almighty and His Church.[38]

After Hadley's letter appeared, more readers spoke out on the subject. A number of correspondents agreed with Hadley, although hardly any of them were willing to sign their names. One anonymous priest in New York claimed that Italians loved to frequent movie theaters during the week and on Sundays, but couldn't seem to get themselves to church on Sundays. Another priest, who signed himself "An Old Pastor," said that his parish included 150 Italians but no more than three ever attended Mass. He concluded his letter on a doleful note: "My Italians never pass any church without saluting the statue of the Virgin in a niche, some even go so far as to cross themselves as they pass by, and this is the extent of their devotion here."[39]

Several clergymen, though, including an Irish-American bishop, rose to Sorrentino's defense. Edward Dunne, Bishop of Peoria, Illinois, had served for seven years as rector of what he claimed was the largest Italian church in the country. His parishioners

> religiously observed the feast of [their] patron saint and a great many more that are not holy days of obligation . . . My experience has been to see the church crowded on the feasts of SS. Peter and Paul, Nativity of St. John the Baptist, SS. Vitus, Roch, Lucy, Sebastian and all the feasts of the Blessed Virgin just the same as on Sunday. As to approaching the Sacraments, I have been kept hearing the confessions of Italian men until after two o'clock Holy Thursday morning.[40]

In a rejoinder to his critics, Sorrentino admitted that Catholic practice among Italians in America was not all that it should be. However, he traced the problem to the treatment that the immigrants had received from their coreligionists: "There are many widespread prejudices in the United States against our Italians, even among Catholics. Much of the evil that may be found among the Italians is due to indifference and neglect on the part of those who should assist them."[41] While he didn't explicitly single out the Irish, presumably they were the prejudiced Catholics to whom he was referring.

After two months of spirited exchanges, the editors of *America* declared that they would not print any more letters on the subject. In an effort to assuage both sides, the editors issued a statement urging all Catholics to show "a little zeal" to help "deepen the Faith that is in them."[42]

America Closes its Doors

After World War I ended, America entered into a strongly nativist phase. Foreigners, especially those from eastern and southern Europe, came to be viewed by much of the general public as dangerous radicals.[43] Starting in 1920, legislation was proposed in Congress to restrict immigration from these regions. In 1924 an Immigration Act was passed which established quotas specifying how many people from each country would be allowed to enter America. The limits were set at 2% of each group's population according to the 1890 census. Since Italians had only started to come to America in the 1880s and '90s, their quota was almost negligible. While as many as 200,000 had been immigrating annually in the years before World War I, from this point on, only 4,000 would be allowed in each year.[44]

With Italian immigration effectively shut off, Italian-American life gradually changed. The law surely increased the rate at which the second and third generations assimilated into American culture. For without the new waves of Italians coming over and settling in Italian neighborhoods in the cities, there was less to remind the children and grandchildren of immigrants about their Italian heritage.[45]

As Italian-Americans assimilated in the 1930s, '40s and '50s, their religious practices became less exotic as well. Many left their urban enclaves for the suburbs and joined non-Italian parishes. Many sent their children to parochial schools—institutions which their parents and grandparents had shown little interest in.[46] Some Italian-Americans even started marrying outside their group.[47] Of course, many still came back once a year to their old churches to celebrate the *festa*. But it too had changed; in many places it had been toned down and stripped of some of its pagan overtones. By the 1940s, Orsi notes that many of the participants in the Mount Carmel *festa* went to confession during the final day of the celebration.[48] That had not been a prominent feature of the *festa* in previous decades. In writing about the Giglio *festa* held each year in Brooklyn to honor St. Paolino,[49] Salvatore Primeggia and Joseph Varacalli make a similar point. They note that by the mid-1950s, the *festa* was clearly controlled by the clergy. Ultimate authority rested with the local pastor and no longer with the laymen from the feast committee.[50] The "Italian problem" seemed to be fast disappearing.

The Postconciliar Problem

Just as Italians were starting to become more regular churchgoers and more reliable supporters of parochial schools, the Church in America began to undergo an identity crisis. The Second Vatican Council (1962-1965) ushered in some liturgical and disciplinary changes and inspired some liberals to press for much more sweeping changes. By the end of the 1960s, the Catholic Church in America and some European countries was starting to unravel. Priests and nuns were resigning in droves, Mass attendance was dropping, Catholic grammar schools were closing and Catholic colleges were severing their ties with Rome and the bishops.[51]

While the Church's position in America began to stabilize in the 1980s, many of the problems that set in after 1965 have yet to be resolved. Mass attendance remains fairly low, and the number of priests, sisters and brothers continues to decline. Enrollment at Catholic colleges is up but just what should be taught at these institutions has not been settled by any means.

The difficulties that have beset the Church in America over the past three decades have affected Italian-Americans just as much as any other group. Their Mass attendance rates are down and their divorce rates are up just like those of the Irish, German and Polish Catholics. As Joseph Varacalli has noted, Italian-Americans have now become thoroughly Americanized—and thus secularized. Italian folk customs no longer have much appeal for them. Instead, they are being charmed by an American culture which is thoroughly materialistic and morally relativist. Indeed, because of the power of American culture, Varacalli fears that the present generation of Italian-Americans is in danger of "repaganizing."[52] Given the magnitude of the present challenge, Catholic Church leaders would be well pleased if Italian-Americans—and Irish-Americans and all other Catholics—would turn once more to the Madonna and the saints seeking their intercession and protection.

JOHN F. QUINN

---

[1] See *Catechism of the Catholic Church* (Washington, DC: Libreria Editrice Vaticana, 1994), 219; *Documents of Vatican II*, ed. Austin P. Flannery, OP (Grand Rapids, MI: Eerdmans, 1984), 411-412.

[2] Kenneth Woodward, *Making Saints: How the Catholic Church Determines Who Becomes A Saint, Who Doesn't and Why* (New York: Simon and Shuster, 1990), 17.

[3] Robert Orsi strongly defends the "Italian" position in his study, *The Madonna of 115th Street* (New Haven, CT: Yale University Press, 1985.)

[4] Woodward, 18.

[5] *Ibid.*, 58.

[6] See Johannes Emminghaus, *The Eucharist: Essence, Form, Celebration* (Collegeville, MN: Liturgical Press, 1978), 170-177.

[7] See Phillip Hughes, *The Church in Crisis: A History of the General Councils, 325-1870* (Garden City, NY: Hanover House, 1961), 145-163.

[8] During a severe thunderstorm in 1505, Luther made a vow to St. Ann that he would join a religious community if she spared his life. Two weeks later, he fulfilled his pledge and joined the Augustinian friars. See Lewis Spitz, *The Protestant Reformation, 1571-1559* (New York: Harper & Row, 1985), 61.

[9] Marvin R. O'Connell, *The Counter Reformation, 1559-1610* (New York: Harper & Row, 1974), 83-118.

[10] Michael P. Carroll, *Madonnas that Maim: Popular Catholicism in Italy Since the Fifteenth Century* (Baltimore: Johns Hopkins University Press, 1992), 114.

[11] St. Francis de Sales, *Introduction to the Devout Life* (the 1613 text) trans. And ed. John K. Ryan (New York: Doubleday, 1989), 106.

[12] Carroll, 115.

[13] See Richard Gambino, *Blood of My Blood* (Garden City, NY: Doubleday, 1974), 214, 219-225; Paul W. McBride, "The Solitary Christians: Italian-Americans and Their Church," *Ethnic Groups* 3 (1981): 335-336.

[14] Rudolph J. Vecoli, "Prelates and Peasants: Italian Immigrants and the Catholic Church," *Journal of Social History* 2 (Spring 1969: 229).

[15] For example, Paul McBride writes, "Italians were possessed of an anti-clericalism which was deeply rooted in their past. The Catholic Church had been an implacable and relentless foe of *Risorimento* and had resisted all efforts to diminish the temporal power of the Vatican" (337-338.) See also Edward Kantowicz, *Corporation Sole: Cardinal Mundelein and Chicago Catholicism* (Notre Dame, IN: University of Notre Dame, 1983).

[16] See, e.g. Gambino, 227f and McBride, 333-350.

[17] Spencer M. Di Scala, *Italy: From Revolution to Republic* (Boulder, CO: Westview Press, 1995), 25-26.

[18] Cavour had died in 1861.

[19] See E.E.Y. Hales, *Pio Nono* (New York: Doubleday, 1962), 327-333.

[20] Denis Mack Smith, *Italy, A Modern History* (Ann Arbor, MI: University of Michigan Press, 1959), 69-73; Di Scala, 122.

[21] O'Connell, 98-102.

[22] Carroll, 94-95.

[23] *Ibid.*, 96.

[24] Jerre Mangione and Ben Morreale, *La Storia: Five Centuries of the Italian-American Experience* (New York: Harper Perennial, 1992), 71-72, 105-106.

[25] See Henry J. Browne, "The "Italian Problem" in the Catholic Church of the United States, 1880-1900," United States Catholic Historical Society *Records and Studies* 25 (1946): 58.

[26] By 1905 the Scalabrini Fathers were operating twenty parishes in America. See Vecoli, 254.

[27] "Pope Leo's Plea for the Italian Immigrants in America," in John Tracy Ellis, ed. *Documents of American Catholic History* (Milwaukee: Bruce Publishing Company, 1962), 464.

[28] Bernard Lynch, *Catholic World* 46 (April 1888), 69-70.

[29] *Ibid.*, 72.

[30] Orsi, 3.

[31] *Ibid.*, 4.

[32] *Ibid.*, 56.

[33] *Ibid.*, 55-56.

[34] On Americanism, see Gerald P. Fogarty, SJ, *The Vatican and the American Hierarchy from 1870 to 1965* (Collegeville, MN: Liturgical Press, 1985), 65-190.

[35] McBride, 345.

[36] Joseph M. Sorrentino, SJ, "Religious Conditions in Italy" *America* 12 (October 17, 1914): 7.

[37] Herbert Hadley, *America* 12 (October 31, 1914), 66. Hadley modified this claim in a later letter. See idem, "Religious Conditions of the Italians" *America* 12 (November 14, 1914.)

[38] Hadley, "Religious Conditions in Italy," 66.

[39] An Old Pastor, "The Italian Question," *America* 12 (December 19, 1914): 244.

[40] Bishop E.M. Dunne, "The Italians Again," *America* 12 (November 21, 1914): 144.

[41] Joseph M. Sorrentino, SJ, "The Italian Question," *America* 12 (December 5, 1914): 194.

[42] "The Italian Question," *America* 12 (December 19, 1914): 246.

[43] Two of the era's most famous radicals were the Italian-born anarchists, Nicola Sacco and Bartolomeo Vanzetti.

[44] Mangione and Morreale, 316; Roger Daniels, *Coming to America* (New York: Harper Perennial, 1990), 282-284.

[45] For a vivid depiction of first and second generation Italian-American life, see Mario Puzo, *The Fortunate Pilgrim* (New York: Atheneum, 1965.)

[46] Gambino, 213.

[47] Will Herberg, *Protestant-Catholic-Jew* (New York: Anchor Books, 1955), 33.

[48] Orsi, 226.

[49] St. Paolino or Paulinus was a fifth-century bishop.

[50] Salvatore Primeggia and Joseph Varacalli, "The Sacred and Profane Among Italian-American Catholics: The Giglio Feast," *International Journal of Politics, Culture and Society* 9 (Spring 1996): 437.

[51] For the Catholic Church's troubles in the 1960s, see Garry Wills, *Bare Ruined Choirs* (New York: Dell Publishing, 1972), 79-272, and Philip Gleason, *Keeping the Faith* (Notre Dame, IN: University of Notre Dame Press, 1987), 82-96, 152-177.

[52] See Joseph Varacalli, "The Changing Nature of the 'Italian Problem' in the Catholic Church of the Untied States," *Faith and Reason* 12 (April 1986): 38-39. 59-70; idem, "Italian-American-Catholic: How Compatible?" *Social Justice Review* 82 (May/June 1992): 84-85.

CHAPTER 6

CHURCH DEDICATIONS OF ITALIAN-AMERICAN
NATIONAL PARISHES:
CHANGING TYPES OF PATRONS 1896-1960

Local and Universal Italian-American Saints: Some Ideal Types

Brendan, Brigid, Finbar, Finnian, Kevin, Kilian, Malachy, and Patrick were strange saints' names to the immigrants from *il Mezzogiorno* who had their own popular canon of venerated men and women. Agata and Lucia were Sicilian females who protected them and their families and into whose company they strove to someday enter. These women, moreover, were dignified by being invoked during the Latin Rite Tridentine Mass of the Faithful. Yet, the English-speaking American, Irish, and Irish-American priests and parishioners whom these Southern Italians encountered often presented obstacles to the veneration of their Marian cults and local saints. Despite the Latin origin of his name, Patrick, the patron of New York's great cathedral, was not Italian, nor was the French patron of the New Orleans Basilica, St. Louis. Oscar Handlin in his beautifully written but theoretically questioned classic, *The Uprooted*, wrote that the Italians moved into residential districts formerly occupied by the Irish. "The result was a struggle, parish by parish, between the old Catholics and the new, a struggle that involved the nationality of the priest, the language to be used, the saints' days to be observed, and even the name of the church."[1] For *contadini*, the canon of saints was not a list of equals if their own special local holy man or woman was not included. If he or she were excluded or if the saint's icon or statue was not near a side altar or at least somewhere in the chancel, narthex, or nave, there was a void. Also, as Handlin wrote, the name of the church could even be an issue.

This paper will use church dedications as the focus for the study of what shall be termed and defined below as *local* and *universal cults*[2] of Italian saints. Catholic ethnic groups vary considerably as to whether or not their churches are dedicated to local saints. Irish churches in the homeland are frequently named for local figures [3] as are those in Southern Italy.[4]

107

In contrast, the Greek rite Ruthenians of pre-World War I northern Hungary had nearly none. [5] If the Southern Italians had nearly none, this paper could not have been written.

The American National Parish

Canon lawyers, prelates, priests, and lay persons surely had interesting debates over whether American national parishes should have been organized. [6] After all, they lacked geographic boundaries which the Council of Trent (1545-1563) had mandated; in a word, they were non-territorial. [7] Many hierarchs assumed that after the second generation had assimilated, these parishes would be phased out and cease to exist, possible exceptions being those for the "Colored" Catholics and those of the Eastern rites. As we now know, the Italians (and other peoples) were not to give up *their* churches without resentment, sadness, and sometimes struggle. In this paper, the term *Italian national parish* will refer to *de jure* non-territorial parishes which are designated for Italians. *De facto* Italian parishes, i.e., those whose congregations possess a great majority of Italians but are territorial will not be the chief source of data. [8]

Definitions of Terms

An *Italian saint* will be defined as one who was either born in or died in Italy or in one of the Italian-speaking regions of countries contiguous to Italy. The latter would include parts of Austria, France, San Marino, Slovenia, Switzerland, and Vatican City. Exceptions will be Biblical figures, such as, St. Peter and persons widely associated with another nation. (A hypothetical example of the latter would be an American cardinal, later canonized, who suddenly died while in Rome.)

A *local Italian Saint's Cult* will be defined as a veneration of an individual in one or several Italian villages prior to the mass migration of Italians to the New World (circa 1880-1920) but was not included in the pre-1970 universal church calendar. A well-known (and controversial) example is St. Philomena (Filomena) (Philumena) whose cult was brought from Sardinia to Port Washington, Long Island, New York and from elsewhere in Italy to Briggsville, Wisconsin. [9] A *Universal Italian Saint's Cult* will refer to a veneration of an Italian saint who was honored in the pre-1970 Calendar of the Universal Church and is thus venerated throughout the world. An obvious example is St. Anthony of Padua whose feast was (and still is) June 13.

Church Dedications of National Parishes

American Catholic national parishes were organized surprisingly early in the history of the Republic. Probably the most vigorous promoters of non-territorial, non-English speaking parishes were the Germans who thought that the Word of God was best understood, that God was most magnificently adored, and the saints were most nobly venerated in the mother tongue.[10] In fact, the first national parish is said to have been organized for Germans in 1789 during Bishop John Carroll's reign.[11] Bohemian (Czech), French, and Polish parishes were also founded quite early. Italian national parishes were to come later.

Silvano M. Tomasi (now Apostolic Nunzio to Ethiopia and Eritrea) notes that the first Italian parish was St. Mary Magdalene de'Pazzi, organized in Philadelphia in 1852. Tomasi states that some other early Italian national parishes were Our Lady of Grace, founded in Hoboken, New Jersey, in 1864, St. Anthony of Padua, New York, in 1866, and Holy Rosary of Jersey City, *circa* the 1860s.[12] However, Sadlier's Catholic Directory for 1872 lists only two national parishes, one in New York and one in Philadelphia.[13] Quite possibly, Tomasi is including both *de facto* and *de jure* parishes in his study, thus blurring this distinction.

The Early Dedications: Pre-1896

The Catholic Directories for the year 1896 (at that time published independently by Hoffman Brothers of Milwaukee and Sadlier of New York)[14] recorded fifteen national parishes in the thirteen cities that were sampled. Their cities and the patrons to whom they were dedicated were:

Baltimore
    None

Boston
    Sacred Heart
    St. Leonard of Port Maurice

Brooklyn
>Our Lady of Loreto
>Sacred Heart of Jesus
>St. Michael the Archangel

Chicago
>Assumption of the Blessed Virgin Mary

Cleveland
>Holy Rosary
>St. Anthony of Padua

Detroit
>None

District of Columbia (Baltimore Archdiocese)
>None

New Orleans
>St. Anthony of Padua

New York
>St. Anthony of Padua
>St. Joachim
>Most Precious Blood
>Our Lady of Loreto
>Our Lady of Mt. Carmel

Philadelphia
>None

Pittsburgh
>St. Peter

St. Louis
>None

San Francisco
>None

Curiously, the church St. Mary Magdalene de'Pazzi of Philadelphia was not listed as an Italian national parish in either 1896 directory, but was listed as such in Sadlier's Catholic Directory for the year 1872.[15] A new church structure had been dedicated by Archbishop Ryan in 1891,[16] but this would not explain the omission. Possibly, the individual submitting the information from the Philadelphia Archdiocese simply made an error of omission. However, we will probably never know for sure the actual cause.

New church dedications of *de jure* Italian-American parishes will be examined and enumerated below for three time periods. Each period approximates a different stage in the Italian-American immigrant experience. The churches studied will be those which are within the city limits of the major cities of the twelve sees listed above. For example, in the New York Archdiocese, churches of the boroughs of the Bronx, Manhattan, and Richmond will be studied but not those of the cities of White Plains and Yonkers; in the Cleveland See, Ashtabula, Lorain, and other locales are excluded. The time periods are:

A.   1896-1920. These dates roughly mark the start of the mass migration to America and the cutoff of immigration from Europe during and shortly after the Great War. It was a time when Italian and other immigrants identified themselves by their village—"the fixed point by which he knew his position in the world."[17] This stage will be termed *The Local Stage.*

B.   1921-1945. In 1921, the restrictive legislation passed by Congress began to erode Italian immigration to a near halt. Italians had built institutionally complete neighborhoods with churches, social clubs, ethnic food stores, newspapers, restaurants, cultural societies, mutual assistance societies and theaters. William Foote Whyte once referred to these neighborhoods as *Gemeinschaft* type neighborhoods due to "their intimate personal relationships."[18] This stage will be termed *The Italian-American Stage* because a consciousness of greater Italian-American identity was formed and other Americans (including the mostly non-Italian church officials in America) did not distinguish among the various regional groups. Humbert S. Nelli has described this process in Italian parishes of Chicago's West Side around 1920:

Despite the eventual loss of adjusting members to American churches or to "old" immigrant churches, the Italian national parish filled a vital need by aiding immigrants to accommodate to their new homeland. In the ethnic parish, newcomers from different localities in Italy found that they had to forget or suppress old-world prejudices against outsiders (that is, anyone from another town or province) in order to form the desired national church. Thus while southern Italians predominated in the West Side community served by Holy Guardian Angel and Our Lady of Pompeii, many Sicilians and some northern Italians also resided in the area, as well as Slavic groups and—after 1910—Mexicans. The mainland "Southerners" themselves formed no homogeneous group, for they arrived from every province, but especially from Cosenza, Aquila, Campobasso, Caserta, Abruzzi and Reggio-Calabria. In Chicago they joined together in the same parish. [19]

C.   1946-1960. This period begins with the end of World War II and closes with the election of the first Roman Catholic American president, John F. Kennedy. It was an Era of migration to the suburbs. Old inner-city neighborhoods such as Boston's West End, Chicago's West Side, and New York's East Harlem and Greenwich Village were experiencing *ethnic succession* and commercial transition. Although Italians did not flee as frequently and swiftly as certain other groups,[20] their exodus was accelerating. Herbert J. Gans reported the resentment of older Boston West End residents when that neighborhood (including the Italian and the Polish churches) were leveled during the urban redevelopment of the later 1950s.[21] This was the epoch of an American religious revival in the larger denominations, reported by Will Herberg and others,[22] producing religious growth in the suburbs and the closing of some national parishes. It will be called *The Suburbanization Stage.*

New Dedications in the Local Stage: 1896-1920

Official Catholic Directories for the year 1896 listed fifteen *de jure* Italian parishes in the sampled cities as of the end of 1895. [23] By 1921, the *Directory*, by then published by P.J. Kenedy and Sons, listed eighty-two.[24] Hence, there were sixty-seven *new* church dedications. Below is a listing of the cities and the patrons of these new dedications:

Baltimore
St. Leo

Boston
Our Lady of Mt. Carmel
Our Lady of Pompeii
St. Lazarus

Brooklyn
Nativity of Our Blessed Lady
Our Lady of Charity
Our Lady of Mt. Carmel
Our Lady of Peace
St. Blaise
St. Francis of Paula
St. Lucy
St. Roch (St. Rocco)
St. Rosalia

Chicago
Holy Guardian Angel
Holy Rosary
Our Lady of Pompeii
St. Anthony
St. Callisto
St. Francis de Paula
St. Mary of Mt. Carmel
St. Michael Archangel
St. Philip Benizi
Sancta Maria Addorata
Sancta Maria Incoronata

Cleveland
St. Marian

Detroit
Holy Family
San Francesco
Santa Maria

District of Columbia
    Holy Rosary

New Orleans
    St. Mary

New York
    Holy Rosary
    Immaculate Conception
    Mary, Help of Christians
    Our Lady of Grace
    Our Lady of Loreto
    Our Lady of Mount Carmel(2)
    Our Lady of Peace
    Our Lady of Pity
    Our Lady of Pompeii
    Our Lady of Sorrows
    Sacred Heart of Jesus and Mary
    St. Anthony
    St. Clare
    St. Joseph
    St. Lucy
    St. Partick
    St. Philip Neri
    St. Rita of Cascia
    St. Roch
    St. Sebastian
    Transfiguration

Philadelphia
    Mater Dolorosa
    Our Lady of Angels
    Our Lady of Good Counsel
    Our Lady of Pompeii
    Our Lady of the Rosary
    St. Donato
    St. Lucy
    St. Mary Magdelene de'Pazzi
    St. Rita's Memorial

Pittsburgh
>Immaculate Conception
>Mary, Help of Christians
>Mother of Good Counsel
>Regina Coeli

St. Louis
>None

San Francisco
>Immaculate Conception
>Sts. Peter and Paul

These new *de jure* Italian parishes were at first classified into five categories based upon a typology of church dedications:

1) *Christological* - churches dedicated to Jesus Christ or His Holy Mysteries, relics, sacramentals, etc., e.g., Transfiguration.
2) *Marian* - churches dedicated to the Mother of God or her mysteries, relics, sacramentals, etc., e.g., Our Lady of Pompeii.
3) *Biblical* - churches dedicated to Biblical figures or those of the Christian Apocrypha, e.g., St. Joachim.
4) *Italian* - churches dedicated to saints defined as Italian according to the definition above, e.g., St. Anthony of Padua.
5) *Non-Italian* - churches dedicated to saints from countries other than Italy, e.g., St. Blaise.

Interestingly, no churches were dedicated to the Holy Spirit or the Holy Trinity, two dedications sometimes used in American Catholicism, Eastern Orthodoxy, Episcopalianism, and Lutheranism.

The results of the quintuple classification of *new* church dedications are shown in Table One.

TABLE ONE
TYPES OF PATRONS IN NEW CHURCH DEDICATIONS
OF Italian-American NATIONAL PARISHES
1896-1920

Christological	Marian	Biblical	Italian	Other Countries
1.5*(3%)	34.5*(52%)	6(8%)	22(33%)	3(5%)
(N=67)				

*One double dedication to the Sacred Hearts of Jesus and Mary.

Source: *The Official Catholic Directory* (New York: P.J. Kenedy and Sons, 1921).

Italian Saints Dedications

The *new* church dedications with Italian patrons numbered twenty-two or thirty-three percent of the sixty-seven churches. Readers will probably find the names of these saints, the frequency distribution of the churches dedicated to them, and some of their biographies to be of interest. The most numerous dedications were to St. Lucy with three (13.6%) of new dedications. The complete list of new Italian saints' dedications (1896-1920) and their frequencies are presented immediately below:

St. Lucy	3
St. Anthony of Padua	2
St. Francis de Paola	2
St. Rita of Cascia	2
St. Rocco (Roch)	2
St. Callisto	1
St. Clare	1
St. Donato	1
St. Francis of Assisi	1
St. Leo the Great	1
St. Mary Magdalene de'Pazzi	1
St. Philip Benizi	1
St. Philip Neri	1

St. Pius V	1
St. Rosalia	1
St. Sebastian	1

New Dedications in the Italian-American Stage: 1921-1945

Not withstanding the Americanization of the Italian-Americans during the inter-war and World War II periods, nineteen new *de jure* Italian national parishes were dedicated in thirteen cities from 1921 through 1945. Of these, eleven were located within the city of New York, four were in Cleveland, and four in Philadelphia. (Several Italian national parishes were either closed or turned into territorial parishes in the thirteen cities that were studied and among them was one in Cleveland, two in Philadelphia, and six in New York.) The frequency distributions and percentages of these new dedications are contained in Table Two.

TABLE TWO
TYPES OF PATRONS IN NEW CHURCH DEDICATIONS
OF Italian-American NATIONAL PARISHES
1921-1945

Christological	Marian	Biblical	Italian	Other Countries
3(16%) (N-19)	8(42%)	3(16%)	5(26%)	0(0%)

Source: *The Official Catholic Directory* (New York: P.J. Kenedy, 1946).

Statistics-oriented sociologists may be seriously troubled by the small sample size and the method of drawing the sample. Still, a comparison with the period 1896-1920 is useful for there were some interesting trends. The percentage of Italian dedications declined from thirty-three to 26 per cent (-7%). Concomitant with this was an increase in the number of Christological dedications from three to 16 percent (+13%) and of Biblical dedications from eight to 16 percent (+8%). (No new dedications were to saints from other countries.) One interpretation of this trend might be that with the new cessation of Italian immigration there was a lessening of identification with Italian culture among Italian-Americans. As Max Ascoli has written, "They became Americans before they ever were Italians."[25] Another might be an incipient trend toward a Christ-centered and Scripture-focused Catholicism which later took hold during the 1960s.

New Dedications in the Suburban Stage: 1946-1960

Of the twelve dioceses studied, only six (Boston, Cleveland, Detroit, New Orleans, Philadelphia, and Pittsburgh) did not eliminate any Italian national parishes during this time. New York's Archbishop Francis Cardinal Spellman's (served 1939-1967) policy apparently was to gradually eliminate them and this may have also been the situation in Brooklyn under Bishop Thomas Malloy (reigned 1921-1957) and later under Bryan J. McEntegart (reigned 1957-1968). Sociologist, Joseph P. Fitzpatrick, writing in 1955, argued that integrating foreign language speakers into territorial parishes would foster cultural and social assimilation in the long run[26] and this was likely one rationale for diocesan policies. Another rationale would simply be a declining number of parishioners due to the migration or the passing on of persons from these neighborhoods. Philadelphia did establish two additional *de jure* Italian parishes within the city limits. Both possessed Marian dedications, their titles being, Our Lady of Consolation and Our Lady of the Rosary. Each was a church that was dedicated in the Nineteenth Century as a territorial parish and subsequently became an Italian national parish. Marian dedications certainly had been quite common prior to the Second Vatican Council, but the results of the present study suggest an incipient decline among Italian national parishes, even prior to 1946. Moreover, with the waning of Italian church dedications to Italian saints, there probably was a decline in dedications to females other than Mary. The present writer suggests this because eight of the twenty-two dedications to Italian saints (36%) which took place between 1896 and 1920 were to women.

New Local Patron Saints: The Local Stage: 1896-1929

Twenty-two Italian *de jure* national parishes that were created during the 1896-1920 period were dedicated to Italian patron saints. Of these, seventeen (77%) were listed on the pre-1970 universal calendar of the American Roman rite Church. [27] Hence, the other five (23%) were dedicated to "local" Italian patrons, following the definition rendered earlier in this paper. Of those *not* in the universal calendar: two were dedicated to St. Rita of Cascia, two to St. Rocco (Roch), and one to St. Rosalia.

New Local Patron Saints: The Italian-American Stage: 1921-1945
Five new dedications during the 1921-1945 period were to (local or universal) Italian saints. Of these patrons, two were to the local saints, Rita of Cascia and Rocco. Clearly, St. Rita and St. Rocco had numerous devotees.

St. Rita of Cascia[28]

Rita was born in 1381 to relatively prosperous peasants at Roccaporena in *Provencia d'Umbria* of south-central Italy, not long before that territory came under Papal rule. Her mother conceived at an advanced age and during childhood and adolescence Rita came to be known by neighbors as being very kind and saintly. However, when she sought entry into an Augustinian convent, her parents ordered her to marry the man of their choice instead. Rita's spouse turned out to be brutal, uncaring, unfaithful, and violent. One day he was discovered dead, covered with wounds inflicted by an assailant. Their two sons sought to avenge their father's death, but Rita prayed that they die before they themselves committed murder. The young men later perished during a plague, but not before each had achieved peace of mind concerning the killing, and had implored God to forgive the killer and themselves.

Soon Rita again sought to enter the convent at Cascia, Umbria. Turned down three times because she was not a virgin, she persisted and subsequently the rules were modified. Thus, Rita was received into the order in 1413. Contemplation concerning Jesus' suffering led to the appearance of a wound on her forehead, said to have been from the Crown of Thorns, hence, her icons and statues depict this *stigmatum*. Rita died at Cascia in 1457.

Prior to her canonization by Pope Leo XIII in 1900, devotion to Rita had spread to other parts of central Italy as well as to Spain, Portugal, Mexico, elsewhere in Latin America, and the Philippines. It diffused into and through the United States during the early twentieth century, especially to the cities of Brooklyn, Chicago, New York, and Philadelphia where her national shrine was dedicated in 1915 and where her devotional society is headquartered. Her cult as "Saint of Desperate Cases" pre-dates the popularity of St. Jude as "Patron of Hopeless Causes," an extremely interesting chronological fact considering Robert A. Orsi's recent contention that devotion to St. Jude, a male saint, brought women refuge from unsatisfactory relationships with their fathers, husbands, boyfriends, brothers, priests, and male physicians.[29] St. Rita's feast day is May 22, but it was not in the pre-1970 calendar of the Universal Church.

St. Rocco (Roch)[30]

Legend holds that St. Rocco (Roch), a native of Montpellier, France, went on pilgrimage to Rome and also visited other Italian cities and towns where he cured many victims of plague by making The Sign of the Cross over them. When he, himself, became ill, he was miraculously fed by a dog.

After Rocco's passing in *circa* 1380, his cult spread to northern Italy. During a pestilence in Venice in 1473, a confraternity was founded in his honor. Devotion to St. Rocco was waning, but it revived in the mid-nineteenth century during European cholera epidemics and Pope Pius IX (reigned, 1846-1878) promoted his cult. Icons and statues sometimes reveal a sore on Rocco's thigh and a dog with a loaf of bread in its mouth. St. Rocco's feast is August 17.

In America it is very possible that the cult of St. Rocco took hold and flourished not merely because of the transplanting of the Italian devotion but, in addition, because of severe health problems in Italian immigrant neighborhoods. Robert F. Foerster described the sordid urban situation of the early twentieth century:

> Pneumonia and bronchopneumonia have taken a fateful hold upon these people, who are in general victims of the infectious maladies, and of rheumatism, but seldom of gastrointestinal diseases. In the children enteritis is common - evidence of ignorant or careless feeding - and diphtheria and measles. In Boston and New York the death rate of Italian children less than five has been very high. Young and old fall a ready prey to tuberculosis; women, it would seem oftener than men, though among other peoples men come first. [31]

Would the Italian immigrants, especially those from the poverty-stricken South invoke St. Rocco in order to ward off future health problems stemming from contagious diseases or to cure present ones? Most likely, the question has more than one answer.

St. Rosalia

St. Rosalia was very possibly an Italo-Greek of the Byzantine (Greek) Rite. Although her background is obscure, she is thought to have been a nun who died on Monte Pellegrino (about three miles from Palermo) during the 1100s. [32]

In the year 1642, an epidemic of plague broke out at Palermo. In accordance, it is said, with a vision of St. Rosalia that appeared to one of the victims, search was made in the cave on Monte Pellegrino and the bones of the maiden were found. They were put into a reliquary and carried in procession throughout the city, and the pestilence was stayed. In their gratitude the people of Palermo honored their principal patron and built a church over her hermitage. [33]

Again a saint helps thwart a plague!

St. Rosalia's Church in Brooklyn was dedicated in 1905.[34] It is located in Borough Park section (near Bensonhurst) where numerous Sicilians settled during the early 1900s. Its founding pastor was Father Paolo Sapienza, a native of Palermo. [35]

St. Vitus (Vito)

Using a different methodological approach than that described earlier in this paper, this writer recorded the patrons of the suburban *de jure* Italian parishes of the thirteen major cities cited above which were listed in the Official Catholic Directory for 1922. Only one Italian saint had more than one church dedicated to her or him. He was St. Vitus (Vito), patron of the churches in Mamaroneck, New York (New York Archdiocese), and New Castle, Pennsylvania (Pittsburgh Archdiocese). St. Vitus, a Sicilian of the third century, is the protector of epileptics and persons suffering from Sydenham's Chorea, the nervous disorder popularly called "St. Vitus Dance."[36] He is, therefore, not usually invoked to prevent illnesses, as are Rocco and Rosalia, but to comfort those already afflicted.

Local and Universal Saints: A Typology

A construct having four types of devotions to Italian-American Saints will now be introduced. The categories will be based upon whether or not the saint's feast day was in the pre-1970 calendar of the Universal (Western) church[36], and whether the saint was venerated by American Catholics of all ethnic backgrounds or merely by Italian-Americans. Previously in this paper saints in the universal calendar have been called "Universal" and others "Local." At this point, the terms "Multi-Ethnic American Venerated," and "Italian-American Venerated" will be added. While these latter terms seem self-explanatory, they do not have such clear-cut indicators as the Universal and Local scheme, and are, therefore, subject to and welcome to be criticized. The four categories are:

   Type A: Universal; Multi-Ethnic American
           Examples: St. Anthony of Padua, St. Francis of Assisi, St. Lucy

   Type B: Universal; Italian-American
           Examples: St. Donatus, St. Francis of Paola, St. Mary Magdalene de'Pazzi

   Type C: Local; Multi-Ethnic American
           Examples: St. Rita of Cascia, St. Francesca Cabrini

   Type D: Local; Italian-American
           Examples: St. Rocco, St. Rosalia, St. Philomena

Interpretations of the Findings

The University of Chicago sociologists of the first half of the twentieth century predicted that Italian, Polish, Slovak, and other predominately Catholic ethnic groups would merge into the general American culture and society. Indeed, some sociologists, a number of whom were active or formerly active Protestant ministers, thought it would benefit the Catholic and Eastern Orthodox Christian newcomers if they embraced Protestantism. [37] As is well known, few abandoned their ancestral church. By the 1970s, advocates for the European-American descendants of the 1880-1924 immigrants such as Geno Baroni[38] and Michael Novak[39] were advising the general public to realize that the "pot didn't melt." What might be asked at the present time is the extent and significance of the immigrants' contribution to American Catholicism's numerous saints' cults. For example, to what extent are the fairly popular devotions to St. Lucy and St. Rita of Cascia the result of Italians showing non-Italian Catholics the comforting and miracle working functions of her veneration?

Nevertheless, the statistical trends concerning patron saints of church dedications which were discovered during the research reported in this paper are assimilationist. Italian-American *de jure* national parishes did manifest a decline in the proportion of new churches dedicated to Italian saints over the years 1896 to 1960, while churches dedicated to Christ or Biblical persons (except for the Mother of God) increased. This is theoretically somewhat similar to the findings of the late Reverend Nicholas John Russo. Father Russo's general findings merit a brief summary and one portion of his evidence is especially close to the findings of the present study.

Russo used several methods to study the religious acculturation of first, second, and third generation Italian-Americans. He found increased weekly attendance at Mass in the second generation, a slight dip from the second to the third, and, on most other indicators, acculturation into the Irish-American practices. Significant for the present paper is an increased frequency of prayer to God with each passing generation to the detriment of prayers to Mary and the saints.[40] Father Russo's empirical findings support one of the responses to Irish-American dominance that Francis X. Femminella[41] suggested some years earlier: "conformity" to Irish-American ways. Russo's discovery of decreased invocation of the Mother of God and other saints is consistent with the decline in Marian and Italian patron saints in newly dedicated Italian-American *de jure* national parishes.

Conclusion

Why were some Italian saints more frequently venerated than others? Local saints like Rocco and Rosalia interceded to cure illnesses as did the universally venerated Lucy. To borrow the concepts and language of Emile Durkheim, they were sacred, held in awe, "set-apart"[42] during a time period when a husband could become physically disabled, a mother's child could leave this world, and even whole communities could be ravaged by cholera, influenza, tuberculosis, or typhoid. They could clarify the absurdities of life and ease the anguish. "Religion is not born out of speculation or reflection, still less out of illusion or misapprehension, but rather out of the real tragedies of human life, out of the conflict bestrewn human plans and realities."[43] Bronislaw Malinowski's well-known interpretation can illuminate the significance of certain saints' cults for immigrants and their children. In addition, we should not totally dismiss the monographs of the psychoanalytically oriented, very skeptical, and (to this writer) highly speculative Freudian anthropologist, Michael P. Carroll, who summarizes well how Malinowski's thesis about protection from natural danger and relief from anxiety can help explain certain Italian devotions.[44]

Why did devotions to Italian saints decline whether measured by patrons of churches in the present study or by the survey research of Father Russo? Perhaps Italian-Americans were becoming more avid and more dedicated Scripture readers years before the Second Vatican Council of 1962 to 1965. This writer, however, sides with the hypothesis of Femminella and Russo concerning "Hibernization" and Max Ascoli's remark on "Americanization." Italian non-territorial national parishes were closing, and few new ones were taking their places. Much that was Italian was being lost.

Some intriguing additional questions might be asked. Why did certain local saints such as Rita and Rocco continue to have flourishing cults among migrants transplanted in the New World? Were they becoming venerated throughout Italy during the nineteenth and twentieth centuries or still only in a few local areas? Which saints never crossed the ocean?[45] What were the cultural, economic, and social characteristics of the parishes where they were honored? A very crucial issue is the identities of and the ethnic and regional backgrounds of the founding pastors of these parishes. In order for a church to be dedicated to a particular saint, the dedication would have required the endorsement of the founding pastor since that was the normative custom at that time.[46] For instance, inquiry might be made concerning the pastors of churches dedicated to Saints Rita, Rocco, or Rosalia. Not all that is Italian among saints' cults is lost as yet. Church names stay the same until the buildings are closed down. Canon 1218 of the Code of Canon Law reads, "Each church is to have its title which cannot be changed after its dedication."[47] However, is this stability just a fading reminiscence, insufficient to keep the numerous Italian saints from being continually pushed out as they have since the 1969 calendar revision became the rule? Father Richard Mazziotta has written in his, "When the Saints Went Marching Out," that "Christ-centered Christianity has compromised an indispensable expression of Catholicism."[48] His suggestions concerning conservation merit deep consideration, but it is difficult to be sanguine about the future of saints' cults in American Catholic life. More and more may be lost before it is recovered.

RICHARD RENOFF

---

[1] Oscar Handlin, *The Uprooted: The Epic Story of the Great Migrations that Made the American People* (Boston: Little, Brown, 1951), 121. A criticism of the "Uprooted" concept is Rudolph J. Vecoli, "Contadini in Chicago: A Critique of the Uprooted," *The Journal of American History*, 51 (December 1964): 404-417.

[2] Cults will be treated simply as devotions to the saints. Traditionally, the Church has distinguished between public and private cults. For the most part, this essay will deal with public cults.

[3] David Hugh Farmer, *The Oxford Dictionary of Saints*, 3rd ed. (New York: Oxford University Press, 1992), xvi. Classic studies of church dedications in the British Isles are Frances Arnold-Forster, *Studies in Church Dedications of England's Patron Saints* (London: Skeffington and Son, 1899), and Francis Bond, *Dedications and Patron Saints of English Churches: Esslesiastical Symbolism: Saints and their Emblems* (London: Humphrey Milford Oxford University Press, 1914).

[4] Consult the index to Aldo Gabrielli, *Santi e santuari d'Italia* (Rome: Edizioni per l' Anno Santo, 1950), 130-135.

[5] This writer counted the patrons of the 185 churches in the Preshov (Hungarian: Eperjes) Diocese as of the year 1876, and found none dedicated to local patrons while over two-thirds had Biblical patrons. (A number were dedicated to St. Nicholas as are some Italian Churches.) See *Schematismus Venerablis Cleri Graeci Ritus Catholicorum Diocesis Eperiessiensis pro Ano Domini 1876* (Kassa: Carol Werfer, 1876).

[6] Cf. Joseph E. Ciesluk, *National Parishes in the United States*, The Catholic University of America Canon Law Studies, 190 (Washington, D.C.: Catholic University of America Press, 1944), 26-37.

[7] *New Catholic Encyclopedia*, s.v., "Parish."

[8] For a clear explanation of this distinction consult Salvatore J. LaGumina, *From Steerage to Suburbs: Long Island Italians* (Staten Island, NY: Center for Migration Studies, 1988), 121.

[9] Concerning the archaeological evidence which prompted the controversy, see

J.B. O'Connel, "The Strange Story of St. Philomena," *The Clergy Review*, 46 (August 1956): 462-471. Hagiographies supporting the cult include Sister Marie Helene Mohr, S.C., *St. Philomenia: Powerful With God* (1953; reprint, Rockford IL: TAN Books, 1988) with a new publisher's preface and Paul O'Sullivan, O.P., *St. Philomena the Wonder Worker* (1927); reprint, Rockford IL: TAN Books, 1993).

[10] Colman J. Barry, *The Catholic Church and German Americans*, Catholic University of America Studies in American Church History, 50 (Washington, D.C.: The Catholic University of America Press, 1953), 251-253; Jay P. Dolan, *The Immigrant Church: New York's Irish and German Catholics, 1815-1865* (Baltimore: The Johns Hopkins University Press, 1975), 70-71.

[11] Ciesluk, 29.

[12] Silvano M. Tomasi, *Piety and Power: The Role of the Italian Parishes in the New York Metropolitan Area, 1980-1930* (Staten Island, NY: Center for Migration Studies, 1975), 62-69.

[13] *Sadlier's Catholic Directory, Almanac, and Ordo for the Year 1872* (New York: D. and J. Sadlier, 1872), 78; 249.

[14] *Hoffman's Catholic Directory, Almanac and Clergy List - Quarterly*, 11 (Milwaukee: Hoffman Brothers, 1896).

[15] See Note 13 above.

[16] *Historical Sketches of the Catholic Churches and Institutions of Philadelphia: A Parish Register and Book of Reference* (Philadelphia: Daniel H. Mahony, 1896) 99-100.

[17] Handlin, 8.

[18] William Foote Whyte, "Social Organization in the Slums," *American Sociological Review*, 8 (February 1943) 34-39.

[19] Humbert S. Nelli, *Italians in Chicago 1880-1930: A Study in Ethnic Mobility* (New York: Oxford University Press, 1970), 194-195.

[20] Concerning Catholic ethnic groups remaining in the cities longer than non-Catholic ones see John T. McGreevy, *Parish Boundaries: The Catholic Encounter with Race in the Twentieth-Century Urban North* (Chicago: University of Chicago Press, 1996), 83-84.

[21] Herbert J. Gans, *The Urban Villagers: Group and Class in the Life of Italian-Americans* (New York: *The Free Press of Glencoe, 1962)*, 304. On ethnic change in Catholic Territorial Parishes consult McGreevy, 77.

[22] Will Herberg, *Protestant-Catholic-Jew: An Essay in American Religious Sociology*, rev. ed. (Garden City, NY: Doubleday Anchor Books, 1960), 46-71. An empirical test of Herberg's thesis was reported in Gerhard Lenski, *The Religious Factor; A Sociological Study of Religion's Impact on Politics, Economics, and Family Life*, rev. ed. (Garden City, NY: Doubleday Anchor Books, 1963), 43-47, which showed increased church attendance among third generation "White Catholics" during the 1950s.

[23] See Note 14 above.

[24] *The Official Catholic Directory* (New York: P.J. Kenedy and Sons, 1921).

[25] Quoted in Nathan Glazer, "Ethnic Groups in America: From National Culture to Ideology," in ed., Morroe Berger, *Freedom and Control in Modern Society* (New York: Van Nostrand, 1954), 166.

[26] Joseph P. Fitzpatrick, "The Integration of Puerto Ricans," *Thought*, 30 (August 1955): 415.

[27] Following a directive in the "Constitution on the Sacred Liturgy," of Vatican II, Pope Paul VI announced a reorganization of the calendar for the Roman rite on May 9, 1969, to take effect on January 1, 1970. Numerous saints feasts were eliminated, many being Italian. See the list in *1970 Catholic Almanac* (Paterson, NJ: St. Anthony's Guild, 1970), 323. The Pope's *Motu Proprio* was printed in *The Pope Speaks*, 14 (June 1969): 181-184. For the pre-1970 calendar cf. *Daily Missal of the Mystical Body*, The Maryknoll Fathers (New York: P.J. Kenedy and Sons, 1959), xlii-lvii.

[28] The following sources have been consulted for this summary of St. Rita's life: *Butler's Lives of the Saints: Complete Edition*, 2, ed. and comp., Herbert Thurston, S.J. and Donald Attwater (New York: P.J. Kenedy and Sons, 1956), 369-370; Farmer, 417-418; Alison Jones, *The Wordsworth Dictionary of Saints* (Ware, Hertfordshire, Great Britain: Cumberland, 1994), 199; *Bibliotheca Sanctorum*, 21 (Rome: Pontifical Lateran University, 1968), 211-221.

[29] Robert A. Orsi, *Thank You, St. Jude: Women's Devotion to the Patron Saint of Hopeless Causes* (New Haven: Yale University Press, 1996). See especially pages 105-107.

[30] On the life of St. Rocco, see Thurston and Attwater, 3:338; Farmer, 420-421; *Bibliotheca Sanctorum*, 11: 264-273.

[31] Robert F. Foerster, *The Italian Emigration of Our Times* (Cambridge: Harvard University Press, 1919), 338.

[32] On St. Rosalia, see Thurston and Attwater, 3:486-484; also, *Bibliotheca Sanctorum*, 11:427-433.

[33] Thurston and Attwater, 3:487.

[34] *Priests and Parishes of the Diocese of Brooklyn: 1820-1990*, vol. 2, ed., Harry M. Culkin (Brooklyn, NY: W. Charles, 1991), 181.

[35] Father Sapienza's obituary appeared in *The Tablet* (Brooklyn) 27 December 1913.

[36] See Note 27 above.

[37] An example of this approach is Jerome Davis, *The Russians and Ruthenians in America: Bolsheviks or Brothers?* (New York: George H. Doran, 1922), 93-103. A Catholic analysis of Protestant proselytization of Italian-Americans if F. Aurelio Palmieri, O.S.A., "Italian Protestantism in the United States," *Catholic World*, 107 (May 1918): 177-189.

[38] Baroni's argument was usually summarized in his basic speech; see, for example, "An Address by Rt. Rev. Mons. Geno Baroni," *Proceedings of the Sixteenth Annual Conference of the Italian-American Historical Association*, ed., Francis X.

Femminella (Staten Island, NY: The Italian-American Historical Association, 1985), 19-25.

[39] Novak's viewpoint is in his "White Ethnic," *Harper's Magazine* (September 1971), 44-50.

[40] Nicholas John Russo, "Three Generations of Italians in New York City: Their Religious Acculturation," in eds. , Silvano M. Tomasi and Madeline Engel, *The Italian Experience in the United States* (Staten Island, NY: Center for Migration Studies, 1970), 195-213.

[41] Francis X. Femminella, "The Impact of Italian Migration and American Catholicism," *The American Catholic Sociological Review*, 22 (Fall 1961): 238-239.

[42] Emile Durkheim, *The Elementary Forms of the Religious Life*, trans., Joseph Ward Swain (London: George Allen and Unwin, 1915), 47.

[43] *Encyclopedia of the Social Sciences*, s.v., "Culture."

[44] Michael P. Carroll, *Madonnas That Maim: Popular Catholicism in Italy Since the Fifteenth Century* (Baltimore: The Johns Hopkins University Press, 1992), 143-145. Carroll's careful ethnography is difficult to fault.

[45] St. Nicholas of Bari is widely venerated in Italy. Anthropologist Giuseppe Galasso reported that he is the patron of 139 of 731 (19.0%) of the communities that he studied in the *Mezzogiorno;* see his *L'altra Europa: Per un'anthropologica storica del Mezzogiorno d'Italia* (Milan: Arnoldo Mondadori, 1982), 113. The devotion in Bari is reported in Michael J.L. La Civita, "Bari's Borrowed Wonder Worker," *Catholic Near-East*, 23 (July-August 1997): 22-25.According to the popular scholar, Martin Ebon who agrees with Charles W. Jones*) the American popularity of St. Nicholas is not directly linked to Dutch settlement in New York City, but represents a nineteenth century New York revival; Martin Ebon, *St. Nicholas, Life and Legend* (New York: Harper and Row, 1975), 87-99.

(St. Nicholas of Myra is the patron of many Eastern rite Christians. St. Nicholas of Bari and St. Nicholas of Myra are the same individual.)

[46] Msgr. George P. Graham, J.C.D., Ph.D., Interview by author, Steubenville, OH, 24 October 1997.

[47] *The Code of Canon Law: A Text and Commentaries*, ed., James A. Coriden (Rahway, NJ: Paulist Press, 1985) 848.

[48] Richard Mazziotta, "When the Saints Went Marching Out," *Commonweal*, 23 October 1992, 16.

*Charles W. Jones, "Kinckerbocker Santa Claus," *New York Historical Society Quarterly* (October 1954): 357-383.

Part III

The Long Island Experience

CHAPTER 7

SAINTS, SUBURBS, AND PARISH LIFE IN LONG ISLAND'S ITALIAN-AMERICAN COMMUNITIES

A major dimension of the cultural baggage transplanted by Italian immigrants to the United States included the Catholic folk religion of their patrimony. Notwithstanding the minority of Italians of old Protestant persuasion such as Waldensians, or those who became Protestant during the early immigrant years, the consensus of immigration historians is that the Italian immigrants were and remained predominantly Catholic, albeit of the Italian Mediterranean mentality. Destined to become one of the largest subgroups within American Catholicism, their assimilation posed a formidable challenge especially since their entry as mass immigrants coincided with the "Americanist" phase of Catholic Church history-a time characterized by vigorous church leadership that was determined to assimilate multiple strains of the European Catholic diaspora, thereby dispelling notions of "foreign" intrusion.[1] Accordingly, American church leadership, which was mainly Irish and largely disposed toward assimilation, was not only inclined to regard resistance to assimilation as undesirable but also damaging to efforts to become acceptable in their new homeland.

The pressure to subordinate Italian folk religious culture proved to be a serious issue in Italian neighborhoods in urban centers where immigrants for the most part tended to settle. Struggles over ethnic religious influence resulted in the emergence of "national parishes"—an accommodation that recognized particular parishes in these neighborhoods, as mother lodes of ethnic cultural patterns as, for example, saint devotions.[2] While this topic has been the focus of numerous studies dealing with urban Italian enclaves, less has been said of the suburban counterpart which is the focus of this essay.[3]

The examination of Italian folk religious characteristics, including saint devotion and the formation of national parishes on Long Island, offers the opportunity to compare experiences between urban and suburban demographic entities and to see wherein similarities and differences exist. The

131

choice of Long Island as the suburban setting is indeed fortuitous because it stands as the prototypical suburban entity in America. Long Island is also home to the largest concentration of Americans of Italian descent in any two contiguous counties in the country outside of New York City.

That religious establishments were the only or most familiar institutions of influence to which immigrants had access was readily evident in the Long Island setting. As such it demonstrates the staying power of a religious heritage, at least nominally, even while accommodation and adjustment to the American social and religious norms developed. The minority of Long Island Italian immigrants that converted to Protestantism did so within the context of Pentecostalism—a movement that held out for these immigrants a degree of intimacy, the formation of close relationships and informality, while it simultaneously provided outlets for emotional releases. Furthermore, the newcomers were influenced by the widespread growth of twentieth-century Pentecostalism which contained provisions for ethnic groups to inculcate aspects of their national culture as, for example, Italian names for some of these churches.[4]

The most significant finding uncovered by a study of the immigrants interfacing with Long Island Catholic religious institutions is that there exists a variety of experiences thereby affirming that pragmatism characterized their religious expression. Thus, in the main they remained Catholic, although, within their transplanted definitions of Catholicism including minimal dogmatic scrupulosity and casualness about church rules. Such attitudes cast them as poor practitioners of their faith compared to more predominant Irish Catholics in their midst.[5] Nevertheless, their attachments to their religious roots encouraged them to stay within the fold either by absorption into extant Catholic parishes when local pastors were understanding and accommodating, or by creating their own diocesan-approved but nevertheless defacto ethnic parishes or actual non-territorial national parishes.

Several explanations have been advanced by scholars who study the nature of the problem presented to the American Catholic Church by the influx of Italian immigrants. Among the explanations are: indifference to these immigrants, controversy over the Americanizing role of the Irish clergy, a heritage of anti- clericalism, aggressive Protestant proselytizing, and the weak formal context of southern Italian culture. The latter point in particular has led to controversy that underscores the complexity inherent in definitions of Italian Catholicism. Some stress the woeful, poor knowledge on the part of Italian peasants regarding formal church doctrine as a key to the problem, while others accept immigrant culture as consonant with Catholicism, albeit on a rudimentary, popular level. Variants of these phenomena could be found in the Long Island suburban atmosphere, although devoid of the extremes of interreligious and intra-religious conflicts that marked the experience in the big cities.[6]

During the immediate post-World War II period, Long Island became the nation's archetypal suburb. Within a short commute from New York City, former city residents sought homes in Nassau and Suffolk counties. Although Long Island physically is comprised of the four counties of Brooklyn, Queens, Nassau and Suffolk, the first two properly are part of New York City, while the latter two eastern counties are regularly referred to as Long Island. All four counties were under the canonical jurisdiction of the Brooklyn Diocese until 1960 when the new diocese of Rockville Centre, made up of Nassau and Suffolk, was created. By the 1990s these two counties boasted of a population of approximately 2.8 million of whom Italian-Americans were the largest single ethnic group numbering approximately 25% of the total. Very few Italian immigrants were to be found on Long Island before the 1880s, a decade which saw the onset of the first sizable Italian immigration. At first modest, the influx increased impressively in succeeding decades. They came, as did others, primarily because they could merge their need to earn a living with their desire for home ownership and land in less congested demographic areas. Indeed, for the overwhelming majority of Italian immigrants who continued to live in large cities, the lure of living close to the soil as they had in the old country and where they could pursue traditional jobs closer to their way of life in Italy persisted and served as a magnet for thousands of New York City residents. In time this old dream became a reality as the exodus to suburbia intensified.[7]

The first-comers saw a late nineteenth century Long Island that was even then beginning to move away from its traditional, bucolic setting, especially as the Long Island Railroad penetrated stretches of the north and south shores. Even if they continued to work in the city it now became feasible to seek a home in suburbia and be a satisfactory distance from their jobs. By the first World War, Italian immigrants and their progeny formed small but distinct enclaves in a number of Long Island communities: Inwood, Westbury, Port Washington, Glen Cove, Copiague, and Patchogue. A review of the social history of these locales and surrounding communities reveals much about the interaction of Italian immigrants and the Church.[8]

Inwood

The hamlet of Inwood in the southwest corner of Nassau County saw a significant entry of Italian immigrants in the 1880s. Exclusively of the proletarian class, they included a significant number of Sicilians but an especially large contingent of Calabrian Albanian Italians whose Balkan ancestry rendered them a unique group within a group. In addition to Inwood, Italians also established enclaves in such nearby towns as Far Rockaway, then still in Queens, where Catholics were served by an Irish-oriented parish of St. Mary Star-of-the-Sea. The 204 Italians residents of Inwood rendered it Nassau County's largest Italian concentration in 1900, a figure that increased to 752 in 1910.[9] Growth in the total Catholic population of the area was such that there ensued considerable pressure to create a Catholic parish in Inwood. This prompted Father Herbert F. Ferrell, pastor of St. Mary Star-of-the-Sea, to provide Sunday school instruction for Inwood's Italian children as well as sewing classes.[10] Thus began the humble origins of Inwood's Our Lady of Good Counsel.

While it was regarded as an "Italian" parish, Our Lady of Good Counsel was in reality a regular diocesan parish whose membership was largely Italian and whose feast celebration and other activities reflected that ethnic background. The first pastor was Father John J. Mahon, of Irish ancestry, as were more than a few of the initial parishioners. Credit must be given to the Irish-Americans from St. Mary Star-of-the-Sea whose names resembled a list of leading marchers in a St. Patrick's Day parade, for supporting the Inwood parish by providing funds for the tabernacle, vestments and other furnishings. Such assistance served as an antidote to the more widely shared experience of confrontation and subordination that Italian Catholics faced elsewhere.[11] The embryonic formation of Our Lady of Good Counsel in 1910 bore impressive fruition in 1915 when, with numerous dignitaries present from the diocese and nearby parishes along with the active participation of several Italian organizations, the formal dedication of the parish took place. Appropriate remarks were offered in English and Italian. Contemporary estimates were that over half of Our Lady of Good Counsel's 1,300 parishioners were of Italian descent—a figure that was soon augmented with a 1918 source indicating the ethnic population of Albano-Americans stood at more than 1,000 out of 1,800. Over the decades numerous Italian-American clergy served as assistant pastors, however, only one, Malta-born Father Francis Agius, served as pastor.

For years *the Italianità* of the parish was to be seen in ethnic activities including an Italian Holy Name Society alongside an American counterpart, and in exuberant saint day festivals celebrating the feasts of St. Michael, St. Audeno and St. Cono. To carry on the religious traditions of their Calabrian ancestors required a conscious effort at transplantation that was facilitated through the organization of the New Mutual Aid Congregation and the Brotherhood of St. Cono, in 1905, and most especially the *Società di San Cono* which was organized shortly afterwards and which began to sponsor the St. Cono Feast in 1906. Typical of Italian feast celebrations, they celebrated with a combination of color, sense and taste of traditional culinary delights, bright illumination, conventional old country music, religious processions through the Italian enclave, and thunderous fireworks. The enthusiastic and joyful participation of first, second and third generation Italian-Americans became spectacles of wonder to non-Italians in the surrounding communities who soon partook of the festivities. A 1923 newspaper coverage of St. Michael's Feast captured the spirit.

> The ceremonies were opened with a parade on Friday evening, in which all the members of the society participated, On Saturday morning the members attended a solemn High Mass at Our Lady of Good Counsel Church . . . almost three thousand members and friends marched through the streets of Lawrence, Inwood and Far Rockaway...The parade was led by the St. Cono Band followed by more than fifty members of the St. Audeno Society . . . Following this came a number of pretty and artistic floats, and members marched in the rear. Red, yellow, blue and pink blazed up and down the streets on Saturday night, as a result of the wonderful display of fireworks ... For miles around, red, yellow and myriad of other colors were seen brilliantly illuminating the sky. It was a night, according to many, that will never be seen again in the old historic town of Inwood . . . It reminded one of the carnivals of Venice, or the yearly fantasies in New Orleans.[12]

The earlier Italian roots of Our Lady of Good Counsel could also be gleaned by an examination of church marriage records which showed that in 1911 all eleven parish marriages were between Italians. However, in 1940, of 26 parish marriages, 16 were between Italians and non-Italians. With the death of Fr. Agius in 1958, non-Italian pastors were appointed, thus signaling the decline of the "Italian era" of the parish.[13] Almost a century later St. Cono Feast continues to be celebrated locally, although the impression is that the Italian-oriented function is no longer the centralizing community event. With at least a third of the parish of Italian descent, Inwood's Italian-American Catholics have accommodated themselves into a mixed parish configuration.

Westbury

Durazzano, Nola and Saviano, mountain towns in the vicinity of Naples (province of Avellino), can be said to have been the origins of Westbury's Italian-American community. Coming from these towns, especially Durazzano, in the late 1880s, the first comers and their descendants became laborers either in the new, burgeoning estates that wealthy families were then constructing, or in the large nurseries in the region. By the early twentieth century they established "the Hill," a distinctive Italian enclave located near St. Brigid. Founded by Irish immigrants in 1856, St. Brigid, which was the oldest Catholic parish in Nassau county, was now to be challenged by the Italian influx. Irish pastors were pressed to deal with newcomers whose tradition and culture differed markedly form those of the Emerald Isle. While the resulting accommodation effectively constrained efforts to start an "Italian" ethnic parish, Westbury's Italian immigrants were insistent that their customs and mores receive due attention, most notably celebration of feast days. This presented a dilemma for the pastor who was confronted with demands from immigrants from each of the three towns of Durazzano, Nola and Saviano, to designate their hometown patron saints for parish-sponsored feasts. Unable to come to agreement among themselves, Italian immigrants accepted the pastor's recommendation to forego those individual saint day celebrations and concentrate on a celebration of the Blessed Mother, a saint most dear to all Italians. Thus, was born Westbury's Feast of the Assumption on August 15. Beginning in 1910, it boasts of being one of one of the most enduring, continuous feasts in the

New York metropolitan area—even older that the better-known St. Gennaro's Feast in Manhattan's "Little Italy." The existence of the *Del l'Assunta*, Durazzano and St. Anthony's societies, all formed by local Italian-Americans, attests to the Catholic orientation of the ethnic group within the existing parish.

Feast-days were the highlights of social activities for Westbury's Italian-Americans. Durazzano Society members exerted themselves in order to put on a gala celebration in honor of St. Anthony of Padua. It was the feast of Our Lady of the Assumption, however, that was the main village attraction, a commemoration in which the entire community joined in a two-day celebration. By the 1940s a regular pattern had developed beginning with High Mass at St. Brigid, followed by a sparkling procession from the church to the feast site, in which marchers dressed in uniform ensembles (white trousers and dark jackets for men and white skirts and blouses and light blue capes for women) processed down Post Avenue, the main thoroughfare. The men's group led followed by the women and then the Junior Auxiliary. In the afternoon athletic events were highlighted by a soap box derby in which youngsters competed with crude, homemade imitations of powerful race cars that competed at the nearby Roosevelt Raceway. Audiences were entertained by local bands or those invited from other communities. The climax of the feast was the biggest fireworks display on Long Island that attracted thousands. Crowds of 10,000 to 30,000 were common, while in one year an estimated 75,000 turned out.[14]

Notwithstanding accommodation in St. Brigid, Westbury's Italian-Americans were sensitive to the absence of Italian curates, especially during the tenure of Fr. James A. Sullivan, a scholarly pastor who lacked the insight required to deal with a congregation of a different cultural background. The Italian-Americans formally registered complaints to the bishop of the diocese. In 1946 Fr. Sullivan responded by importuning Fr. Anthony DeLaura, fresh out of the service where he had served as chaplain, to accept a post assistant pastor. Agreeing to serve in behalf of all parishioners Fr. DeLaura was the first clergyman of his nationality at St. Brigid.[15] During the 1970s and 1980s a visiting priest celebrated masses in Italian. In 1989 Italian-American Fr. Frank Gaeta became St. Brigid's first pastor of Italian descent. Although Italian-Americans still make up a significant portion of the parishioners, the congregation is much more of a hybrid with important segments representing a variety of ethnic groups including Irish, Hispanic, and Italians. Indeed, masses are said in Haitian and Korean.

Port Washington

Sand-mining, one of the largest industries on Long Island, served as a magnet for some 120 Italians to Port Washington, by 1900. Bountiful, local deposits of the mineral made an excellent ingredient for cement mixing, then in large demands for the construction of New York City skyscrapers and subways. Italians, largely from the province of Avellino and a smaller number from Sardinia, provided the bulk of the labor force. At its height the sand-mining industry included several firms that employed hundreds of men in various manual tasks. While most immigrants remained laborers, some like industrialist/publisher Generoso Pope became mine operators.

Although the majority of Port Washington's Italians remained laborers inured to hard work, they were not docile, but rather determined to fight for their rights. Faced with bitterly low wages and with exhausting labor conditions that left them physically and mentally fatigued, in 1908 they joined other nationalities to agitate for a union. In May of that year 150 Italians went out on strike to bolster their demands for a 25 cents a day wage increase that would earn them a daily wage of $1.75. It was a bitter strike that landed some leaders in jail, nevertheless a union was recognized. Thirty years later, a repetition of this scenario occurred.[16]

Ethnic-oriented life was evident in numerous organizational activities of a social, political, fraternal, educational and religious nature. Remaining overwhelmingly Catholic, Port Washington's Italians seemed to eschew a desire to establish an ethnic parish, but rather accepted accommodation within the existing territorial parish of St. Peter of Alcantara. The absence of demands for an ethnic church did not reflect apathy about their heritage. In fact, the plethora of ethnic activities and the existence of so many ethnic organizations, including extensive coverage in the local press, revealed one of the liveliest ethnic communities. By the 1930s, Italian-American assistant pastors began to be assigned to the parish.

Early in their tenure Port Washington Italian-Americans began to celebrate their heritage by creating societies that organized feasts in honor of Our Lady of the Assumption and St. Anna and creating societies. The latter had special meaning to local Italians since so many had come from Avellino where St. Anna was hailed as the patron saint. By 1913, the feast of St. Anna, which had become a fixture in the community also exhibited a nationalistic streak which was clearly reflected in a spectacular fireworks demonstration depicting the bombardment of Tripoli and subsequent landing of Italian troops in North Africa. Another fireworks feature commemorated Guglielmo Marconi's wireless invention.[17] The community in the main responded favorably to these celebrations, however, there were some demurrers as expressed in an irate letter of 1910.

> If our Italian neighbors desire to worship with so much fervor,
> enthusiasm and noise, if requested they will doubtless be willing to
> do so at a time and place that will not be an annoyance to a large
> number of citizens who wish to spend their Sundays in quietness and
> peace.[18]

The Italian Mutual Aid Society continued to sponsor these feasts into the 1920s and 1930s. In the post World War era a new parish with an early strong Italian identification, Our Lady of Fatima was created in Manorhaven, previously known as old Port Washington.

Glen Cove

Sturno, a mountain town near Naples was the origin for most early Italian settlers to Glen Cove. Seeking employment in small-size factories, small retail establishments, and in the blossoming local estates, Italians started coming in the 1880s and 1890s. Population growth was so spectacular that by 1910 Glen Cove had the largest concentration of Italians east of New York City.[19]

From the outset religion held a paramount place in the lives of these new Americans. "A man holds dear what is left. When much is lost, there is no risking the remainder," was the way immigration historian Oscar Handlin described the attachment of immigrant peoples to familiar religious heritages of their ancestors. This truism applied to Glen Cove where southern Italians satisfied their religious prompting within the context of an ancestral peasant culture which contained an admixture of pagan folkways and magical practices along with more traditional Catholic customs. Thus, they appeared to be more likely to attend weekly services, while simultaneously promoting the cult of St. Rocco with its lighthearted socialization. Notwithstanding a small number who became Protestants, Glen Cove's Italians remained sufficiently loyal Catholics. They rapidly formed the Society of St. Rocco, named in honor of Sturno's patron saint, and soon aspired to have their own national ethnic church. Thus, although they attended Glen Cove's St. Patrick's Church, which was founded by Irish immigrants, they hungered for religious expressions that bespoke of their old world traditions. Faced with an unsympathetic pastor, they were heartened by the efforts of the Irish pastor of nearby St. Dominic's Church in nearby Oyster Bay who offered services by his own Italian-American assistant pastor. Indeed Oyster Bay's Italian colony, which was the first to conduct the St. Rocco Feast in the area, so impressed the normally staid native population that the events elicited rare positive press coverage.

> It takes the Italians to set the pace for the ordinary Oyster Bay American. For two days and two nights Italians have given the residents of Oyster Bay some food for thought. Oyster Bay is a quaint, old-fashioned country town; they do not believe in giving much toward making a show—their forte being in making a show at the bank. Not so with the Italian populace. These people are patriotic. They believe in their patriotic saint, St. Rocco, and are willing to place their earnings in support of their ideas, and as a consequence they did things which should bring the blush of shame to the American populace, because of their liberality. "What is a dollar in comparison to the support of what we think if for our own benefit" has been their motto. [20]

The creation of St. Hyacinth by local Polish Catholics served as a further encouragement for Italians to establish their own ethnic parish, a long-held desire that was to achieve fruition slowly. An important step was the acquisition of property in Glen Cove on the part of the St. Rocco and San Marino Societies. On this land a temporary chapel was constructed and occasional masses were celebrated, however, the issue of legitimization was raised since diocesan authorization had not been obtained. Although this is not to suggest that a schismatic church was in the offing, the concern likely entered Bishop Thomas Molloy's mind since he was experiencing a trying period with "independent" churches in other parts of the diocese. With little movement towards a resolution of a potential schism, St. Rocco and San Marino leaders took matters in their own hands by circulating a petition signed by thousands that requested a church of their own. They seized the propitious opportunity of a 1936 visit to Long Island by Cardinal Eugenio Pacelli, who received the delegation from the Italian societies.[21] Apparently the future pope interceded because within months Bishop Molloy acceded to their demands and approved the creation of St. Rocco's Church. Virtually the entire Italian colony contributed to the church's fundraising drive either with cash or labor in kind such as digging the foundation and setting stones.

As was the custom, the St. Rocco Society organized in 1910 and the San Marino Society organized in 1922, planned and implemented the celebration of the Feast of St. Rocco in August and the San Marino Feast in July. The formation of the San Marino Society reflected Calabrian influx into Glen Cove. By the 1940s these feasts were so stupendous that they dwarfed those conducted by Italians in nearby towns. Members of both societies frequently intermingled efforts. Over the years the original societies became extinct. However, a new St. Rocco Society endures into the 1990s and continues to sponsor the annual St. Rocco Feast, increasing the number of days of celebration. Unfortunately the noise factor over an extended period has alienated many in the community, even causing some former supporters to no longer become involved.[22]

Glen Cove's St. Rocco's Church opened for the first mass on Christmas Eve 1937 to a standing room only congregation. A true national parish, it has, on occasion, served as the convocation center for representatives throughout the Brooklyn Diocese. Italian-Americans have been pastors continuously and the St. Rocco feast continues to be one of the major celebrations of its kind in the general area. Italian masses and weddings are available along with English liturgy. The string of Italian pastors was broken in 1998 when Father Aaron T. Vellaramparampil, a native of India, became pastor. He is, however, fluent in Italian.[23] St. Rocco stands as the only true ongoing national parish on Long Island.

Copiague

A humble hamlet on the south shore of western Suffolk, Copiague is an unincorporated village that is located between better known communities. The Italian influx, including a healthy sprinkling of northern Italians from Emilia-Romagna, began at the turn of the century. One of them, John Campagnoli, became a catalyst for an upsurge of Italians into the area. A graduate mining engineer and real estate promoter, Campagnoli utilized his friendship with former classmate and world-famous inventor Guglielmo Marconi, to promote the "Italian" community of "Marconiville," then a synonym for Copiague.[24] By the First World War Marconiville had expanded to the point where local residents, tired of traveling to the adjoining town of Amityville for Mass and other Catholic services, began to pressure to have their own local church. Even before action was taken, native Italians began to celebrate the Feast of Our Lady of the Assumption. The well-connected Campagnoli was said to have used his influence with Bishop Molloy to endorse the notion of a separate parish with the result that in 1929 ground was broken for Copiague's own Catholic Church of Our Lady of the Assumption.[25]

Despite the involvement of local Italian-Americans, Our Lady of the Assumption, from the beginning was to be a territorial parish rather than a national, ethnic parish, a fact underscored by a diocesan loan of $40,000. Despite the assistance, the impact of the Great Depression on the low income community rendered construction of the church a gradual development. In the meantime the congregation worshiped in a basement church that leaked constantly. The reality of the demographic makeup of the community reinforced an impression of Italian orientation, an opinion that was further underscored by the designation of a succession of Italian-American pastors. One of them, Fr. Francis Del Vecchio, energized the community to complete the church structure, even donning overalls and mixing cement to see it come into being. In 1942 his heroic efforts bore fruit when Our Lady of the Assumption was formally consecrated. That it was popularly considered an "Italian" parish was evident in numerous ways: the clergy that staffed the parish, officers of church organizations, frequency of visits and support by Italian-Americans in nearby towns, and most especially Italian feast celebrations.[26]

As in other Long Island Italian enclaves, the feast was celebrated with strings of bright lights surrounded by streamers of vibrant colors strung across, the streets, booths of gastronomic delights from which emanated wonderful aromas, and whose scent drew people close as if a magnet, lively bands that provided medleys of old Italian melodies, and of course loud fireworks. The latter sometimes brought reaction from neighbors who complained not only because of the noise, but also because the incendiary works caused fires in nearby residential areas. In time the fireworks aspect diminished and eventually was discontinued.[27] On the whole non-Italian neighbors found the feast celebrations extraordinary. Copiague resident Ronald Barry, of Irish descent and the first parishioner to be ordained a priest from Our Lady of the Assumption, fondly recalled the events.

> I remember the big Our Lady of Assumption feasts which were very impressive. It was like the San Gennaro's feast in New York City. It was strange to a kid like me because I had never experienced things like the parading of a statue and the big fireworks, and good odors from the cooking stands with all the Italian food. I had never seen anything like that. It was entrenched when our family moved in. It was novel to me and I came to enjoy it a great deal. When we would go across the tracks, it was like being in a different world. There were people who cultivated their gardens. I always remember the times when grapes ripened. You were entering a different kind of world, yet we lived only a couple of blocks south of the tracks in a totally different environment. [28]

It was during the tenure of Monsignor Anthony DeLaura, the last Italian-American pastor of Our Lady of the Assumption, that changes in the demographic makeup of the community became discernible. Although the congregation was still predominantly of Italian ancestry, they were increasingly of second and third generations for whom Italian-speaking services were not essential. Furthermore, the late 1950s and the 1960s saw the influx of non-Italians into the area. By the mid-1960s the narrowly Italian phase of parish life was over.[29] Indeed even the use of the old Italian name of Marconiville fell into disuse until by the end of the century it had become virtually extinct. The naming of a non-Italian pastor in 1967 further illustrated the territorial integration of Our Lady of the Assumption with little evidence of its earlier unique Italian flavor.

Patchogue

Motivated by a desire for land and a healthier climate than in the congested areas of New York City's Little Italy, Italian immigrants moved into Patchogue and its environs, including East Patchogue, Bellport and Hagerman, in the 1870s and 1880s. Seventy miles east of the city, Patchogue was regarded as the commercial and industrial center of Suffolk County, offering farming possibilities and employment in small industries. The several Italian families already resident in Patchogue by 1900, worshiped in St. Francis de Sales, a parish with a distinctive Hibernian hue. These early Italian residents could discern the Irish ethnic background in talks sponsored by the parish as, for example, "The Irish Influence on the Church," and in the roster of names in classes for Communion and Confirmation. When Fr. James J. Cronin, pastor of St. Francis de Sales, recognized the Italian influx as part of a growing trend, he called upon a young Italian priest, Fr. Raphael A. Cioffi, to start a new parish to serve the needs of the newcomers. Thus was born the "Italian" parish of SS. Felicitas and Perpetua in 1922. Financially the new parish would have to make it on its own.

Built in the heart of the Italian colony in west Patchogue, the church became the focal point for numerous activities of a social and religious nature. Although it was abundantly clear that what Cioffi had wrought was ostensibly an Italian national parish, it was not exclusively Italian. From the outset there was a minority of non-Italians as indicated by church records that showed that whereas 88 percent of confirmands in 1922 were of Italian ancestry, they formed less than 68 percent in 1951.[30] Marriage records implied a similar pattern of Italian name declivity over these years. For his notable efforts in starting the parish, Fr. Cioffi was rewarded with the pastorate of one of the largest parishes in Brooklyn.

Over the next 42 years Italian-Americans were regularly appointed pastors to the parish, whose name had been changed to Our Lady of Mount Carmel. While each of these pastors made his own imprint, that of Fr. Cyrus Tortora (1943-53) deserves special mention. He literally energized the poor Italian community, exhorting people to take pride in their heritage and religion, not in a chauvinistic way, but in a way that enabled them to overcome the stigma attached to them in the larger community. The prevailing demeaning attitude was largely of socioeconomic derivation. As people on "the other side of the tracks," Italians suffered in the esteem of native

Patchogue residents. During Tortora's tenure, Our Lady of Mount Carmel was host to a major Diocesan Eucharistic Congress that drew 18,000 people into town. Normally a church event reserved for prestigious large city parishes, this raised the status of the Italian parish. Fr. Tortora's ministry as wartime chaplain to soldiers of all faiths in nearby Camp Upton during the Second World War won due praise. Long before Vatican II, Fr. Tortora practiced a degree of ecumenism as was evident in his support of the efforts of a local rabbi for a sufficient living wage. Fr. Tortora was especially concerned with Italian prisoners of war stationed in Camp Upton and was able to arrange visits with local Italian families.[31]

Feast day celebrations were major part of life among local Italians. These were events in which laymen played prominent roles even to point of organizing, funding and sponsoring feasts. Perhaps the best of examples, is that of Carmine Bianco, who for decades was the catalyst behind the feast of St. Liberata, a famous virgin martyr whose memory was especially revered in the Parenti region of Italy, the birthplace of many Patchogue Italians. Born in Parenti in 1869, Bianco's deep love for the saint was transplanted to the United States with his immigration in 1891 and subsequently to Patchogue into which he moved in 1916 and where he became a greenhouse worker. In 1919, Bianco built with his own hands a one-room chapel in the saint's honor and in the fall of that year the St. Liberata Society, of which he was chairman, held a festival. The society raised funds to help defray feast-incurred expenses and some of the costs of building the chapel. The St. Liberata feast continued to be celebrated for more than forty years before its demise in 1963. In that year Carmine Bianco, feast founder had passed away, and old age was catching up with Joseph Cardamone, stalwart feast supporter. The religious devotion of some Italian immigrants continued to be manifest. For example, Naples-born Crescenzo Vigliotta, a parishioner of Our Lady of Mount Carmel and resident of the adjacent village of Blue Point, had such strong devotion to the Blessed Mother that he donated 70 acres of land in Eastport to the Montfort Fathers, where a beautiful shrine of Our Lady of the Island is housed. Notwithstanding such devotional acts, third generation Italian-Americans were unwilling to make the effort to continue to conduct the elaborate preparations required for the feast celebration of St. Liberata. Moreover, the administration of Our Lady of Mount Carmel had acquired an enlarged focus, which seemed to relegate such festivals to the periphery.[32]

The Patchogue vicinity underwent major change in the post-World War II period as population growth and demographic changes impacted the area. The old parish of Our Lady of Mount Carmel in the heart of the Italian area was no longer adequate to accommodate the congregation with the result that a new church was constructed in another part of town.[33] The appointment of Fr. Alexander Sledzous as pastor of Our Lady of Mount Carmel in 1966 marked the end of the distinctively Italian phase of parish life. No longer regarded a defacto ethnic, national parish, it became a traditional geographic-based parish. A similar transition took place in St. Joseph the Worker parish in East Patchogue which had its origins in serving an ethnic Italian congregation, but which by the 1960s also functioned to serve the wider community on a geographic not an ethnic basis.

Conclusion

A review of Long Island Italian enclaves provides a number of insights regarding the interaction between Italian immigrants and the Church, the most important of which is the continued association with Catholicism. For some it was nominal as reflected in infrequent mass attendance and participation in other services, conforming to Joseph A. Varacalli's description of the typical immigrant as "the average turn-of-the-century contadino . . . very religious, . . . marginally Catholic and Christian."[34] However valid this portrayal may be for Long Island Italian-Americans of the first generation, it is also evident that succeeding generations of the suburbanized ethnic group increasingly acculturated to Irish religious norms with respect to cooperation with the clergy, financial parish support and decreasing interest in private devotion.[35] In general the sustained evangelization of Italian and non-Italian sisters and priests helped bring about a transformation "and Italian-Americans became the strong supporter of many a 20th century Catholic parish," to use the words of historian James Hennessey.[36]

The history of Italian-Americans on Long Island confirms the role played by ethnic religious organizations, with loose ties to existing parishes yet existing as separate entities. Variants of mutual aid societies, these organizations were created by laymen who became active promoters of feast and saint day celebrations in remembrance of the religious practices transplanted from their home towns in Italy. The dedication of a Carmine

Bianco of Patchogue, who assumed a heroic obligation as a form of a private vow to foster commemoration of St. Liberata, was indeed extraordinary. To undertake the expense and sacrifice demanded annually in organizing feast committees, collecting funds from local townspeople, locating festival sites, obtaining the cooperation of local pastors and public officials, inviting bands from outside the community, housing and maintaining feast shrines and other paraphernalia on their own property, and in general overseeing festivities that attracted tens of thousands was a daunting challenge—one that could only be met by those who had the deepest commitment. Bianco, for example, maintained—next to his house for thirty years until his passing at age 80—a one room chapel that housed the statue of St. Liberata that was the centerpiece of a procession through the Italian area of town.[37]

With the passing of these dedicated individuals feast celebrations declined and in some instances ceased altogether. With the exceptions of Glen Cove and Westbury, the era of laymen devoted to the tasks of commemorating local saints from the old country while not entirely over, is definitely waning. Interestingly, in recent years, new generically Italian feasts, some unconnected with particular saints, have emerged and still dot the Long Island landscape.

In sum, three models of integrating Italian Catholic immigrants developed: accommodation and assimilation into existing Irish-oriented parishes, creation of defacto "Italian" national or ethnic parishes, and the creation of national parishes functioning outside of traditional geographic boundaries. Of the latter only Glen Cove's St. Rocco Church was from the outset a national parish—furthermore, it still functions as such. The defacto Italian parishes of Our Lady of Mount Carmel in Patchogue, Our Lady of the Assumption in Copiague, and Our Lady of Good Counsel in Inwood, while originally dedicated as extra-territorial Italian national parishes, have since become integrated into the traditional diocesan structure in which they serve a given geographical area regardless of nationality. Based on the

Long Island communities examined, it can therefore be said that while ethnic religious cultural patterns persist in some locales, in most places they have been diluted and integration into the mainstream of Catholicism has occurred.

SALVATORE J. LAGUMINA

[1] Andrew M. Greeley, *The Catholic Experience* (Garden City, 1969), p. 186.

[2] See Jay P. Dolan, *The Immigrant Church, New York's Irish and German Catholics, 1815-1865* (Annapolis, 1975), p. 22.

[3] See Randall Miller and Thomas Marzik, eds., *Immigrants and Religion in Urban America* (Philadelphia, 1977); Silvano M. Tomasi, *Piety and Power, The Role of Italian Parishes in the New York Metropolitan Area* (Staten Island, 1975); Robert A. Orsi, *The Madonna of 115th Street: Faith and Community in Italian Harlem, 1880-1950* (New Haven, 1985); Daniel S. Buczek, *Immigrant Pastor: The Life of the Right Reverend Monsignor Lucyan Bojowski of New Britain* (Waterbury, 1974).

[4] On Pentecostalism see Winthrop S. Hudson, *American Protestantism* (Chicago, 1961), p. 160.

[5] Scholarly attention on the Catholicism of Italian immigrants can be found in Tomasi, *Piety and Power*; Orsi, *The Madonna of 115th Street*; Henry J. Browne, "The Italian Problem in the Catholic Church of the United States, 1880-1900," *Historical Records and Studies*, Vol. XXXV, 1946, pp. 46-72; Rudolph J. Vecoli, "Prelates and Peasants: Italian Immigrants and the Catholic Church," *Journal of Social History*, Vol. 2, #3, Spring, 1969, pp. 217-268; Francis X. Femminella, "The Impact of Italian Migration on American Catholicism," *The American Catholic Sociological Review*, Vol. XXII, Fall, 1961, pp. 233-241; Joseph A. Varacalli, "The Changing Nature of the Italian Problem in the Catholic Church of the United States," *Faith and Reason*, Vol. XII, No. 1, pp. 38-73.

[6] See Tomasi, *Piety and Power*, pp. 47-50, 148-153 on Protestant Christianizing.

[7] Extrapolated from data in United States Census, 80-1C p. 34, New York; other references Brooklyn and Queens with a larger aggregate estimate Italian-American population. See Edward J. Miranda and Ino J. Rossi, *New York City's Italians* (New York, 1976), p. 20.

[8] Salvatore J. LaGumina, *From Steerage to Suburb, Long Island Italians* (Staten Island, 1989). See also LaGumina, "Long Island Italians and the Labor Movement, Part I" *Long Island Forum* (January 1985), pp. 4-10, and Part II (February 1985) pp. 31-38.

[9] *United States Census, Street Schedules*, 1900, 1910.

[10] Alfred H. Bellot, *History of the Rockaways* (Far Rockaway, 1918), p. 56.

[11] Rockaway *News*, April 28, 1910.

[12] Far Rockaway *Journal*, May 11, 1923. For examples of other early feast cele-

brations, see Rockaway *News*, September 12, 1913 and May 13, 1915. The loudness of the fireworks display split the community by the mid-1920s. While demands to lower the decibel levels eventually were heeded, the issue served to promote Italian organization life that for a time presented a united front advocating better attention to the Italian areas locally. See Rockaway *News*, August 26 and 30, 1926. See also "The Albanese and Italian Community of Inwood, Long Island (co-authored by Angela Danzi, Richard Renoff and Joseph A. Varacalli), *Italian-Americans: The Search for A Usable Past*, Edited by Richard N. Juliani and Philip Cannistraro (Staten Island, New York: American Italian Historical Association, 1989.)

[13] *Marriage Register, Our Lady of Good Counsel*, Inwood, New York.

[14] See Westbury *Times*, August 21, 1936, September 13, 1937, and August 12, 1938, for examples of the Feast of the Assumption celebrations.

[15] Interview, Monsignor Anthony DeLaura, March 23, 1982.

[16] Information on the sand mines and strikes may be found in Port Washington *News*, May 23, 1908; Mitch Carucci, "The Sand Pits of Port Washington," *Long Island Heritage,* October, 1981; Salvatore J. LaGumina, "Long Island Italians and the labor Movement, *Long Island Forum*, February 1985, pp.31-38.

[17] Port Washington *News*, August 16, September 13, 1913.

[18] Port Washington *News*, October 3, 1910.

[19] *United States Census,* Street Schedules, Nassau County, 1900.

[20] Oyster Bay *Guardian*, August 25,1911.

[21] "Petition" in *Angelo Cocchiola Papers,* in possession of Catherine Cocchiola. *Minutes of Societa de Mutuo Succorso,1925-32*, passim. *St. Rocco Anniversary Booklet,* Oct. 21-23, 1937.

[22] *Newsday,* January 23, 1985.

[23] *The Long Island Catholic*, May 13, 1998.

[24] LaGumina, "Marconiville, U.S.A.: The Rise of An Italian-American Suburban Community," *The Family and Community Life of Italian-Americans,* Richard J. Juliani, ed., pp. 81-93.

[25] Interview, Fr. Francis Dell Vecchio, March 31, 1976.

[26] Amityville *Record*, October 5, 1950.

[27] See Amityville *Record*, June 21, July 12, 1951.

[28] Interview, Fr. Ronald Barry, September 20, 1982.

[29] Interview, Monsignor DeLaura.

[30] *Marriage Register, Our Lady of Mount Carmel, Patchogue, St. Joseph, Hagerman, and St. Sylvester, Medford.*

[31] Interview, Frank Mooney, October 19, 1984, Interview, Marie Cantino, April 9, 1985.

[32] Interview, Rose Pascuzzo, June 26, 1985.

[33] Long Island *Catholic*, January 19, 1967.

[34] Joseph A. Varacalli, "The Changing Nature of the Italian Problem," *Faith and Reason.*

[35] This is in keeping with the findings of Nicholas John Russo, "Three Generations of Italians in New York City: Their Religious Acculturation," *The Italian Experience in the United States*, Silvano Tomasi and Madeline Engel, eds. (Staten Island, 1970), pp. 195-202.

[36] James Hennessey, *American Catholics*, (New York, 1983), p. 174.

[37] The suburban experience of these lay organizations with local churches was apparently more harmonious than the more frequent conflict that existed in urban centers. See Vecoli, "Cult and Occult in Italian-American Culture," *Immigrants and Religion in Urban America*.

Part IV

Analytical Reflections

CHAPTER 8

THE VIEW FROM THE OUTSIDE: PERCEPTIONS OF
ITALIAN-AMERICAN RELIGIOSITY

Jacob Riis spoke better than he knew when in 1899 he said of the Feast of San Donato in New York City: "The religious fervor of our Italians is not to be pent up within brick walls."[1] It was that the irrepressible expressiveness of Italian-American religiosity, a seemingly innate urge to externalize and materialize spiritual impulses in art, architecture, music, and elaborate ceremony, clashed mightily with the religious habits of turn-of-the-century Americans, both Protestant and Catholic. For as much as the piety of the *contadini* (the peasantry of Southern Italy, or *Mezzogiorno*, who made up the bulk of Italian immigration to America) was external and exuberant, that of Anglo- and Irish-Americans was internal and reserved.[2] So it is not all that surprising that the latter would view with alarm the ubiquitous public *festas* (*feste* or feast days), processions, and pageants of the South Italians in honor of various saints and the Madonna. The one described in the following advertisement displayed in the store windows of New York's Little Italy earlier this century is typical.

> *Annual Festival in Honor of S. Gandolfo*
> *Protector of Polizzi Generosa*
> Program of the Feast

On Saturday the 14th of September, at ten a.m., the feast will begin with a performance of the famous musical band, led by the renowned Maestro Domenico A____. In the evening there will be a magnificent display of lights from Prince to Bleeker Streets and from Mott Street through Prince Street as far as the Bowery. A concert will take place on a special stand. EXTRA! Grand concert with singing by the following artists: ... On Sunday the 15th there will be High Mass in the Church of Loreto in Elizabeth Street with a Eulogy. The evening program will be similar to that of the preceding day. On Monday the 16th a band will be parading through the streets. In the evening at 7:30 the grand procession will take place in which compatriots and the faithful will join. On the return of the procession there will be a flight of angels, fireworks, and drawing of prizes; followed by the band concert with singing as on Saturday.[3]

Writing in a 1938 handbook for social workers, visiting nurses, school teachers, and physicians who served the *contadini*, Phyllis H. Williams had a startlingly rationalistic view of what was perhaps the most singular event of the San Gandolfo feast previewed above, "the flight of angels," achieved by tying rope from one fire-escape to another one across the street, and lowering on pulleys two young girls costumed as angels who then hover just above the statue of San Gandolfo as it passes in procession. At which point the procession stops for the angels to recite poems in honor of San Gandolfo. Williams's only comment on this scene: "Although this act lasts but ten minutes, the children must be under considerable physical strain; the twenty-five dollars that each receives does not, therefore seem excessive."[4]

Protestant missionaries' response to the sight of such "gaudy" public festivals as the San Gandolfo feast were less pragmatic and restrained. To many of them the Italian immigrants were "just as ignorant of the true Christ and of the [Christian] way of life as any heathen in darkest Africa." Italian saints' festivals were "nothing more than sensual orgies with music and fireworks." Some Irish-American Catholics rallied against such attacks on Catholics, but others shared in common with Protestants the view of the *festa* as a flamboyant paganization of true Christianity.[5]

An American Tradition of Spiritual Reserve

D. W. Brogan once observed that the condition of Roman Catholicism in America was highly ambiguous, in part because America is "a Protestant country." More than a platitude, he meant, "not that the majority of Americans are adherents, more or less active, of Protestant churches, it is that the historical background, the historical tradition, the folkways, the whole national idea of the 'right thing' is deeply and almost exclusively Protestant." Accordingly, to understand more deeply some of the American antagonism to the Italian-Americans' *feste* and other of their public expressions of piety, it is useful to examine closely a central element of the American Protestant tradition: the profoundly private and reserved character of its piety. As we shall see, it is a characteristic associated in some degree also with the Catholicism of nineteenth-century Irish immigrants, and it partly explains why some Irish-Catholics were as repulsed as Protestants over the spectacle of the Italian-American religious feste.[6]

It is well known that American Protestantism has been informed deeply by the Calvinism of the New England Puritans. Calvinism was a profoundly introspective religion, it held that only by tireless self-searching could one tend to know whether or not he or she was saved. Thus things like personal diaries became indispensable aids for tracking the record of one's soul. New England Calvinists violently rejected "the ancient pageantry of Catholic worship," which they saw as a collection of unwarranted, non-Biblical accretions. Along with their proscription of the elaborate liturgical practices of the Roman Catholics and the Anglicans went a conscious disruption of the Catholic rhythms of fast and feast, and the distinction between sacred and profane spaces, which were long-standing ways of ordering time and space, and the essence of the Italian-American feste. As David D. Hall has said in his study of the religious practices of the New England Puritans, the Puritans' repertory of public ritual was confined to "collective rites like fast days and thanksgivings." Fast days were the most important; they included "prayer, the practice of [public] confession, and the ceremony of public execution," the last being mainly for the benefit of the living who witnessed it. In this intensely reformist religious culture "the people had to do without the Christian calendar and its days of high significance: no Christmas, Easter, or Ascension." In an extreme departure from nearly all traditional religious practice, Christian or other, the Puritans had severed their year from the cycles of nature, refusing to mark in any way the changes in season. Even such traditional rites of passage as marriage and death were turned into nondescript civil ceremonies devoid of merriment. It must be said, however, that the ministers and magistrates of early New England found it difficult to enforce these prohibitions.[7]

Calvinist Puritanism in early America suffered periods of decline, but renewed itself by way of two major Awakenings. Jonathan Edwards led the first in the early 1700s; Charles Grandison Finney, Lyman Beecher, and others, led the second in the early 1800s. The revivals that advanced

Calvinism westward during the latter period often generated a religious enthusiasm that manifested itself in outward emotional expressiveness. But these ecstatic expressions of the spirit, no matter how demonstrative, were short-lived and they rarely, if ever, manifested themselves in anything concrete and durable, such as religious art works or sustained and expressive public liturgies. Rather, Protestant ministers in the nineteenth century channeled the enthusiasm of those who had the experience of sudden conversion into established churches in order to "nurture" their interior growth. Many, especially women, also found an outlet in the numerous missionary societies of the nineteenth century that carried on an extensive range of social work and social reforms. The enthusiasm and massive conversions brought on by this Great Awakening led ministers and theologians to reconsider the fundamental relation of sudden conversion and the gradual disciplining of the interior life. The influential Congregational minister and theologian of Hartford, Connecticut, Horace Bushnell suggested in his *Christian Nurture* (1847) that Christian formation was achieved more certainly by gradual self-discipline than by a reliance on the evanescent seasons of awakenings. "The appealing simplicity of Bushnell's logic," writes the historian Anne C. Rose, "belies how radically he questioned the central tenet of the evangelical tradition in America: the need for a single conversion experience." For purposes of our discussion Bushnell's insistence on step by step spiritual "nurture" over enthusiastic conversions underscores the high importance that nineteenth-century Protestant leaders like Bushnell placed on close attention to the interior life, thereby strengthening the American tradition of private religion.[8]

The case for an American Catholic tradition of private religion runs up against the obvious objection that Catholicism, with its Mass and other devotional liturgies, and its long tradition of religious art in Churches, is nothing if not a religion of external expression. And it must have certainly appeared as such to American Protestants when the first great wave of Irish Catholic immigrants of the nineteenth century began practicing their religion. Granted, the Catholicism of the Irish immigrants was more external than Protestantism, but it was never so external that it burst out of the church and into the city streets. What external expressiveness there was was contained within the walls of the church building, and for the most part it stayed out of the public eye. But more important there are positive convergences in the realm of personal religion between nineteenth-century

Protestantism and Catholicism that are often overlooked because their violent clashes, doctrinally and socially, distract us from seeing them.

It is well-established that the great many Irish-Catholic immigrants to America in the 1830s and 1840s met with extreme intolerance from the Protestant majority which thought of them as superstitious, and subversives in the service of the Roman Pope. In Lyman Beecher's terms, they were the "locusts of Egypt." A good part of Protestant Americans' prejudice against the Catholic Irish rested on the ground of politics as much as anything else. Protestants feared Catholics for the threat they posed to the comparatively new American republic. Samuel F.B. Morse, the inventor of the telegraph, spoke for many when he said in 1835 that he was unconcerned with "the religious tenets properly so called of the Roman Catholic," but rather with "the foreign political conspiracy . . . identified with that creed." But what is more relevant to the point at hand—staking out the common ground of Protestants and Catholics in the realm of private religiosity—is that Irish-American Catholicism, in part through its contact with American Evangelical Protestantism, took on some of its features. Samuel Eliot Morison points to the basis for this common ground in his discussion of seventeenth-century Puritan theology. Like Catholicism, he said, Puritan Calvinism held "that man existed for the glory of God, and that his first concern in life should be to do God's will and so receive future happiness." In her history of early nineteenth century America, Rose extends the similarities. Then, she says, "Catholic parishes . . . were similar to contemporary Protestant congregations. Parish and mission work both stressed the need for interior conversion of heart and spiritual discipline. The Irish-Catholic immigrants' "taste for devotions, rituals performed by *individuals*, corresponded to the attachment of Victorian Protestants to religious nurture and feeling. Literate Catholics studied manuals of instruction in devotions in an effort to enhance their *personal piety* through a routine of observances and prayers."[9]

During this period Jesuits, Redemptorists, and other Catholic orders stormed the country on parish missions. Their purpose was to bring about the reinvigoration of American Catholicism by way of "personal conversion." To be sure, these missions may have, as Jay Dolan has argued, "rivaled the theater," and encouraged "homage to the saints through the public display and application of their relics." But just as Protestant enthusiasm had to be channeled into a personal plan of life, so too *The Mission Book*, the handbook of the Catholic mission movement, was unequivocal about what social expression the converted heart had to take: its fulfillment lay "in the church through the observance of orthodox religious practices." Such expression, despite its root in an enthusiastic theatrical experience, did not unleash froward and sustained public displays of religiosity such as the Italian immigrant's *feste*.[10]

Finally, one popular form of last century's antipathy to Catholicism, the expose, offers an ironic reversal of the position of Italian immigrant Catholics in this century. The *raison d'etre* of the expose is to bring out before the public eye in a provocative way that which it cannot readily see. As Rose points out, "Maria Monk's *Awful Disclosures of the Hotel Dieu Nunnery of Montreal* (1836) titillated readers with intimations of illicit sexual relations and infanticide in monastic communities." Such books created an atmosphere conducive to the mob violence that resulted in the torching of the Ursuline Convent in Charlestown, Massachusetts in 1834.[11]

The point of the foregoing case for an American tradition of private, reserved religion is to emphasize that American Protestants and Catholics rejected the immigrant Italians' religiosity more because of the strangeness of its elaborate external expression than because of its Catholicism *per se*. For before the arrival of the *contadini*, both Protestants and Catholics in America had become used to a Christianity that stressed interiority over exteriority.

The Festa and the Faith

With this long American tradition of private, reserved religion in place, we are now in a better position to appreciate why American Catholics advanced criticisms of Italian-American religiosity along similar lines as Protestants did. The *feste* of the immigrant Italians, some American Catholics thought, reflected "very little love of the faith, and very little knowledge of it." Some others complained that Italian religion, "what there is of it, is exterior." And, finally, there was this comprehensive indictment from a Jesuit writing in a 1914 number of *America*:

> Piety does not consist in processions or carrying candles, in prostrations
> before a statue of the Madonna, in processions in honor of patron saints of
> villages, but true piety consists in the daily fulfillment of the religious
> duties exacted of us by God Almighty and His Church, and it consists in a

love for that Church and her ministers. In these points, no matter how numerous be the Italian processions, no matter how heavy the candles, no matter how many lights they carry, the Italian immigrant seems very deficient.[12]

But it must be said that it was not only the native Protestant and Catholic Americans who criticized harshly the *feste* of the *contadini*, other more established Italian-Americans, the *connazionali*, the more educated and nationalistic Italian immigrants usually from the north of Italy, joined in as well. Jane Addams' Hull House benefitted from a reputation for sustaining good relations "not only with the Neapolitans and the Sicilians of the immediate neighborhood, but [also] with the educated *connazionali* through the city." Addams' gratifying experience with the *connazionali* in their relation to the *contadini* reminded her of John Ruskin's celebration of the former as "the 'companion people' because of their power for swift sympathy." The *connazionali* may have speedily moved to celebrate Garibaldi and the ideal of Italian nationalism but they were far less sympathetic to the indigenous culture of their compatriots from the *Mezzogiorno*, at least in the view of Caroline Ware. Her reading of the Italian immigrants from Genoa and other places in the North who settled in New York's Greenwich Village is quite at odds with Addams's Chicago experience. The Northerners, wrote Ware in 1935, "had established themselves in a position from which they could look down with scorn upon the 'low' Italians, could take pains neither to know or to be classed with them, and could dominate the affairs of the Italian community from a lofty distance." The position they took from on high manifested itself especially in their view of the *feste*. Educated Italian immigrants, as Rudolph J. Vecoli says, found their "humiliating religious display," and their "theatrical vulgarity" embarrassing. The more bourgeois Italian-Americans seemed averse not so much to the religiosity of the feste, but to the Italians behaving crassly in public, perhaps forgetting that colorful and flamboyant, sacred and profane public feste are emblematic of the entire Italian peninsula. As Carol Fields has recently written in *Celebrating Italy*, the phenomenon of the festival, when "the world is hung with banners," occurs "all over Italy." There was among educated Italians, it seems, strict limits to their sympathy for sentimental religious expression, whether it be that of their own people or that of others. As Theodore Maynard writes, Mother Francesca Cabrini of Lombardy in the North, the saintly missionary to Italian immigrants in the Americas, in a letter to one of her sisters expressed her distaste for certain expressions of Spanish piety that she saw in Lima, Peru.[13]

The fiercely anti-clerical wing of the *connazionali* denounced the religious *feste* for raising the saints above Italy's national heroes. An article in the August 13, 1907 edition of *La Tribuna Italiana* put it this way:

> Why do not our countrymen instead of spending so much money in use-
> less illuminations, processions, and festivals, now for a saint, again for
> a madonna, demonstrate their patriotism by commemorating the great
> men....who fought for the holy cause of liberty for the people? Up,
> Countrymen, first be patriots and then religious.[14]

A few Italian churchmen objected to the *feste* for their materialism. After visiting America from Italy and viewing a *festa*, Don Luigi Guanella favored prohibiting them for their reckless admixture of the sacred and the profane, and the mixing of the profit motive with what for him amounted to mere entertainment under the cover of a religious event.[15]

Curiously, some Italian-American historians of the late twentieth century have interpreted the *festa* and Italian-American religiosity in general, in line with early twentieth-century Americans' perceptions of them as essentially pagan and un-Christian, insofar as they had little to do with doctrinal Christianity. Vecoli, for example, sees the *festa* as "the most authentic expression of South Italian culture transplanted to the New World." But although religion is a part of that culture, he does not see it as necessarily associated with the Roman Catholic Church. Indeed, Vecoli says that for most of the *contadini* "religion continued to be what it had been in their *paesi* (villages): a belief in the efficacy of magic and devotions to their saints and madonnas coupled with a basic indifference to and distrust of the institutional church." Robert A. Orsi's influential study of Italian Harlem's annual Feast of the Madonna of Mount Carmel, opens by confronting the long-standing American perception of Italian-American pious practices like the feast as "exotic and pagan." He rejects Vecoli's interpretation of Italian-American religiosity because even though Vecoli stresses Southern Italian immigrants' disaffection from the Catholic Church, he still has viewed their religious practices "only from the perspective of the church." Orsi's interpretation lines up with current historiographical fashion which follows an essentially sociological mental construct that distinguishes sharply between an "institutional church," on the one hand, and "the people," on the other. Orsi's work on *La Madonna del Carmine* starts from the perspective of the "people's perceptions, values, needs, and history," from which he develops a "theology of the streets." His point of view, of course, sidesteps the original historical question; and, moreover, by characterizing Catholicism strictly in terms of the pre-Christian paganistic religious practices, of the *Mezzogiorno*—where, Orsi following Carlo Levi asserts Christ "never reached," *The Madonna of 115th Street* has the effect of providing an elegant ethnographical justification for the crude invectives of the early twentieth Protestant missionaries.[16]

Contra Vecoli and Orsi, Giovanni Schiavo, a historian writing in 1949, insists that "at no time did his [the Italian immigrant's] belief in God and in the Roman Catholic Church ever waiver." Quoting with approval, the observation of a Bostonian in 1899, Schiavo writes: "The piety of the Italian though frequently of the highest order, has peculiarities that distinguish it from that of other races. The Irishman or the Belgian does not burn candles to his patron saint years after he had given up the practice of churchgoing—though he may be as inconsistent in other respects. On the other hand, it is only in Italian churches that one may expect to find at any hour penitents prostrated before the crucifix or the stations of the cross, passionately lamenting their errors."[17] Even, more recently, Mark Woman in his book about European immigrants to America who returned to Europe during the period from 1880-1930 writes that Catholics in general, but especially those who immigrated to less sparsely populated parts of America, became disillusioned with America in large part because they could not hear Mass or attend other forms of Catholic devotions. Italians "traveling between two Italian communities tied together by immigration and return migration—Roseto Valfortore, Italy, and Roseto, Pennsylvania—put their disillusionment into a song":

What can we find in America?
Mountains of gold and mountains of work,
A gold cross, but still a cross,
A diamond cross is still a cross.[18]

However, as Vecoli concludes, the weight of contemporary criticism notwithstanding, "the observance of the feast-days was too deeply ingrained in the Southern Italian culture to be easily eradicated."[19]

Protestant Italian-American ministers on the piety of the Contadini

The drama and the spectacle of the *feste* were obvious and emphatically public expressions of Italian-American religiosity, which, because they intermixed religious ceremonies with the spirit of the carnival, were interpreted in a variety of ways. But the ebullient expressivity of Italian-American religiosity, which as I have been arguing made them stand out starkly in an American culture steeped in private religion, was evident to some American observers in the more privates spaces of the Italian churches. Two prominent Italian-American Protestant ministers, Antonio Mangano and F.C. Capozzi, who had first hand experience with the richness of Italian Catholic exteriority and the more internalized religiosity of Protestantism, were especially sharp-eyed observers of the singular expressiveness of Italian churches, which they both thought was indispensable to Italian piety.

Mangano, a Calabrian-American Baptist minister and Director of the Italian Department of Colgate Theological Seminary, wrote prolifically on the condition of the Italian immigrant in America. In one of his more well-known pieces on the "Associated Life of the Italians in New York City," which first appeared in a 1904 number of the social work magazine, *Charities*, Mangano said nothing about the orthodoxy of the *feste*, because he understood them to be not primarily religious events at all, but instead mere "amusements." Writing with a most respectful tone, he saw the feste as occasions for the Italian-American to show "his love for show and pomp, uniforms, banners, music, elaborate discourse. Eating and drinking are the chief features." Religious holidays, many of which had to be rearranged to accommodate the temperate climate of the United States and thereby not so seriously religious, were just "the most extravagant" of these public events. Italian immigrants packed into the feasts— fifteen thousand men a day" during the week of one festival—not out of any passionate religious fervor, but because of their natural conviviality, and their "strong desire for companionship." For "nothing" is more pleasurable to them than meeting with friends."[20]

Mangano treats the religiosity of his fellow *contadini* under a completely separate heading from the one under which he treated the *feste*. And here we find an eye tempered by the experience of American Protestantism, and keenly sensitive to the more ornate quality of the "23 Roman Catholic churches" in Manhattan that served Italian immigrants. Saying little about the efforts of these congregations and their pastors on behalf of the social needs of the Italian immigrants, Mangano's commentary centered on the church buildings themselves in which he found an uncommon "warmth and artistic display." He attributed this uniqueness to the long Italian tradition of "artistic cathedral decorations," and to the historical reality that much of the lives of Italians had been centered in the church. It is but natural that his places of worship should embody all that art and aesthetic natures can contribute."[21]

F.C. Capozzi, the Rector of Saint Mary's Episcopal Church in Wind Gap, Pennsylvania, was even more emphatic than Mangano on the centrality of expressiveness in Italian-American churches and their rituals. "Worship, without a rich and pompous ceremonial, is to them something almost devoid of meaning, the church building itself, if there be not a profusion of art, to them is incapable of breathing religion and devotion; they would feel within its wall as though they were in a cold and chilly Place." Capozzi was among the many Protestants who sought to attract Italian-American Catholics to Protestantism; he differed from most in that he envisioned this attraction taking place within a wider restoration of Christendom, one that included a "self-reformed" and not a destroyed Catholic Church. He held out Anglicanism as the principle, imperfect as it was, by which a new Christian unity could thrive. It had the right blend of "Catholic tradition and intellectual freedom," "order and liberty," which "might eventually bring about the equilibrium between the objective reality of Christian truth and the subjective exigencies of Christian souls."[22]

Capozzi's fascinating book, *Protestantism and the Latin Soul*, examines why it was that fin-de-siecle Protestantism had failed to reach the Italian immigrants. He argued that part of the reason for this failure lay in the inexpressive character of Italian evangelical churches. Barren and cold, they "look like places of public meetings, and suitable for the discussion of worldly and commercial matters." How could they attract "a people endowed with such a lively imagination as Italians?" That "the excessive formalism of the Roman Catholic Church distracts and lulls the spiritual energies, by pleasing the senses and exciting fancy and curiosity, does not mean that the church buildings should lack something able to dispose souls to meditation, prayer, something to make them feel that they are not in ordinary places, but in the house of God." By way of contrast, a Protestant can in the most spartan of surroundings "raise himself above sensible things, to concentrate his attention upon the inward world and revive before his own spirit the idea of God." But the Italian cannot "dissociate himself from the exterior world," and is unable to approach God "but by means that appeal to his senses and arouse his emotions." Capozzi concluded that Anglicanism had preserved a sufficient amount of Catholic artist expression in its liturgies to be appealing to the Latin soul. But Calvinism and other Protestant sects that reviled religious art and ceremony, were "too austere for the Latin temper. The pure religion of spirit, for which [they] plead, is something unsuited to them [Italians]."[23]

Traversing Private and Public

Italians' churches and their *feste* as exemplars of an historic Italian preference for external worship and splendid artistic expression do not exhaust the range of Italian-American religiosity. There is a rich piety centered in the privacy of the home. Saints' pictures and crucifixes bedecked immigrant Italian homes; votive candles flickered before homemade shrines to various saints, the Virgin Mary, and the suffering Christ. The rhythms of family life followed the liturgical calendar, with appropriate foods prepared and prayers said for the feast days of important saints. The size of one's house or one's earnings were no impediments to celebrating such feasts, as Jerre Mangione recalls from his boyhood lived amid a large, extended family of Sicilian immigrants in Rochester, New York. "On any Sunday or holiday a score of relatives would crowd into our tiny house at the invitation of my father, whose capacity for hospitality far exceeded his income, to partake of a Lucullan banquet consisting of at least three meat courses, and at Christmas and Easter, *cannoli*, the masterpiece of his art as a pastry maker."[24]

The calendar of feasting in the Italian-American home moved with and complemented the yearly regime of public religious festivals in the streets, creating a rhythm of life, of work and feasting unhampered by the strict division of private and public realms that had become the hallmark of American culture since the 1830s. In America the private sphere of the home had become a protected refuge from the harsh realities of a public sphere dominated by cut-throat competition. This separation led to a debilitating division within the individual which many Progressive intellectuals and artists felt deeply. The *festa* appealed to many of them, Jane Addams, Lewis Mumford, Randolph Bourne, Jacob Riis, Claude Bragdon and others—precisely because its participants moved effortlessly between private and public spheres, and in so doing enjoyed an authentic sense of community. Disaffected from their Protestant American families and the Victorian culture in which they grew up, they looked upon the *festa* as providing the "wholeness" and "organic experience" they longed for. They desired to participate in some way in the experience of the Italian immigrant, who, as Riis wrote, looked to the saints *feste* as "the rallying-point in his civic and domestic life to the end of his days."[25]

One American Progressive, the architect Claude Bragdon, tried to recreate the spirit of the *feste* in massive public Festivals of Song and Light which he staged in Rochester, Syracuse, Buffalo, and New York City during 1915, 1916, and 1917. Ostensibly secular in nature, Bragdon's festivals were deeply informed by the late nineteenth-century spiritualist cults. Festival evenings drew thousands of Americans who listened and sang with their city's large amateur choruses, which typically were accompanied by a symphony orchestra. The musical offerings, as in the Italian *feste*, mingled classical and operatic compositions and traditional folk tunes. The Italian *feste* created a world "hung with banners"; Bragdon's festival world stressed light. He hung lanterns with multicolored glass shades that used innovative arrangements of geometrical patterns, which were continuous with "his efforts to create a new system of architectural ornamentation rooted in occult science." By way of his wife's communications with the spiritual world, Bragdon was informed that light would "revolutionize the art of man." In Bragdon's formulation his lantern lighting acted upon the unconscious mind of its viewer "as does the mesmerist's crystal ball, tranquilizing the body and awakening the soul." For him these Festivals of Song and Light were intended to be more like "a religious ceremony" than the usual public concert, they were portents, says Wayne Willis of "an exalted, popular, participatory art of the future."[26]

What Bragdon sought to create by rational planning was in essence what the South Italians in America had achieved naturally in the *feste*, not just in the way of spectacle and artistic expression, but in the effortless way in which they brought about community—that elusive goal of twentieth-century American social life. For Jacob Riis the Italian *festa* exemplified neighborly affection by way of an unselfconscious intermingling of public and private spheres. With a masterful style, Riis, in his famous description of the San Donato festival, made the reader keenly aware of how the *festa* blurred the boundaries of the public and the private. Unlike the lavish spectacle of the gigantic New York feasts in honor of San Gandolfo, San Gennaro, and others, the Festival of San Donato was tucked away in a side alley off Elizabeth Street in lower Manhattan. Riis discovered it seemingly by accident by falling in behind a procession moving in tow behind some policemen. He was led into a space that was ambiguously public and private. Entering "through a gap in the brick wall that passed for an alley," he came into a backyard where "the village of Auletta feast[ed] its patron saint." Hung banners and sheets hid the squalor, "it was a yard no longer, but a temple. All the sheets of the tenement had been stretched so as to cover the ugly sheds and outhouses." And there "against the dark rear tenement the shrine of the saint had been erected." Riis conveyed with unexampled vividness an extraordinary visual texture of kitchens, fire-escapes, and neighborhood alleys. "The fire-escapes of the tenement had, with the aid of some cheap muslin draperies a little tinsel, and the strange artistic genius of this people, been transformed into beautiful balconies, upon which the tenants of the front house had reserved seats." The climax of this *festa* was the raffling of a live sheep, which a family could feast on for weeks. The eventual winner of the lottery, which Riis suggests had been fixed in favor of a poor family, had been watching the public drawing with anticipation from high above. "'Philomeno Motso,' read the man with the bag, and there was an answering shriek from that third-floor fire-escape behind the shrine. The widow up there had won the prize. Such luck was undreamed of. She came down forthwith and hugged the sheep rapturously, while the children kissed it and wept for joy." And so it was that the public *festa* tangibly extended its joyousness into the privacy of the family. Let it be said that Riis's reading of the San Donato feast places it squarely at odds with the Catholic Church. The people keep the saint's statue in the neighborhood saloon, it "belonged to the people, not to the church." For Riis the whole point of this and the other feste one finds on Mulberry, Mott, and Thompson streets, is that they awakened neighborly affection, a feeling intensified by the fact that the Italian immigrants were bound together by being strangers in the land. Each *festa* in its own way replied vivaciously to the question central to the Progressive intellectual's social thinking: "Who is my neighbor?"[27]

Such facile intermingling of the public and private was not restricted to congested lower Manhattan. In *An Ethnic at Large*, Jerre Mangione's matchless memoir of Italian-American life in early twentieth-century America, we again see how easily the Italian immigrants moved between private and public places. It was a practice that, as a "mindless[ly] conformist" boy, caused him great embarrassment before "the sons of Polish, German, and Russian Jewish immigrants" who lived in his neighborhood. As a boy Mangione enjoyed family gatherings at which he delighted in hearing tales of Sicily just so long as they remained private. But he became "tormented" with the worry that they were making a bad impression on the Americans around us "when during the summer his and other Sicilian families took to serenading one another in the dead of night, waking up their non-Sicilian neighbors with their songs and mandolins, or when they invaded the public parks with their exuberant festivals." Mangione came to see later in his life that there was a link between the Sicilian immigrants' bold projection of their ethnicity into public places and the hostility and antagonism they suffered at the hands of other ethnics and the white Protestant majority. "I learned long afterward (not from them)," writes Mangione, "that at one point the public's image of Sicilians in Rochester was so sinister that the immigrants had felt compelled to prove that they were a civilized and moral people, not criminals involved with the Mafia or the Black Hand, as the press would have the community believe."[28]

So on Columbus day in 1908 the Sicilians in Rochester mounted an elaborate Passion Play—the drama of the trial and crucifixion of Jesus—to prove their moral worth to the larger community of Rochester. Included in the play's large cast were milkmen, masons, ditch diggers, shoemakers, bakers, tailors, and factory hands. Although the play's Sicilian-American producers mailed hundreds of invitations to leaders of the Anglo-American community and their wives, only a few showed up. Fortunately, the enthusiasm of these few for the quality of the production generated so much excitement that the Sicilians were encouraged to stage a second performance. At the second performance of the Passion Play the auditorium in which they staged it was packed with both Italians and non-Italians. Mangione's parents were there at the performance and they gave him an eye witness account of it. The lines in the Passion Play were spoken in Italian but the Americans were as deeply moved by the performance as the Italians in the audience, joining in the prolonged applause. The next day came the big payoff, writes Mangione, "the same newspapers that had been headlining Sicilian crime on their front pages devoted the same kind of space to praising the Sicilian community for making such an impressive contribution to the city's cultural life."[29]

Even though it turned out that the good will produced by the Passion Play wore off and within the year the press was back to demonizing the Sicilian immigrants, the public play struck a "mystic chord of memory" that temporarily affected the wider Protestant American culture, forming a ground for unity between the two cultures. The Passion Play evoked the memory of a common Christian heritage, of the united Christendom that Minister Capozzi sought to restore. But what is more significant is that the Passion Play is a historical instance of the interconnectedness of cultures that has been mostly overlooked in the scholarly literature on ethnicity in America until quite recently. With the popularity of Antonio Gramschi's idea of studying culture—the totality of a people's thought and customs—as a means to understand how subcultures congeal and find their corporate identity within the context of larger, dominant cultures, scholars' emphasis over the past thirty years has been on the distinctiveness of disparate cultures. In part this stress was to underscore the viability and strength of minority groups living under trying and oppressive conditions. What therefore has emerged from the massive amounts of writing on ethnicity in America is the centrality of difference and cultural clash, a view which obscures the elements that different cultures share in common, such as a common Christian tradition. Without insisting on a new "consensus" view of America that slights cultural differences, historians, sociologists, and others are beginning to correct the imbalance in the literature on ethnicity that everywhere has seen irreconcilable cultural traditions.[30]

The historian Patricia Nelson Limerick has recently addressed this distorted view of ethnic relations in America. "Excited by the recognition of how well the concept of culture has worked to explain difference, we have let the concept of culture evolve into a powerful piece of earthmoving equipment, digging away at what might have been common ground." To return to the story of the Rochester Sicilians' Passion Play, the fact that it only achieved a temporary peace in cultural relations, would receive the only achieved a temporary peace in cultural relations, would receive the stress in the prevailing academic fashion of overemphasizing cultural difference. But in the process of doing so, as Limerick says, we "cut the ground out from under intergroup empathy, compassion, fellow feeling and understanding." Limerick encourages scholars to serve the public good now by spreading the news outside of the academy of an emerging new vision of our "interrelatedness, of our intertwined destinies." Limerick remains grateful to the "concept of culture" for taking people "a long way down the road toward seeing each other 'face to face'." But at the turn of the twenty-first century she also takes new hope that some part of St. Paul's prophecy will be realized in earthly time: "Now we see each other through a glass, darkly; now I know in part . . . But then shall I know even as also I am known."[31]

Jane Addams expressed a similar hope for the rapprochement of ethnic groups at the start of this century as she ruminated on various theories of cultural relations. "I believe," she wrote "that we may get, and should get, something of that revivifying and up springing of culture from our contact with the groups who come to us from foreign countries, and that we can get it in no other way." Like Limerick, she turned to a saint for her hope. The Italian immigrants she lived among had a saying from St. Francis of Assisi that she had become fond of: "The poor little brethren gathered with us under the Madonna's cloak, keep us warm quite as much as the great blue mantle itself."[32]

DOMINIC A. AQUILA

---

[1] Jacob Riis, "Feast Days in Little Italy" in *A Documentary History of the Italian-Americans*, ed. Wayne Moquin with Charles Van Doren (New York: Praeger Publishers, 1974), 315.

[2] The *contadini* refers to the Italian peasantry, but it also includes fisherman, artisans, and unskilled urban poor. *Mezzogiorno* refers to the six Italian provinces of Abruzzi, Campania, Apulia, Lucania (or Basilicata), Calabria, and Sicily; it connotes the land that time forgot. See Richard Gambino, *Blood of My Blood: The Dilemma of the Italian-Americans* (Toronto and New York: Guernica Press, 1996).

[3] Quoted in Phyllis H. Williams, *South Italian Folkways in Europe and America: A Handbook for Social Workers, Visiting Nurses, School Teachers, and Physicians* (New York: Russell & Russell,, 1938), 150-1.

[4] Williams, *South Italian Folkways*, 151.

[5] Quoted in Rudolph J. Vecoli, "Prelates and Peasants: Italian Immigrants and the Catholic Church," *Journal of Social History* 2 (Spring 1969): 233-34.

[6] Dan Herr and Joel Wells, eds., *Through Other Eyes: Some Impressions of American Catholicism by Foreign Visitors from 1777 to the Present* (Westminster, Maryland: The Newman Press, 1965), 166.

[7] Samuel Eliot Morison, *The Oxford History of the American People, Volume One: Prehistory to 1789* (New York: Meridian Books, 1972), 102-3; David D. Hall, *Worlds of Wonder, Days of Judgement: Popular Religious Belief in Early New England* (Cambridge, Massachusetts: Harvard University Press, 1989), 166-212.

[8] Anne C. Rose, *Voices of the Marketplace: American Thought and Culture, 1830-1860* (New York: Twayne Publishers, 1995), 5.

[9] Rose, *Voices of the Marketplace*, 9-10. My emphasis. Morison, *The Oxford History*, 102.

[10] Jay P. Dolan, *Catholic Revivalism: The American Experience, 1830-1900* (Notre Dame, Indiana: University of Notre Dame Press, 1968), 11, 170.

[11] Rose, *Voices of the Marketplace*, 9.

[12] Quoted in Vecoli, "Prelates and Peasants," 234.

[13] Jane Addams, *Twenty Years at Hull-House* (New York: The Macmillan Company, 1916), 232, 256; Caroline F. Ware, *Greenwich Village, 1920-1930: A Comment on American Civilization in the Post-War Years* (New York: Harper & Row, Publishers, 1935), 152-3; Theodore Maynard, *Too Small a World: The Life of Francesca Cabrini* (Milwaukee: The Bruce Publishing Company, 1945), 198.

[14] Quoted in Vecoli, "Prelates and Peasants," 234.

[15] Ibid., 234-5.

[16] Vecoli, "Prelates and Peasants,"232, 268; Robert Anthony Orsi, *The Madonna of 115th Street: Faith and Community in Italian Harlem, 1880-1950* (New Haven and London: Yale University Press, 1985), xiii-xxiii; Carlo Levi, *Christ Stopped at Eboli* (New York: Farrar, Straus and Giroux, 1977).

[17] Giovanni Schiavo, *Italian-American History, Volume II: The Italian Contribution to the Catholic Church in America* (New York: The Vigo Press, 1949), 474-5.

[18] Mark Woman, *Round-Trip to America: The Immigrants Return to Europe, 1880-1930* (Ithaca and London: Cornell University Press, 1993), 88-9.

[19] Vecoli, "Prelates and Peasants, " 235.

[20] Antonio Mangano, "The Associated Life of the Italians in New York City" in *The Italian in America: The Progressive View, 1891-1914*, ed., Lydio F. Tomasi (New York: Center for Migration Studies, 1972), 110, 112.

[21] Ibid.

[22] F.C. Capozzi, *Protestantism and the Latin Soul* (Philadelphia: The John C. Winston Company, 1918), 3-4, 221-3. For more on Protestant evangelization of

Italian-Americans see Salvatore Mondello, "Protestant Proselytism Among the Italians in the USA as Reported in American Magazines," *Social Science* 41 (April 1966): 84-90.

[23] Capozzi, *Protestantism and the Latin Soul*, 173, 176-77.

[24] Jerre Mangione, *An Ethnic at Large: A Memoir of America in the Thirties and Forties* (New York: Putnam's Sons, 1978), 15.

[25] For the Progressive search for authentic community see Casey Blake, *Beloved Community: The Cultural Criticism of Randolph Bourne, Van Wyck Brooks, Waldo Frank, and Lewis Mumford* (Chapel Hill, orth Carolina: The University of North Carolina Press, 1990). For the domestic calendar of Italian feast days see Helen Barolini, *Festa: Recipes and Recollections of Italian Holidays* (New York: Harcourt Brace Jovanovich, Publishers, 1988). The quote from Jacob Riis is from *A Documentary History of the Italian-Americans*, 316.

[26] Wayne Willis, "'Caliban, not Ariel': Claude Bragdon and the Progressive Quest for Cultural Democracy," (paper presented at the annual meeting of the Organization of American Historians, Louisville, Kentucky, 12 April 1991).

[27] Riis, "Feast Days in Little Italy" in *A Documentary History of the Italian-Americans*, 313-15.

[28] Mangione, *An Ethnic at Large*, 15-16.

[29] Ibid.

[30] For Gramschi's influence on historians see T.J. Jackson Lears, "The Concept of Cultural Hegemony: Problems and Possibilities," *American Historical Review* (June 1985): 567-93.

[31] Patricia Nelson Limerick, "The Startling Ability of Culture to Bring Critical Inquiry to a Halt," *The Chronicle of Higher Education*, 24 October 1997, A76.

[32] Quoted in *The Social Thought of Jane Addams*, ed., Christopher Lasch (Indianapolis: The Bobbs-Merrill Company, Inc.,1965), 215.

CHAPTER 9

FROM ETHNICITY TO IDEOLOGY: THE SHIFTING BATTLE OVER THE DEVOTION TO THE SAINTS

More than half way through the Acts of the Apostles, Saint Luke has the Apostle Paul standing in the middle of the Athenian areopagus addressing the citizens in this way:

> Men of Athens, I perceive that in every way you are very religious. For as I passed along, and observed the objects of your worship, I found also an altar with the inscription, 'To an unknown god.' What therefore you worship as unknown, this I proclaim to you...[We] ought not to think that the Deity is like gold, or silver, or stone, a representation by the art and imagination of man (Acts 17:22-23, 29).

Paul of Tarsus was an outstanding evangelist in every way. Not only could he go to places like Athens where Christianity was hitherto unknown and manage to win converts like Dionysius and Damaris (Acts 17:34), but he showed two other qualities important for any good evangelist. First, he demonstrated resourcefulness and creativity in his proclamation without diluting its message. Second, he lacked timidity in criticizing what the local culture thought to be authentically religious. The resourcefulness and creativity were evident in taking what the culture characterized as "unknown" and rendering it intelligible by way of Christian explanation. His courage was reflected in daring to tell the Athenians that their "thinking" about the Deity was all wrong.

172

In every age, an imaginative and creative presentation of salvation in Christ is needed. From the very beginning, the Church has had this in what Catholics call the communion of saints. The saints are men and women whose earthly lives so transparently reflected Christ's that the Church proclaims confidently, even infallibly, that these men and women are already in heaven. It might be said of these saintly men and women that they now form a gorgeous mosaic in heaven. They come from varied epochs, they come from all corners of the globe. And it is in and through their unique earthly circumstances that they all arrive at a common eternal destiny.

With remarkably disparate earthly lives, the saints show that imitation of Christ is possible in any and every culture. We can even say of the saints that they incarnate the faith in a specific set of historical circumstances. They make concrete and attainable an intense way of following Christ in times and places very much removed from the first century Palestinian culture of the earthly Jesus. By doing so, the saints have had an enormous impact on evangelization. Indeed, in the lives of the saints, the gospel is announced anew. In and through their heroic virtue, the word of Christ at once ancient and contemporaneous is spoken again. In the cult that develops around the saints, the gospel continues to be announced and a model for imitation by others is established. In the canonization of the saints, the proclamation of the gospel reaches a new level when the faithful have new intercessors alongside the one Mediator.

Down through the centuries, saints have been honored at the places of their births and at the sites of their deaths, and sometimes in both. In some cases, like that of pre-modern southern Italy, the renown of saints is limited to a village or region. In other cases, their acclaim is much wider, extending perhaps to a whole nation or even across national boundaries. The Church, as we have seen above, has every reason to encourage a veneration of the saints. But when saints are venerated as they are by the faithful, care must be exercised. Pope Paul VI sounds a note of caution in his apostolic exhortation *Evangelii Nuntiandi* (1975). There he writes that popular religiosity "is often subject to penetration by many distortions of religion and even superstitions. It frequently remains at the level of forms of worship not involving a true acceptance by faith. It can even lead to the creation of sects and endanger the true ecclesial community."[1]

We are a long way from first-century Athens but not very far from Pope Paul VI (1963-78) and his rightful concern about popular religiosity and the distortion of religion. Today, the word *culture* is a highly contentious topic in some circles, and the word *inculturation* is similarly controversial in some quarters of the Church. Against this backdrop of contentiousness and controversy, another Paul speaks. Not his given name at birth but his chosen one upon election as Pope, John Paul II (1978-) is a man of culture and a man of faith. Indeed, few others are as qualified as he to speak to matters of culture and faith. As Successor of Peter, John Paul II is charged with the mandate of announcing the gospel in its entirety (Acts 20:27). A son of Poland who speaks multiple languages fluently as well as the most traveled Pope in history, John Paul II is deeply sensitive to culture as a medium of faith.

In his 1990 encyclical letter *Redemptoris Missio*, Pope John Paul II addressed himself to the twin themes of faith and culture. He notes that as the Church carries out missionary activity among the nations, she invariably encounters different cultures and becomes involved in the process of inculturation.[2] Calling inculturation a profound and difficult process, the Pope cautions that care must be taken not to compromise the distinctiveness and integrity of the Christian faith.[3] As inculturation takes place, the Church transmits her own values to the different cultures, taking the good elements that already exist in them and renewing them from within.[4] The Pope concludes that inculturation must be guided by two principles. The first is compatibility with the gospel and the second is communion with the universal church.[5] Responsibility for insuring that inculturation takes place in accord with the gospel and the universal church belongs to the bishops in their role as guardians of the deposit of faith.[6] If proper vigilance is not exercised by the bishops, the Pope warns that there is a risk of passing uncritically from a form of alienation from culture to an overestimation of it. The Pope adds that culture, as a human creation marked by sin, needs to be healed, ennobled and perfected.[7]

The Saints and the Italian-Americans

Consideration of devotion to the saints among Italian-Americans touches upon the few issues already raised in this essay. Clearly, it involves the issue of evangelization. When Italians migrated to the United States, they needed to be evangelized. As we shall see later in this essay, their formation in the Catholic faith in Italy was weak, and there was little practice of it there too. It also involves the issue of popular religiosity, for Italian immigrants brought with them to the United States a strong sense of allegiance to the saint or saints of their particular region in Italy. This was expressed in the *festa* with its colorful processions and elaborate pageantry. For the first generation Italian in America, the carrier of the concept of sainthood was not the Church but ethnicity. But this drew the criticism of other Catholics here in the United States, especially the Irish-dominated hierarchy. Criticism of Italian religiosity no doubt needed to be made, but as we shall see, the criticism could have been offered more delicately.

Devotion to the saints among Italian-Americans very definitely touches on culture, whether defined in terms of ethnicity, nationality or ideology. When the Italians came to the United States, they were like a lot of other immigrants in a land of immigrants. The Italians sought to preserve what was distinctively Italian as they raised their families in American cities, sent their children to American schools and worked at American jobs. The longer Italians remained in the United States, however, they had to determine just how American they were going to become. In addition, how much assimilation would there be? And what kind of effect would assimilation have on Italian devotion to the saints?

This essay is an attempt to chronicle the changes which have taken place in Italian devotion to the saints over several generations. The early period of this devotion in the United States is marked by a pronounced ethnic influence. But as the vast majority of Italians assimilated, just as the Irish, Germans and Poles did, devotion to the saints changed, too. We might say that something of a shift in the direction of ideology and away from ethnicity has occurred regarding Italian devotion to the saints. Today, devotion (or non-devotion) to the saints on the part of Italian-American Catholics represents what sociologists refer to as a *symbolic marker*. Devotion or non-devotion signifies one divide between contemporary orthodox and liberal interpretations of the faith.

Ethnic Devotion to the Saints
   When Italians migrated to the United States most heavily, between 1880 and 1920, they came upon a country whose Catholic hierarchy was

dominated by the Irish. In tone and character, according to Francis X. Femminella, Italian immigrants encountered something totally unlike what they were accustomed to in their country of origin. Not surprisingly, this created difficulty for the Italians. Rather than warm, personal relationships with the saints as they experienced them back in Italy, for example, the Italian immigrants found importance attached to creedal tenets.[8] Nicholas J. Russo says the Italians resented the Irish domination of the American Church. Even as many Italian immigrants were indifferent to American-Irish customs, they still were, in the words of Russo, subjected to Hiberni-zation.[9]

In his book *Piety and Power*, Silvano Tomasi explains that "at first, an attempt was made to include the Italian immigrant in the existing Irish par-ishes."[10] However, this proved to be a very unworkable situation. The Irish parishes were perceived by the Italians as inhospitable and hostile and soon "[a] situation of open conflict began to develop between the Irish pastors and Italian priests, Irish and Italian parishioners."[11] In an effort to change this, national parishes came on the scene. With national parishes, the Ital-ians, the Germans or other ethnic groups could have their own parish, pray in their own language, be ministered to by their own priests and not have to be subservient to another ethnic group. National parishes afforded Catho-lics independence at the most local level. However, it never really removed the antagonism altogether as long as the Irish controlled the American episcopacy. With the arrival of national parishes, the Italians were not under the thumb of the Irish as much, but their customs were never far from scrutiny, either.

The piety of the Italian immigrants to the United States was not fully and authentically Catholic. Rudolph J. Vecoli explains that the Italian immigrants practiced a folk religion, a fusion of Christian and pre-Christian elements, of animism, polytheism, and sorcery with the sacraments of the Church. Their beliefs and practices did not conform to the doctrines and liturgy of the Church.[12] Not only was there a lack of conformity to norma-tive expressions of Catholic piety, the Italian immigrants were also consid-ered little better than pagans and idolaters. As Vecoli notes, being held in such disfavor had little remedial effect upon the Italians. They continued defiantly to have their own folk celebrations, not bothering to even try and find some acceptable accommodation with the dominant ecclesial culture.[13]

The religiosity of the Italian immigrants infuriated their more assimilationalist-minded co-religionists here in the United States. One critic, writing in *The Catholic World*, faulted the Italian immigrants for being fed on pilgrimages, shrines, holy cards and devotions to the neglect of the truths of Catholicism.[14] But the Catholic Church in the United States, dominated of course by the Irish, was in a difficult position. If the American Church was to forbid Italian popular devotion, thought prelates like Archbishop Michael Corrigan (1885-1902) and John Cardinal Farley (1902-18) in New York, the Italians could be lost to the Protestants. In view of the potential of losing the Italians to the Protestants, Robert A. Orsi concludes that the Italian *festa* was to be tolerated only as a transitional stage in Italian progress toward a more American Catholicism and only under the careful supervision of the clergy.[15]

Instead of labeling Italian religiosity superstitious and sacrilegious[16] and having nothing to do with it or in other instances only tolerating it, one can speculate what the Irish would have accomplished if they had used a different tack. The Irish could have, for example, looked upon the Italian *festa* as an opportunity to evangelize. In their study of the *giglio* feast, Salvatore Primeggia and Joseph Varacalli consider the annual feast centered around Our Lady of Mount Carmel Parish in Williamsburg, Brooklyn. As the authors describe it, the celebration takes place over a 15-18 day period in July. During this period, there is a continuous celebration of religious activities in the church (masses, novenas and processions) and secular activities in the streets (social events, food concessions and games of chance).[17] Primeggia and Varacalli raise the question of "to what degree has the religious leadership of Our Lady of Mount Carmel shrine Church been able to employ the feast as an agent of evangelization."[18] They note that "historically it is clear that the feast has been an important mechanism to bring a somewhat 'unchurched' Italian-American population into the tenets and practices of the Catholic faith."[19] Primeggia and Varacalli are dubious, though, that many unchurched Italian-Americans become devout Catholics because of the long-standing separation in the Italian mind between religion and church.[20] The doubt expressed by Primeggia and Varacalli on converting Italian church non-attendance into an authentic practice of Catholicism is predicated on a chronic history of non-practice as we shall soon explore. This notwithstanding, it would be interesting to imagine what the Irish could have done for Italian practice of Catholicism if the Irish attitude was different. Realistically however, if the Italian leadership of the *festa* could not expect to do much about Italian non-practice of Catholicism, we must consider some other factors.

In the early part of the twentieth century, the Jesuit magazine *America* was reporting on the state of Catholicism among the Italian people. Father Joseph Sorrentino described the situation in Italy thus:

> The Catholic spirit is keenly alive today among the Italian people; it hovers over you wherever you go; it is felt in their feasts and in their mournings, in their public joys and public calamities; it asserts itself in their homes...The Italians do not content themselves with what we might call acting unconsciously under the influence of the Catholic spirit; they go farther; they practice their religion...{F}aith is not dead or dormant, but emphatically active and living, blossoming and bearing fruit throughout all the length and breadth of Italy.[21]

Over the next several weeks in 1914, Father Sorrentino's assessment of Italian Catholicism drew sharp dissent in the letters to the editor of the Jesuit journal. One priest, who signed his letter "An Old Pastor" and did not give his name, wrote on the basis of fifteen years' experience with the Italians of his parish. He complained that for fifteen years he tried and tried and tried in vain to get them [the Italians] to attend church. This priest concluded that the religious lethargy of the Italians he knew was due to poor instruction they had received in Italy before coming to the United States. Besides their anemic attendance at church, this priest also criticized the depth of faith or, more properly, the lack of it among the Italian Catholics. At one point in his letter, the priest opined, "[W]e were told by some of your writers within the past month that they [the Italians] have a special devotion for the Blessed Virgin and her feast days. If they have, they do not show it in this parish. Their religion, what there is of it, is exterior."[22] Another letter writer, agreeing with this priest, paraphrased one Bishop Bonomelli on piety. Piety, the letter writer observed, "does not consist in processions or carrying lighted candles, in prostrations before a statue of the

Madonna, in processions in honor of the patron saints of villages...[T]rue piety consists in the daily fulfillment of religious duties exacted of us by God Almighty and His Church and it consists in a love for that Church and her ministers. In these points, no matter how numerous be the Italian processions, no matter how heavy the candles, no matter how many lights they carry, the Italian immigrant seems very deficient."[23] That the religious observances of the street merit a respect in Catholic life thus went unacknowledged by such critics.

Assessments of the state of Catholicism among the Italian immigrants to the United States continued to show up in the pages of *America*. In 1931, Joseph Lagnese published a piece which conceded the Italian Catholic's "non-attendance at church" but argued that the Catholic faith was "deeply rooted in him."[24] Like others evaluating the Catholicism of the Italian who immigrated to the United States, Lagnese attributed Italian non-practice of the faith to a faulty religious education.[25] At the end of his essay, Lagnese somewhat paternalistically cautions against "condemning the Italian too sweepingly or harshly. If, instead of criticism, they would take him in hand, they would find him as a child. The Italian's passionate nobleness of soul would be brought out; as he understands things, conditions would be bettered; and there would be an advancement of the Faith along the lines of unity and consolidated strength."[26] Might Lagnese have been suggesting, then, a different approach in evangelizing the Italian Catholics? Quite possibly. Four years later, in 1935, M. J. Hillenbrand began his assessment of Catholicism among the Italians with the provocative title, "Has the Immigrant Kept the Faith?"[27] The author tried to answer the question by considering the Italian immigrants of Camden, New Jersey. Arguing that Camden's Italians were typical of America's Italians, Hillenbrand writes that he was not able to find "a single Italian [male] under thirty who by any stretch of meaning might be classified as a practicing Catholic."[28] Hillenbrand went on to conclude that, quite obviously, the Italian has not kept the faith in America.[29] He, too, muses at the end of his article about what if things were different. If the methods, circumstances and limitation on resources[30] were different, might the question which introduced Hillenbrand's essay been answered in the affirmative. Without directly using the word "evangelization," Hillenbrand may very well have been recommending a different tack also, a tack which might have started by building on what was true and valid in the Italian immigrant experience.

Immigration has handed the Church in the United States historic opportunities to evangelize. Unlike Paul, whose Athenian mission was to announce the gospel to those who had never heard of Christ, the Church in the United States for the most part has evangelized those who have at least heard of Christ. In the case of southern Italians, Christ's name had already been preached, albeit inadequately, in this European nation for centuries. Yet, the preaching of Christ's name is no guarantee of a conscientious practice of Catholicism. Paul's evangelization of the Athenians was circumstantially and substantively different from an American evangelization of the Italians. As for difficulty, we would have to say that Paul had the rougher mission. The Americans, after all, had the advantage of announcing the gospel to people who were already baptized and had at least a nominal commitment to Catholicism.

While Baptism afforded an advantage of sorts for the American evangelization of the Italians, it was hindered by the immigrants' unstinting devotion to the traditions of southern Italy. The Italians had immigrated to a land where another ethnic group, the Irish, did not have much of a social edge over the Italians but clearly had an ecclesial advantage. As previously mentioned, the Irish ran things in the Church in the United States for a very long time. By the middle of the twentieth century, this was no longer true and Irish domination of ecclesiastical affairs had clearly subsided. But during the periods of heaviest Italian immigration, the Irish were in charge of the major ecclesial structures.

With the Irish who sought a more Americanized Catholicism from the Italians, evangelization did not satisfactorily take hold and deepen. Italians who eventually received their own national parishes were left to make good on their own in many instances. The criticism that Paul made of the Athenians was surely made of the Italians by the Irish. In retrospect, it was not the right kind of criticism, unfortunately. It may have been a correct criticism of Italian "thinking" as far as true worship is concerned, but it was not sensitive to Italian ways. When Pope Paul VI criticizes wrongful popular religiosity in *Evangelii Nuntiandi*, he also writes that "pastoral charity must dictate to all those whom the Lord has placed as leaders of the ecclesial communities the proper attitude...Above all one must be sensitive... know[ing] how to perceive [popular religiosity's] interior dimensions and undeniable values [and] be ready to help it to overcome its risks of deviation."[31]

With the bishops unable or unwilling to exercise a proper vigilance over Italian devotion to the saints, the potential for abuse was quite considerable. The potential was realized too, as others have attested earlier in this essay. The abuses had a life-span, happily. Changes, ecclesial and social, were coming and this would make the abuses in devotional life less likely. As abuses declined, however, so did, unfortunately, public devotion itself fall to the wayside.

The Saints in the Post-Vatican II Church

Pope John XXIII stunned the Catholic world in 1959 when he announced that the Church would hold a Second Vatican Council not quite a century after Vatican I (1870). For a part of four years (1962-65), the bishops of the Catholic Church met in Rome for the twenty-first ecumenical council. Early at Vatican II, the bishops approved by a vote of 2,162 to 46 a document on the liturgy called *Sacrosanctum Concilium*. In this constitution, promulgated on December 4, 1963, the Fathers of the Second Vatican Council called for a full, conscious and active participation in the Church's liturgy by the faithful.[32] The full, conscious and active participation prescribed by *Sacrosanctum Concilium* would be tried almost right away in the vernacular.

Actually, the *Constitution on the Sacred Liturgy* called for a retention of the Latin language at mass. But it also said that the "mother tongue...frequently may be of great advantage to the people [and] the limits of its employment may be extended."[33] It left to "the competent territorial ecclesiastical authority"[34] the decision on the extent to which the vernacular language was to be used in the liturgy. The American bishops, like their confreres all over the world, made maximum use of the language concessions and proposed changes on April 2, 1964. The Vatican Liturgical Commission approved the proposed changes on May 1st of the same year. Very quickly then, the new liturgy sounded altogether different with the vernacular now completely replacing the Latin which had been in use for hundreds of years in the Catholic world. *Sacrosanctum Concilium* treats many different aspects of Catholic worship. Among the varied aspects treated are: the sacraments and sacramentals; the divine office; the liturgical year; sacred music; and sacred art and furnishings. The central emphasis of *Sacrosanctum Concilium* is unmistakable, however. It is centered above all on the mystery of the Holy Eucharist which *Sacrosanctum Concilium* calls a sacrament of love, a sign of unity, a bond of charity, a paschal banquet in which Christ is consumed, the mind is filled with grace, and a pledge of future glory is given to us.[35]

Even as *Sacrosanctum Concilium* is concerned preeminently with the eucharistic liturgy, it does offer some comments on popular devotions. Early in the document, it mentions that popular devotions are "highly recommended" as long as they are used in accord with the laws and norms of the Church.[36] Concerning the devotions of particular churches, that is, the Church in a certain nation or region of the world, *Sacrosanctum Concilium* indicates that these devotions have a special dignity if they are conducted by order of the bishops.[37] The constitution further instructs that popular devotions should "harmonize with the liturgical seasons, accord with the sacred liturgy, in some fashion derive from it and lead the people to it."[38] This is necessary, it maintains, because the sacred liturgy far surpasses any popular devotion.[39] Toward the end of *Sacrosanctum Concilium*, the Council Fathers teach that

> [t]he Church has also included in the annualcycle days devoted to the memory of the martyrs and the other saints. Raised up toperfection by the manifold grace of God,and already in possession of eternal salvation, they sing God's perfect praise inheaven and offer prayers for us. By celebrating the passage of these saints from earth to heaven the Church proclaims the paschal mystery as achieved in thesaints who have suffered and been glorified with Christ; she proposes them to the faithful as examples who draw all to the Father through Christ, and through their merits she pleads for God's favors.[40]

A little bit further along, the Council Fathers declare:

> The saints have been traditionally honored inthe Church and their authentic relics and images held in veneration. For the feasts of the saints proclaim the wonderful works of Christ in His servants, and display to the faithful fitting examples for their imitation.[41]

Once again, there is a recommendation that many of the feasts of the saints should be left to be celebrated by a particular church or nation or religious community.[42] Here, too, there is a concern that the feasts of the saints not overshadow "the very mysteries of salvation."[43]

Liturgical and Cultural Change

Two factors must be considered at this point regarding the shift in devotion to the saints among the Italian-Americans. The first is liturgical and pertains to the document cited multiple times above (SC). The second is cultural and pertains to the sociological phenomenon of assimilation. Allow me to consider these factors in this order.

The Impact of Vatican II on Liturgy

The sixteen documents of Vatican II were drawn up in Rome by bishops and their *periti* assembled from all over the world. The documents conceived there would then have to be implemented later on in the various nations by the bishops who voted on and approved them. It is surely not difficult to imagine the problems associated with taking sixteen documents of several different grades of authority and supervise their enactment structurally and otherwise. The bishops could count, of course, on the parishes within their dioceses. The parishes were a way, a means by which Catholic people could learn about the new liturgy and its demands. The parishioners, of course, could be instructed by their pastors in the theology of the new liturgy and its mechanics. Given the inherent weaknesses of communicating with millions of people all over the world about such a sensitive topic as how Catholics worship God and honor the saints, the bishops would have fared very badly without a system or network of parishes on which to rely. However, there were also not a few problems in parishes concerning the implementation of the new liturgy.

The implementation of the reforms of the Second Vatican Council is a much written about topic, and we cannot say a great deal about it here. Scholars from many different vantage points have analyzed and evaluated the reforms called for by *Sacrosanctum Concilium* and their implementation in parishes. Thoughtful commentators are in agreement that liturgical reform has not come about easily in the post-conciliar era for many Catholics. Some have complained, for example, that liturgical reform was not needed in the Catholic Church. Others have complained that it was not only long overdue but was not far-reaching enough. Some, conceding the need for liturgical reform, have objected to how it was carried out in American parishes. Here, such varied things as pace, balance and judgment have been questioned as far as implementation is concerned.

Not unimportant factors in parish liturgical reform following Vatican II are authority and office. As previously mentioned, the diocesan bishops relied upon the pastors to carry out liturgical reform in parishes. Many of the pastors, men ordained before Vatican II, learned of liturgical changes at the same time their parishioners did and sought to make adjustments where they could. The adjustments, however, were not merely mechanical and rubrical; they were much deeper and more profound. Adjustments and shifts were needed mentally and attitudinally. Pastors, for the most part, accepted the conceptual and attitudinal shifts which accompanied the change from the Tridentine Mass to the *novus ordo*. There were, of course, some pastors, albeit relatively few in number, who for various reasons could not subscribe to the liturgical reform initiated by the Second Vatican Council. The unwillingness of certain pastors to accept enthusiastically the liturgical changes wrought by Vatican II was never really an impediment to implementing reforms in parishes, however. Pastors retire, are demoted or transferred, and other arrangements are made. Liturgical reform, an idea decades old by the mid-to-late 1960s, had ripened and the Church in the United States was about to see the idea come to fruition.

To implement an idea well, there must be a correct grasp of it. Before correctly applying an idea, there must be an accurate apprehension of it. In many American parishes after Vatican II, there were poor attempts at implementing liturgical reform because there was a misunderstanding of what *Sacrosanctum Concilium* really says. As we have seen already, *Sacrosanctum Concilium* did *not* seek to eliminate devotion to the saints. What it did was subordinate the veneration of the saints to the clearly higher purpose of celebrating the paschal mystery of Christ. The idea of the eucharistic liturgy as the summit and fount[44] of Catholic life was never intended to be the practical halt to an outward, public devotion to the saints. The latter did occur, though, in many American parishes with Italian populations. Instead of promoting the Holy Eucharist above all devotions while leaving room in parishes for an outward, public veneration of the saints, popular piety declined and eventually disappeared in all but the most ethnic enclaves. If the idea of *Sacrosanctum Concilium* was to situate popular devotions properly in the life of the Church, we ought not to conclude that the idea was a failure. It could be that the idea was not tried properly, or worse yet, was manipulated. For some, devotion to the saints is an idea whose time has come and gone. The veneration of the saints expresses a continuity with the past; it is traditional. For those seeking a break with the past, a liberation from tradition's stranglehold, it is better not to acknowledge the saints in an outward, public way. Ideas can be executed, that is, discharged carefully and wisely, and action then is the result. Of course, they can be wiped out, snuffed out as an ideological concession to the mainstream secular mind-set. Then there is no action, no outward, public display of honor for the saints.

Assimilation to Secular Culture

The second idea is not really new at all. In fact, it is an idea which has been around for a long time—as long as individuals and groups have moved geographically, psychologically and socially from marginality toward integration. This transition, occurring on so many different levels, is referred to as assimilation. Most of the time, assimilation is considered a process, and it most assuredly is that. Echoing what Pope John Paul II said concerning inculturation, assimilation is a profound and difficult process.

Every individual and group which moves from one culture to another for longer than a vacation or short period of study must decide just how much and in what way he or they will assimilate. What makes assimilation an important issue to address is the fact that so many Italians willingly accept the idea now and become actively involved in the process now. This was not always so. The earliest Italian immigrants were slow to assimilate. Previously, Italian immigrants could manage on their own because that is what every ethnic group did—initially at least. Eventually, though, the customs, mores and traditions of an ethnic group are tested by such things as increased financial prosperity, ethnically mixed marriages and the move away from urban neighborhoods to the ethnically undifferentiated suburbs. Now, assimilation is passed on generationally.

Silvano Tomasi contends that "the ethnic parish was born as a compromise between the demands of immediate assimilation and the resistance of immigrants to abandon their traditional religiosity."[45] What happens, however, when the national parish is not there like it was in the past? Perhaps it has been closed or merged with another non-national parish. The pluralism of the Catholic landscape today does not favor the viability of ethnically homogeneous parishes, with some exceptions of course.

There is also a sense in which assimilation is embraced so eagerly that it is not merely a working accommodation to the larger society which is sought but nothing less than the outright dismissal of everything, saints included, associated with the first culture. The basis for such conformity is not the critical appraisal of competing ideas about culture but a reflexive ideological conformity to present mainstream culture. There is also embarrassment that an Old World culture can occasionally encroach upon a modern, progressive one. Outward, public devotion to the saints is embarrassing because it reflects an incomplete domination by the presumably more sophisticated American culture. When Italian-Americans today continue to honor their saints in an outwardly public way, it reflects an other-than mechanical acceptance of the American credo that religion is and should be a private matter. Devotion to the saints Italian style means that religion is a matter for the public square too. Unfortunately, too many contemporary Italian-Americans have passively conformed to the privatization of religion. As a consequence, the saints have been pushed to the margins of the Italian-American religious consciousness.

Conclusion

Devotion to the saints, troubled as it was when first brought to the United States by Italian immigrants, has survived with all the changes in the Church and the American culture, albeit in muted form. Gone are the abuses which characterized this kind of religiosity just a few generations ago. At the same time, it must be acknowledged that an outward, public devotion to the saints has not been a very effective tool in challenging the non-practice of the Catholic faith by Italian-Americans and most other

Catholic groups for that matter. Abuses deriving from ethnicity have been replaced by abuses deriving from secular ideology. The demise of outward, public devotion to the saints, while hailed in some quarters, is really a net loss for the Church and the culture. For according to Pope Paul VI in *Evangelii Nuntiandi,* a well-oriented popular piety "is rich in values. It manifests a thirst for God which only the simple and poor can know. It makes people capable of generosity and sacrifice even to the point of heroism, when it is a question of manifesting belief. It involves an acute awareness of profound attributes of God: fatherhood, providence, loving and constant presence. It engenders interior attitudes rarely observed in the same degree elsewhere: patience, the sense of the cross in daily life, detachment [and] openness to others."[46] When Catholics witness to these values, the culture in turn, in the words of another Paul, John Paul II, is healed, ennobled and perfected.[47] This is what the first Paul, Paul of Tarsus, was doing in the Athenian areopagus so long ago.

REV. ROBERT J. BATULE

---

[1] Pope Paul VI, *Evangelii Nuntiandi,* (Boston: Saint Paul Books and Media, 1975), p. 28.

[2] Pope John Paul II, "Redemptoris Missio," *Origins,* 20:34 (1991), 556.

[3] *Ibid.*

[4] *Ibid.*

[5] *Ibid.,* p. 557.

[6] *Ibid.*

[7] *Ibid.*

[8] Francis X. Femminella, "The Impact of Italian Migration and American Catholicism," *The American Sociological Review,* 22 (Fall, 1961), 236.

[9] Nicholas J. Russo, "Three Generations of Italians in New York: Their Religious Acculturation," in *The Italian Experience in the United States,* ed. Silvano M. Tomasi and Madeline H. Engel. (New York: Center for Migration Studies, Inc., 1977), p. 198.

[10] Silvano M. Tomasi, *Piety and Power: The Role of the Italian Parishes in the New York Metropolitan Area, 1880-1930* (Staten Island, New York: The Center for Migration Studies of New York, Inc., 1975), p. 62.

[11] *Ibid.,* p. 81.

[12] Rudolph J. Vecoli, "Prelates and Peasants: Italian Immigrants and the Catholic Church," *Journal of Social History,* II (Spring, 1969), 228.

[13] *Ibid.,* p. 235.

[14] Bernard J. Lynch, "The Italians in New York," *Catholic World,* 47 (1888), 70.

[15] Robert A. Orsi, *The Madonna of 115th Street: Faith and Community in Italian Harlem, 1880-1950* (New Haven, Connecticut: Yale University Press, 1985), p. 56.

[16] *Ibid.,* p. 57.

[17] Salvatore Primeggia and Joseph A. Varacalli, "The Sacred and Profane Among Italian-American Catholics: The Giglio Feast," *International Journal of Politics, Culture and Society,* Vol. IX (Spring, 1996), 426.

[18] *Ibid.,* p. 437.

[19] *Ibid.*

[20] *Ibid.*

[21] Joseph Sorrentino, "Religious Conditions in Italy," *America,* Vol. XII:1 (1914), 6.

[22] Letter to the Editor, *America,* Vol. XII:10 (1914), 244.

[23] Herbert Hadley, Letter to the Editor, *America,* Vol. XII:3 (1914), 66.

[24] Joseph G. Lagnese, "The Italian Catholic," *America,* 44 (1931), 475.

[25] *Ibid.,* p. 476.

[26] *Ibid.*

[27] M. J. Hillenbrand, "Has the Immigrant Kept the Faith?," *America,* 54 (1935), 153.

[28] *Ibid.,* p. 154.

[29] *Ibid.*

[30] *Ibid.*

[31] Pope Paul VI, p. 29.

[32] Austin Flannery, ed. *Vatican Council II: The Conciliar and Post Conciliar Documents,* revised ed. Vol. 1 (Boston: Daughters of Saint Paul, 1988), p. 7.

[33] *Ibid.,* p. 13.

[34] *Ibid.*

[35] *Ibid.,* p. 16.

[36] *Ibid.,* p. 7

[37] *Ibid.*

[38] *Ibid.*

[39] *Ibid.*

[40] *Ibid.,* p. 29.

[41] *Ibid.,* p. 31.

[42] *Ibid.*
[43] *Ibid.*
[44] *Ibid.,* p. 6.
[45] Tomasi, p. 2.
[46] Pope Paul VI, p. 28.
[47] Pope John Paul II, p. 557.

CHAPTER 10

THE SAINTS AND OUR PSYCHOLOGICAL WELL BEING: A PSYCHOLOGIST'S PERSPECTIVE ON AN ITALIAN-AMERICAN LEGACY

"In the search for new forms and models of holiness in our pluralistic and multicultural society, one cannot ignore the great figures who throughout the centuries have given vivid witness to the holiness of the Church. Neither can one ignore the socio-anthropological influence of the saints, since the choice of heroes, models and leaders can have a lasting effect on the development of one's personality. Of course, the hero and model par excellence is Jesus Christ, and the Christian life consists essentially in the...imitation of Christ."[1]

Early Experiences as a Practitioner

Vigorous internship training disciplines the mental health professional to keep the needs of the client in perspective. Patient assessment, diagnosis and intervention are guided by methodology and technique that has a scientific basis. Clinical practice has a stylistic component, in which the psychologist utilizes his or her own background, experience and personality strengths in interaction with those of his clients, as a means of better serving the task at hand. Cultural features are often part and parcel of this process and an awareness of the cultural influences on a patient has been aggressively promoted by most mental health professional organizations. They have required that these cultural factors be incorporated into internship training and even into the ethical codes of the various professions, simply because an awareness of cultural factors can facilitate treatment, while insensitivity to them can be harmful. In addition, a strong case can be made for tapping into the faith convictions of the client, as an adjunct to their treatment. There is now a growing body of evidence that a sensitivity to the religious devotions of the client facilitates treatment[2] and may even be a requirement within the arena of patient rights.[3]

Early in my career, I received excellent training that helped me to be respectful of the cultural, ethnic and regional influences that shaped the lives of my patients. I was also especially comfortable with the faith lives of those I served, even before that was a popular position. Most clinicians, especially psychologists, tend to be respectful of people's faith but are uncomfortable with the notion of dealing directly with that aspect of their life experience, even as polls consistently show that about 90% of the American population believes in God and over 70% report that religion is the most important issue in their lives.

I have been atypical. Among the three highly valuable gifts my fourth-grade educated, immigrant parents gave me, were a belief in education, a love of the Catholic Church and a conviction that God was always with us. Although at times dormant during my graduate school career, the lessons had never completely left me and no amount of mental health training grounded in secular thinking seemed to eradicate these convictions. When I entered the clinical field, I brought with me a comfort with clients who were influenced by strongly held beliefs that involved ideas like faith, charity, grace, and Judeo-Christian traditions. Contrary to the popular so-cial science wisdom of the day, it seemed to me that for every client whose religious devotion carried feelings of anxiety and guilt, there were many, many more for whom feelings about God, church and spirituality brought meaning and a sense of well being to their lives. As a person with one foot in the Italian heritage, the saints were unavoidably part of the package.

It is well established that for many of the immigrants, Jesus, Mary and Joseph were a reassuring presence to their routine lives, along with the lives and example of the Church's numerous saints. It was part of the Italian-American experience.[4] The same seemed to be true of the Poles, Ukrainians, Portuguese, and Irish who inhabited the Northern New Jersey of my origins during the 1940s and 1950s. The Protestants may have heard a beautiful solo sang to them by virtue of their faith in God, but the Catho-lics, especially the Roman Catholic immigrants in America, seemed to have all of that and the saints, as well. If the well acculturated Catholic Ameri-cans in the early twentieth century allowed a gentle duet by Jesus and Mary to sooth their lives, the Poles and Irish sought soft accompaniment from a chorus of select saints, while the Italians, with all their ostentation, brought in the opera, and everybody was invited to sing. Christ saved us but his Mother could be counted upon to put in a good word and her husband, Joseph, *il protettore della famiglia*, (protector of the family) was there to safeguard his, as well as our, family. After all, there was strong biblical precedent for this. Mary told her son of the need of the newlyweds at Cana, and Joseph sought refuge for his family under the threat of Herod's men. There are also the numerous biblical accounts of the deeds of the Apostles and their successors. Finally, the Roman Calendar, a fixture in almost every Italian immigrant household, provided a daily reminder of the phrase in the Apostles Creed that goes "...I believe in the communion of saints,..."

Each of the saints had a role and there was a saint for every task or dilemma that life might deliver. There was a typology of saints that classified them as martyrs, pastors, doctors, virgins, or just men and women of Christ. There were parish saints to be paraded through the streets on their calendar days, namesake or patron saints to give one a sense of unique identity and regional saints that required special devotion or loyalty. After all, they were all once mortal like ourselves and, because they were also conceived in original sin, they could demonstrate for us the transcendental value of sacramental grace and the Christian virtues of temperance and fortitude to help mere mortals in the quest for heaven.

When I began to practice in Washington, D.C. and in nearby southern Maryland, all these almost forgotten traces of memory came alive for me as my patients brought similar devotions into their clinical material. I was practicing and teaching in an internationally known, public service psychiatric hospital and training center, as well as maintaining a busy, private practice in the suburbs. In the hospital setting, an Afro-American patient, with a Baptist background, would see an image of Christ in a projective test (e.g. the Rorschach or ink blot test) or speak of the importance of his church activities on weekend visits home, and somehow they would sense that I understood the relationship of these images and pastimes to the healthy side of their adjustment. I believe it is an intuitive talent within us all to sense the world-view and even belief system of those with whom we become interpersonally intimate, often without anything being said directly.[5] Sometimes these patients would complain that these expressions of faith were not validated or were even punished in the past by other mental health practitioners, so they learned quickly to leave them out, even though such ideas were dear to their heart. With respect to saintly preoccupations in that setting, I frequently observed that both patients and staff, Catholic and Protestant, would be fascinated by the display of Saint Elizabeth of Hungary that was a central exhibit in the hospital's museum and within its well documented historical record.

In the private practice setting, there were similar quests among patients who sought a therapist who might at least respect their faith. A Caucasian, southern Maryland, evangelical couple would tell me that they searched high and low to locate a "Christian therapist". Failing that, they would find my Italian name in a directory and decide that I was probably Roman Catholic. Perhaps, I would at least understand their belief "that Jesus Christ was the son of Go" and the source of salvation (these words were actually said to me on a number of occasions), even as they had some misgivings about my allegiance to Rome. Jews who ardently practiced their faith seemed also to intuitively sense that I would have a respect for and even a grounding in the sacred history and tradition of their faith. I was honored to have been consulted by them. Although, sometimes initially cautious about my views, they seemed somehow to know that I was comfortable with God or Yahweh, the Creator of the universe.

In time, some parish priests discovered my practice (there were very few psychologists in the under-served areas of Maryland in the early 1970s) and old southern Maryland farm families began coming to me. They were often of English stock, who had been on the land, sometimes all the way back to the time that Father White came in on the Ark and the Dove, bringing "papists" to the colonies. Some were the direct descendants of commonly known historical figures within our American heritage. There were also descendants of Ireland and Germany, as well. With these folks, Our Blessed Mother was included in their expressions of faith. This is poignantly forwarded by a concerned parent who stated: "My husband found some marijuana in my youngest son's bedroom and I can only pray to God and Mary that we haven't lost him to drugs."

But when the word got out through the son of a successful, Italian-American specialty foods producer and distributer, the small but solid local Italian community discovered my practice and all the saints came marching in. Once again I heard the opera. "My mother has cancer, we have been lighting candles to Saint Jude"; "My son is in the Air Force and being shipped to Germany. Saint Christopher (who was dying hard among them) is with him"; they prayed to Saint Anthony, to find lost objects or to care for children in need; to Saint Francis of Assisi for the poor; to San Giorgio to bear up against suffering and to overcome evil (Saint George defeating the dragon is also spoken of in south eastern Sicily); to Saint Joseph the worker, for the ordinary man who toiled with his hands.

Female saints populated the psychological lives of clients as well. Since many of the Washington, D.C. immigrants and their second-genera-tion American offspring gravitated toward the Holy Rosary Church (for Italians), La Madonna (the real one) was never to be forgotten. But Santa Lucia and Santa Maria Goretti also visited my treatment sessions, when issues of chastity or virginity were at issue (not exclusively from Italians or women) and there was often a veneration of Mother Seton, the first American-born saint, that came up around themes of widowhood or by women whose husbands had left.

A substantial number of Poles, Irish and even, Afro-American Catho-lics were also referred through parish sources. In recent years, a young priest from northern Virginia was reported to have been associated with local statues of the Virgin Mary secreting water, as one might shed tears. This occurred on many occasions before many parishioners and witnesses and the phenomena drew the attention and even examination from medical doctors, scientists and psychiatrists. It was covered several times in the *Washington Post*, with a blend of skepticism and wonderment. On one occasion, the young priest visited a parish that was several minutes from my practice and he reportedly drew tears from the eyes of Our Blessed Mother when he touched her image on a stained glass window. Two Afro-American children, who were students at the parish school, were brought to me for consultation regarding school achievement and other adjustment issues. Both had observed the phenomenon, along with many of their class-mates, and that was as much an issue within their therapy as the presenting problems. Even their parents had a strong need to discuss their wonderment about this event. I know nothing of the current status of this manifestation by the young priest, but I do know that those who spoke to me of it, bore a sense of joy on their faces that seemed very special.

Among the Italians-Americans, from time to time, there were intru-sions of unbridled, superstitious thinking regarding the saints, that were more a vestige of pagan idolatry and psychologically primitive, magical thinking, than of religion, as in the case of *il malocchio* ("The evil eye"). But unlike the experiences and observations described by Bianco in *The*

Two Rosettos,[6] such religiosity and distorted thinking around faith issues were rare and were considered to be an expression of ignorance and superstition by even the less educated among my community acquaintances and patients. Rather, there was an appreciation of sainthood that was consistent with traditional Church teachings. In his scholarly article on the saints in the Italian-American experience, Quinn[7] points out that in the Second Council of Nicaea, in the eighth century, the bishops declared that the saints were worthy of veneration (*dulia*) but not worship (*latria*). It seemed to me a tribute to Church and clergy both in Italy and America during the first part of the twentieth century that these basic tenets of the faith were in the awareness and discernment of even the most modestly educated Italians and Italian Americans that I encountered. To them, the saints carried no special magical forces of good or evil and should not be worshiped like junior deities. They in no way replaced or stood as equals to Jesus but were merely examples of *poveri cristiani* who tried to emulate the life of Christ. They represented what we should strive to be and by virtue of their canonization, we knew that they were surely in heaven. In that privileged place, perhaps they could, through our Savior, bring some good to their sometimes stressful lives, much like guardian angels.

Interestingly, the more senior Italians or Italian-Americans, those who were approaching 50 or older in the early 1970s, were openly devoted to saints. This was true of the Italians I had known from my youth in New Jersey, as well as those I met from Washington, D.C., Maryland, and Virginia, both as acquaintances and clients. The generations that followed were, in times of need, more likely to invoke only the name of Jesus, Mary or possibly the saint after which their church was named. Sadly, the richness of the devotion to saints seemed to be fading with each generation and among the youngest Italian-American adults (who where often blended with other ethnic identities through marriage), topics concerning the saints had become material for recollection, that helped them describe the religious devotions of their parents and grandparents. It had become, for many, part of the family history, if you will, which, like the very language of the country from which their ancestors emigrated, came to be spoken about, but was no longer spoken. Now, many years after I made these observations, Mary Brown[8], in her authoritative history, traces the decline of the veneration of saints in America to the period after World War I, when legislative changes ended mass migration from Italy. In addition, the booming, post-war economy after World War II brought many Italian-Americans to the suburbs, thus ending the era of ethnically organized churches and further stemming the devotion to saints. The Italian-Americans from Washington, D.C. seemed to have been somewhat of an exception, in this regard, as they often massed together in certain areas in the suburbs, thus retaining the strong vestiges of their ethnicity for perhaps one additional generation.

From Practical Experience to Theoretical Considerations

Many of the modern, psychoanalytic theories of personality were developed out of the long-term observation and treatment of a limited number of clinical cases. Early analytic personality theorists focused on the key family figures of the clients they studied and treated. They noted that family figures who occupied pivotal roles within the family structure of their clients seemed to surface as subject matter within a therapy session, as if they were dynamic, dramatic characters within the patient's personality that shaped both his or her emotions and view of the world. Freud[9] identified parental figures as the key characters in shaping the development, particularly the psychosexual development of his clients. Through these parental figures, individuals learned the patterns and rules of satisfying their basic instinctual and emotional drives, while also attending to reality demands and social mores. Sometimes the task became distorted and the patient developed a "neurosis" or an adjustment problem. Heavily influenced by the Greek myths, Freud developed his own myths around family life and the challenges of development. The myths he tapped and embellished were also reflections of the sociology and culture of his country and his time. Eventually, those myths and stories were imported into most western, industrialized nations and in some ways, then shaped the very cultures that adopted these views. Most educated people in our American culture are familiar with the paternal and maternal roles in the Oedipal situation and its hypothesized impact on the individual's view of self.

Alfred Adler[10] added theoretical themes that addressed siblings and Jung[11] talked about general human archetypes that take on the unique trappings of one's culture but that are actually part of one's deeply imprinted character, yearning for psychological expression. There were many others who followed, but they goes beyond our scope for this paper. A common thread in nearly all of the well-established psychological theories is that there are psychodynamic representations within the personality that are treated as if they were characters woven into the shadowy parts of one's unconscious and preconscious personality. They are theorized to predispose us to some form of irresistible drama that creates in us areas of tensions that must eventually be worked through in order to achieve psychological well being. There are, accordingly, almost what one might think of as internalized stories working within us, that dominate one's life. The Oedipal situation is the most widely subscribed to and written about psychological themes along these lines. One can never have his primary love object and one must always fear the threatening parental figure of the same sex, so life is a sublimated compromise. One can be healthy but never totally and completely fulfilled and safe. Likewise, in Adlerian psychology, a younger sibling might always be overcoming the dominance of his more senior sibling, which becomes played out in many other relations in life; at school; on the sports field; at work. And the stories never seem to be totally resolved. For Jung, our life's journey becomes scripted by our archetypes that are never totally realized.

Paul Vitz[12] has written extensively on this topic and has challenged the great psychologists of the past by introducing the story of the life, death and resurrection of Christ as the only internalized drama that ends with complete psychological (and spiritual) resolution and hope. The epic drama resolves for the individual those aspects of psychological development which are always incomplete and compromised in Freud's oedipal situation, Adler's sibling rivalry, and Jung's archetypical quest for self discovery. And for Vitz, the Christian message is at once psychological and real, hence offering the possibility that both aspects of our existence can be resolved through the Christian experience.

In a similar vein, I have lectured on the secular journey that occurs in most psychological treatment and have contrasted it to the journey in Christian-oriented treatment.[13] Briefly, secular psychological treatment squires and assists the patient through the various stages of symptom relief and relief from emotional suffering. As stabilization takes place, the patient is helped to carry out routine daily functions, to work and to relate better to loved ones. Finally, if therapy is pursued to its logical extremes, the patient achieves "self-actualization and autonomy", with the greatest emphasis on "self".

In partial contrast, I propose that the psychological journey in Christian or Catholic-oriented treatment ends in a much different place. The early stages of symptom relief, freedom from pathological emotional suffering, the ability to function in work and relationships, are nearly identical to secular therapy (although the means to obtain these might be guided by different moral mandates). However, as the Catholic therapist helps to free the client from emotional impediments to emotional freedom and autonomy, the ideals that one strives for are not self-centered but other-centered, i.e. "love God above all others and love thy neighbor as thyself", and accordingly, the psychologically healthy Christian might choose, not worldly self-fulfillment and pleasure, but to have less for oneself for the sake of someone else. "I will not divorce, even though my marriage is difficult. For the sake of others, I will sacrifice to find a way to make it better, if I can." "I will not abort my child because it will delay my career. I will make room for her in my life at the expense of what I want now." For the Christian, these are signs of strength and health and are in line with the true earthly ends of our journey, because, after all, where does the ultimate journey take us? To eternal salvation, which cannot be conceived of by the secular therapist or client, because it doesn't exist for them. Moreover, who are the quintessential examples of this, the Christian itinerary through life? The answer is the saints.

What is widely accepted by most developmentally-oriented personality theorists is that within the process of development of ego, conscience, morality and character, there is not only a need for delay of gratification, restraint and restriction, but there is also the need for ideals, and the content of these ideals are best captured by the psychological incorporation of external characters or personalities. The male child identifies with father and becomes a man; possibly a well-suited man, if the object of identification and the circumstances are correct. The female child has mother as an object of identification, although the route to identification is different. As we develop, we emulate certain figures in our immediate life circumstances, in history, in literature, and in myths that personify admirable characteristics that might assist us in our adjustment. Vitz [14] has written of the strong role of Christ in the identification process of both males and females. Any well educated Catholic can tell you that the saints personified

Christ in their own lives. And if there is any validity to Vitz's thesis that Christ's example offers us not only spiritual resolution to our human dilemma but also psychological resolution, then the saints also act as both historical and psychological witnesses to this reality. They have value to us because they are about folks just like us, trying to go the way of Christ. And for the Italian immigrant, often uneducated, and earning his keep with his or her hands, ordinary was very important.

Beyond Psychology: The need for example and a life of Grace

If there is any accuracy to sociological generalizations about groups, then maybe there is an accuracy to characterizing the early Italian immigrants and their second generation offspring as often extraverted and other-directed, who under stress, looked to other family, friends, and community to explain their difficulties, provide the support that was necessary to help them through, and yes, from time to time, to take the blame, whether it was deserved or not. After all, they were Italian. Obviously, these were a people who acted upon life in work and in their relationships and although they were not devoid of reflection and introspection, it was secondary to interpersonal validation. It was very important for Concetta to feel that Mario and Giovanna were in agreement with her, because truth had to be spelled out in public and within the awareness of the community, and not just privately felt, within the silent assessment of one's own introspection. Accordingly, the saints were extensions of the Church community to whom one could also appeal. What better friends can one hope for to understand your plight than those who are in heaven and close to God. But if there is a lesson to be taken from these simpler people from a simpler time, when devotion to the saints was still in flower, it is that they knew the value of witnesses and of role models and those they chose, sometimes not always for the purist of motives, were nevertheless, Christ-like. D'Elia[15] makes the case that modernism has worked against this wonderful sociological dynamic.

If we ever needed people images to improve our plight, we need them today. The immigrants of the early twentieth century had Joe Dimaggio to demonstrated the art of consistent hitting in baseball or Joe Lewis to show us how to lose and then come back to win for one's country. Today, Michael Jordon shows black and white youngsters that a superstar can also be a good father and husband. However, we are also in an age where media figures often do not capture the kind of virtues that a reasonable person of times past might want to emulate. Often, we get an unabashed portrayal of things that are contrary to good sense. This is a serious matter because dramatically presented characters have been shown to be extremely powerful shapers of behavior and forgers of values. Children have been found to mimic violent and sexual acting out, after viewing idealized, dramatic examples of such.[16] There is also evidence of this for adults. Organizational and industrial psychology have many examples of how leadership shapes the behavior and values of employees within a company. We are all better imitators than reasoners. We seem to readily adopt the styles of dress, grooming and even speech of the actors and characters in popular movies and this has been going on consistently since the late 1920s, from Valentino to Gable to Cruise. We even imitate their mores. In the 1940s, kissing became an acceptable, casual expression of romantic love. By the 1970s, it became stylish to go "all the way" and by the 1980s, eros was a casual emotion. Now in the 1990s, we are becoming a jaded bunch, looking for variations that challenge the natural plan.

Humankind craves examples of what humanity is. We follow the leaders. Yet, there still remains, as always, an upside to all this, about which writers and media people and even church people give too little attention. There seems to be a unique and remarkable phenomena that occurs whenever a really special kind of somebody comes along and we morally ragged group of citizens somehow recognize the truth in him or her. The closer the individual is to our time or, at least our experience of reality, the more powerful. Witness the overwhelming devotion to Mother Theresa or to John Paul II by people from all faiths, all cultures and all lifestyles, even those from lifestyles that are antithetical to how they live or have lived. There is something about authentic virtue and authentic faith that always rings true because it is universally and absolutely true. We need a standard to follow that makes a distinction between a person who takes a stand for virtue and a person who just takes a stand. Devotion to the saints is not simply an Italian thing, it is a thing for all humanity that once was manifested in virtually every civilized nation and culture in the world that came to know Christ. We need the saints and we need them made as real to us as possible because we need to learn to be like them. We need them not to replace God but to bring us closer to Him.

PHILIP J. SCROFANI

---

[1] Lodi, Enzo, *Saints Of The Roman Calendar*, translated and adapted by Jordan Aumann, OP, Alba House, Staten Island, NY, 1992.

[2] Larson, D. "A Survey of Mental Health Research on Religion and Spirituality." In *Spiritual Issues in Clinical Practice: The Faith Factor*, Sponsored by Human Sciences International, Feb. 21, 1997.

[3] Scrofani, P. J. "Moral Relativism and Psychotherapy." *New Oxford Review*, Vol. 5, June, 1996.

[4] See the essay in this volume by Mary E. Brown entitled: "Italian-Americans and Their Saints: Historical Considerations" (Chapter 3); also see the essay in this volume by John Quinn entitled: "Saints Over Sacraments? Italian and Italian-American Spiritual Traditions" (Chapter 5).

[5] Refer to footnote 3, i.e. Scrofani, P.J.

[6] Bianco, Carla *The Two Rosettos*, Indiana University Press, Bloomington and London, 1974.

[7] Refer to footnote 4, i.e. Quinn, John.

[8] Refer to footnote 4, i.e. Mary E. Brown.

[9] See Chapter Twelve of Robert A. Baron (Editor), entitled: "Personality: The Uniqueness and Consistency of Individual Behavior," *Psychology: The Essential Science*. Allyn and Bacon Publishing, Boston, 1989.

[10] See footnote 9, i.e. Baron, Robert A.

[11] See footnote 9, i.e. Baron, Robert A.

[12] Vitz, P.C. & Gartner, J., "Christianity and Psychoanalysis, Part 1: Jesus as the Anti-Oedipus," *Journal of Psychology and Theology*, 1984, Vol. 12, No 1, 4-14; and Vitz, P.C. & Gartner, J., "Christianity and Psychoanalysis, Part 2: Jesus as the Anti-Oedipus," *Journal of Psychology and Theology*, 1984, Vol. 12, No 2, 82-90.

[13] Scrofani, "Strengthening Families in Christ: Building The House on the Rock of Hope," *Bishop O'Connell Lectures*, 1996.

[14] Vitz, P.C. "Support from Psychology for the Fatherhood of God," *Homiletic and Pastoral Review*, 1997, Feb., Vol. 97, No. 5.

[15] See the essay in this volume by D.J. D'Elia, entitled: "People of the *Festa*: The Incarnational Realism of the Italian-Americans" (Chapter 11).

[16] Bandura, A. *Principles of Behavior Modification*. New York: Holt, Rinehart & Winston, 1969; and also Bandura, A. *Aggression: Social Learning Analysis*. Englewood Cliffs, N.J.: Prentice-Hall, 1973

CHAPTER 11

PEOPLE OF THE *FESTA*:
THE INCARNATIONAL REALISM OF THE
ITALIAN-AMERICANS

It is my belief that the religious and moral greatness of the future of the Italian immigrants is bound to blend with the political and material greatness of the United States. The result will abound in blessings from God and great achievements for civilization. It will reveal the secrets of a new era to the twentieth century—Blessed Giovanni Scalabrini, *L'Araldo Italiano*, October 24, 1901 .

Introduction

    One thing is certain, the Italian American *festa* was not what that old devil Screwtape perversely said of the fasts and feasts of the Church's spiritual year, that it was "the Same Old Thing," over and over again. Nor was it, some of us remember, an end in itself. And no amount of subtle historicizing now will make it into that.

    La festa was not a response of displaced peasants, caught in the violent transition from status to contract and jealous of higher class status, to a growing *petit-bourgeois* demand for "absolute novelty,"—which C. S. Lewis and others have seen as characteristic of Modern mass society.[1] It was deeply rooted in custom, summoned up from the *trés ancien régime* of pagan and Christian memory to confront the new, disintegrating society of Modern nineteenth-century America.[2] It was a doxology, a *Te Deum*, a protest against the bourgeois rationalization and routinization of life in industrial society. The *festa* was for southern Italians, in its yet undegraded, pure form a *communio*, a Roman Catholic affirmation of God's plan for man in Jesus Christ, subject only to the self-understanding and limitations of the people themselves.[3] It was a dynamic, paraliturgical gathering in procession toward the altar and the Eucharistic banquet, the eternal *festa.* But it was also profoundly human, Biblical in its understanding of man-in-community—as true religion must be—deeply rooted in the material world like the celebrants themselves. La *festa*, the "Great Sanctus" of southern Italian worship, was incarnational and sensual in the best tradition of Mediterranean Catholicism (the food, the wine, the music, the rites, the overall embrace of the material world). Sensual symbols or hierophanies were everywhere, like the ancient God of these people of the *Mezzogiorno* who had become man and was still among them in the saints. They lifted the saints' statues high above them in the *festa* procession; and the saints—"other Christs"—led them into the Churches of "Little Italies" where the infinite God Whom the universe could not contain, humbly awaited them as a broken contadino in the Holy Eucharist, the *pasch,* the ultimate Transcendence. These *contadini*, with their physical and spiritual stamina, were a late Medieval people, still living in the pre-Enlightenment world in which everything was "immersed in the transcendent," as it should be, and open to God's deeper reality. Their sensual symbols, their sacramentals, including the *festa* itself—had not yet lost their "transparency for transcendental reality," had not yet become opaque to the transcendent, reduced along with the liberating dogmas of Catholicism to the categories of the Age of Rationalism. For them, Christianity had not yet been historicized. The world was still the Creation—continuous and dynamic—still from the hand of God and whole. For them, the world and the body itself were images and signs of God.[4]

The lifting of the statues of the saint, more often than not *la Madonna,* San Giuseppe, Sant' Antonio, San Rocco, San Gennaro, or, the *gigli* (wood or metal structures topped by a statue of San Paolino) in the *Giglio* Feast of Brooklyn celebrated every July since 1903, provides the defining symbolism of la *festa*, that of transcendence, but not at the expense of the horizontal dimension of the sensual. The "Image of Elevation" in all religions, Mircea Eliade reminds us, is a symbol of man's mystical experience.[5]

But before we can say anything more about the *festa* and the saints in Italian-American life, and the *Weltanschauung* of the first generation, we need to emphasize what so many writers these days often do not even notice. And here, once again, the great Rumanian student of *homo religious* will be our guide "For religious man, nature is never only 'natural'; it is always fraught with a religious value. This is easy to understand, for the cosmos is a divine creation; coming from the hands of the gods, the world is impregnated with sacredness....We must not forget that for religious man the supernatural is indissolubly connected with the natural, that nature always expresses something that *transcends* it (my italics)....a sacred stone is venerated because it is *sacred*, not because it is a stone; it is the sacrality manifested through the mode of being of the stone that reveals its true essence. "That is why," Eliade continues, "we cannot speak of naturism or of natural religion in the sense that the nineteenth century gave to these terms; for it is 'supernature' that the religious man apprehends through the natural aspects of the world."[6]

Much of what is still being written about the religion of southern Italians in the late nineteenth-century is seriously compromised by its pre-critical, rationalistic, speculative, and really unscientific character, for the most part dating from that overcredulous period itself, i.e., scientism. A notorious example is the continuing influence of Sir James G. Frazer's *Golden Bough; A Study in Magic and Religion* (1890), which in addition to its unscientific confounding of religion and magic, relies much too much on what are now recognized as naive evolutionary schemes, even conceits, peculiar to Darwin's century. Sigmund Freud's case is more ambiguous, but his cavalier dismissal of religious belief as illusion has also lost its credibility in the light of more probing work by Carl Jung and others.[7]

Even so intelligent, sensitive, and perceptive a student as Leonard Covello seems to fall victim to what Eliade calls the reductionism of nineteenth-century thinkers like Marx, Nietzsche, and Freud. Writing in his day, he simply did not have the benefit of the more empirical, objective knowledge that scientific study of the history of man's religious experience was soon to make available in the work of Eliade, Van der Leeuw, and other writers on the phenomenology of religion. The recognition of the legitimate Christianization of pagan religious traditions— an early casualty to nineteenth and twentieth-century reductionism, despite the thought of John Henry Newman—and a much greater understanding of the important differences between Christianity and Gnosticism, have given a whole new dimension today to the study of man's religious experience.[8]

Ultimately, the problem, no doubt, is a much larger one; one really for the student of the sociology of religion; and we shall have a little more to say about this later on. But space, in the end, permits us merely to recommend to the reader the seminal work of the Catholic sociologist, Werner Stark.[9]

Finally, by way of these preliminary observations, it seems strange indeed that in today's mass consumer society without absolutes, when so many of history's victims are being acknowledged and even compensated in some instances, and when the universal standard is individual choice, the first-generation Italians continue to be seen, for the most part, as second-rate and representative of an inferior humanity in their religious, intellectual, social, and other values.[10]

Gnosticism and the Mysticism of Contracted Existence

"Opaqueness"—one cannot think of a more fitting metaphor to suggest modern man's blindness to the transcendent. Voegelin, Eliade, and Fr. Louis Bouyer of the Oratory all use it. Also Voegelin, notably, has shown how the opaqueness to the transcendent is closely associated with magic, sorcery, and totalitarian movements of the twentieth century. It was this opaqueness, this blindness, this counter-reality of what Voegelin calls Gnosticism in the Modern world that confronted the southern Italians in the United States as a hostile *Weltanschauung*.

This Christian heresy, which is a heresy of too much rather than too little belief, sees the world as alien, corrupt, and evil; but man by his own initiatives can acquire the knowledge to create a different and better world and even achieve self-divinization. This absolute knowledge (*gnosis*) is what will save men in the end—not Judaeo-Christian Revelation. It alone (scientism) gives man power over nature, as in the empiricism of that master Gnostic and prophet of the Modern world, Francis Bacon, and his nineteenth-century counterparts, Auguste Comte (positivism) and John Dewey (Instrumentalism, radical empiricism).[11]

The Modern revolt of *gnosis* against "belief" (*pistis*), Hans Jonas has pointed out, has striking parallels with twentieth-century existentialism and nihilism, especially the rejection of any objective norm of conduct (Natural Law). This antinomianism follows from the Gnostic and existentialist view of man as isolated and threatened by a fallen nature which has no opening to the transcendence of God, let alone His redemption. Man's present state, accordingly, is deformed by being reduced to what Voegelin calls "the contracted existence":

> The death of the spirit is the price of progress...the more fervently all human energies are thrown into the great enterprise of salvation through world-immanent action, the farther the human beings who engage in this enterprise move away from the life of the spirit. And since the life of the spirit is the source of order in man and society, the very success of a Gnostic civilization is the cause of its decline. Only by recovering the traditional wisdom of classical philosophy (especially Plato and Aristotle) and of the original sources of early Christianity—lost to progressive immanentization— can we hope to transcend the narrow limits of Modern thought and of contracted existence and reveal the true being of man in a comprehensive philosophy.[12]

Now it was into this "Gnostic civilization" of late nineteenth-century industrial America that the southern Italian came. At the time these pre-Modern, agrarian people arrived, society was already in an advanced industrial Gnostic state—in Voegelin's words, possessed like certain parts of Northern Europe by the "magic dream of creating the Superman, the man-made Being that will succeed the sorry creature of God's making." This is, he continues, "the great dream that first appeared imaginatively in the work of Condorcet, Comte, Marx and Nietzsche and later pragmatically in the Communist and National Socialist movements." Man in Western culture, except for pre-Modern peasants like the southern Italians, was in Promethean revolt against the divine order in the cosmos, in a sinful condition, against transcendence, against man's need in this life for spiritual formation (true culture), which can only come by surrendering to divine grace.[13]

Voegelin defined "economic materialism, racist biology, corrupt psychology, scientism, and technological ruthlessness" as "modernity without restraint," and all of these ideologies were powerfully at work when the southern Italian immigration began.[14] These and other ideologies, (e.g., William James' Pragmatism or John Dewey's Instrumentalism) were the result of Modernity's radical immanentism, the seeing of nature's symbols as "opaque," mere objects, closed to transcendence, and understandable only by the impoverished Gnostic categories of Enlightenment (bourgeois) rationalism. When this happens, when symbols and language become opaque and no longer "function transparently to point into transcendence," man is condemned to a "closed universe of pure immanence."[15] This is the "mysticism of the contracted existence," from which the southern Italian Catholic immigrants were spared—and which is our bane.

Romano Guardini, in his *The End of the Modern World* (1968), described Modernity as having three presuppositions in an analysis similar to Voegelin's, that will also shed light on the nineteenth-century southern Italian experience in America. The Modern world, he wrote, rests on the presuppositions that man, nature, and culture are autonomous, not having and not requiring a transcendent dimension.[16]

Now, southern Italians as pre-Modern people believed that they, nature, and culture had meaning only in relation to God—only as they opened to the transcendent. The *festa* was the great symbol of this belief, "the light of the world....a city set on a hill" shining their light to the world.(Matt. 5, 14-16) There was no opaqueness in their world, which was not the Gnostic world of evil, demonic powers, but the redeemed Creation of the Father. The contadini love of nature, of God's Handiwork, was the Christian *agape* of surrender, not the Modern Baconian and Gnostic *eros* of domination. (Max Scheler). How else to understand the Neapolitan family custom at the annual festa in honor of *la Madonna del Carmine*, (Our Lady of Mount Carmel) of a woman of the household abasing herself by licking the stones of the Church floor? The southern Italian love of nature was Franciscan, that of St. Francis of Assisi, not Promethean, and with the "most Italian of saints, and the most saintly of Italians" they still sang of Sister water and Brother fire in the *Canticle of Creation*." [17]

The southern Italian villagers or *paesani*, most of them illiterate or semi-literate, had no or very little experience of typical elitist-led, Gnostic movements like the Enlightenment and the French Revolution; nor had they any historical memory of Calvinism and the Scientific Revolution (worldly saints). In America all of these were powerful agents of change--which later the American immanentist philosopher, John Dewey, was to declare the ultimate Reality or god. The Scientific Revolution and the eighteenth-century Enlightenment promised the industrial masses utopia, the fulfillment of man in the world by means of reason and science (*gnosis*). The legacy of the French Revolution was also that of man's sal vation through world-immanent action; while the American culture of narcissistic antinomianism, which in the beginning of the Nation had been Calvinist orthodoxy, was at the end of the century spreading to all classes the Gnostic doctrine of self-deification, without the need of the Church founded by Christ. [18]

Not Divine Invaders or Experts—But Saints

The Modern "expert" in America, the secularized version of the Calvinist saint or elect, the "pneumatic" or saint of Gnostic anthropology, the intellectual, and bourgeois technocrat intent upon revolutionizing society and now in the process of creating this brave new world, was not the saint of the *domus* and the *festa*. The Madonna, Saint Anthony and Saint Rocco, beloved of old parishes like Holy Rosary in Jersey City, did not have a day set aside on the calendar of positivistic saints in Auguste Comte's "Religion of Humanity." The saint of the *festa*—unlike the American Thorstein Veblen's engineer or social technician—was a hierphant, making known sacred things, rather than a maker of some Gnostic dream world in the West. Southern Italian saints lovingly surrendered to the Creation in *agape.* They were not Modern experts, Gnostic godlings, divine invaders among the common people, or Ph.D.s. They were not revolutionaries, but witnesses to the *contadini* and all men and women that this once fallen world has been redeemed by Jesus Christ, the Second Person of the Holy Trinity, and that the poor and down-trodden (Heb. *anawim*) as well as emperors and kings may by divine grace be brothers and sisters of Christ. They were witnesses to the fact that man is *capax Dei* (capable of God) here and now! No less a theologian than Saint Thomas Aquinas, himself born of a southern Italian woman, taught in the name of the Church the ancient doctrine that "the soul is made like to God by grace."[19]

> The determination of the true and genuine ends of human life [the philosopher Jacques Maritain wrote near the end of his life, just before he joined the Little Brothers of Jesus] is not within the province of science. It is within the province of wisdom. In other words, it is within the province of philosophy—and, to tell the truth, not of philosophical wisdom alone, but also of God-given wisdom. Society needs philosophers in this connection. It needs saints even more.[20]

Society needs saints, men and women need saints, and southern Italian life and the *festa* were about saints, not Gnostic supermen (*perfecti.*) Indeed, the saints were so central in the lives of the *paesani*, that the Danish reformer and journalist, Jacob Riis, remarked in 1899 that you could tell a "real Italian man...when he is at home with the saint in the backyard, the church or wherever it may be." Riis was right in this—the uneducated southern Italian immigrant agreed with Maritain—but Riis observed without really seeing when he went on to draw the typical Protestant and Docetic (i.e., Gnostic, anti-papal, and anti-sacramental) conclusion that *paesani* held that "the saint belonged to the people, not to the church" and that somehow the two were in opposition.[21]

No, the saints in the southern Italian understanding were in the Church, not themselves the Church; made saints by the Church, by the two greatest gifts of Jesus Christ, Pentacost (the Church Herself) and Holy Eucharist. While they may have not been able to explain it this way, the southern Italians' faith was Christocentric and ecclesiocentric—certainly not idolatrous—as their great devotion to *la Madonna* shows; especially in the favorite prayer of the holy women of the Confraternity of the Holy Rosary, in novenas always before the Blessed Sacrament, with its meditations on the life of Christ and Mary and humble openness to contemplative prayer.[22]

The candle burning at the shrine in the home (*domus*) before the statue of the saint, made it one with the sacred space of the Church, the home of God, just as all men and women were called to be one with Christ in the Mystical Body, according to Catholic teaching.(Rom. 12,5) In the village Church, the home of God, Paradise itself, the Sacrament of Sacraments, the Holy Eucharist descended to the little poor men, women, and children in the Person of Jesus Christ reserved in the Tabernacle.[23]

The error that so many writers on southern Italians make is to see the saint as a kind of super-hero or semi-divine, Gnostic "angel," and then to play the saint against the Church. It will be readily conceded that the *paesani* were not apologists for the Catholic faith and could not technically account for the role of the saints in their lives. Many college-educated Catholics, even with the recently issued *Catechism of the Catholic Church,* cannot or do not chose to do so today. But often non-Catholic writers, then as now, were too quick to label as crass superstition what for good reason has a long history in Jewish and Christian thought. The southern Italians knew that saints are men and women who do the will of God in imitation of Jesus Christ, true God and true man; and that to do the will of God here and now is Heaven. They knew that Christianity is nothing more than the imitation of Christ, and that the saints are Christ's complements. For all their lack of theological instruction, these child-like people somehow understood what Saint Catherine of Siena, Patroness of Italy and Doctor of the Church, meant when she said that "all the way to heaven is Heaven."[24] The angels, who were said to hover over their Churches and after whom Arcangela Santello and many other *paesani* were named in baptism, seemed to be their tutors.

The Problem of the "Four Romes"

The true historian must be capable of some degree of empathy, of looking at things from the perspective of the *paesani*. Not only were they in a strange country, without the English language and illiterate or semi-literate. They were living in urban centers and were looked down upon both by the Protestant majority and the Catholic minority as coming from one of the most backward areas of the Western world. Moreover, at the time of their coming, anti-Mediterranean racial theories like Aryanism abounded, and Social Darwinism was promoting vicious Nativistic and anti-immigration movements.

The very Catholic Church to which the southern Italians belonged hardly welcomed them, and many of the American clergy seemed to be cold or indifferent to their plight, more concerned with winning acceptance themselves from influential Protestant Christians than sharing the one true ancient faith with the pope's own countrymen. Many of the *contadini*, it is true, made clear that they did not intend to stay in the United States. As for the southern Italian *festa*, the American hierarchy in general looked upon it, at best, as an embarrassment, only confirming the Anglo-Saxon Protestant view that the papist religion degraded men by catering to saint "worship."

As if this psychic trauma were not enough, the *paesani* soon found themselves smack in the middle of the Americanist crisis, the struggle between Pope Leo XIII and powerful elements in the American hierarchy over the degree to which the Church in the United States should adapt to

American conditions, i.e., Modernism. From the vantage-point of the 1990's, we now know that this was no "phantom heresy," as was once widely believed. This is not the place to discuss Americanism. But it is important to point out that the religious practice of the southern Italians, whose Catholic faith was wholly Incarnational and traditional, i.e., Roman, was championed by the Italian Pope Leo XIII. It was this Supreme Pontiff, the author of the anti-Americanist encyclicals *Longinqua oceani* (1895) and *Testem Benevolentiae* (1899), who also sent Mother Frances Xavier Cabrini and Bishop Giovanni Scalabrini to aid the immigrants, especially to strengthen their Roman Catholic faith in a hostile environment. And it was this Pope who in 1904 elevated the shrine of Our Lady of Mount Carmel in Italian Harlem to the rank of a sanctuary, making it one of only three Marian sanctuaries in the New World, in an obvious rebuff to the American hierarchy and preserving the integrity of the southern Italian *festa* as consistent with sound Catholic doctrine.[25]

The *paesani* as late Medieval people still, for all intents and purposes, were living in Christendom, and thus had little sympathy for the Modern ideology of the nation-state and national religions, i.e., Erastianism. After all, late Antiquity and the Middle Ages were in their blood—had not Saint Thomas Aquinas, the architect of Medieval Christian culture, Gregory VII and other popes come from their ancient land. They were "Romans" and Catholics, universal men.

In the *paese*, before they came to these shores, they had begun to feel the pain of a new oppressor, the government of the North, of the *Risorgimento,* with its capital in the Rome of the Caesars. When Garibaldi's troops stormed Porta Pia and seized the Eternal City in 1870, every Italian was soon forced to take his stand for one Rome or the other: the Rome of Peter and Paul, or the Rome of the Republic. The problem of dual loyalty followed the *contadini* to America, as did the new government's agents, for many of the Italians had come for bread rather than to stay. In the United States, at the height of the Americanist crisis in the 1890's, the problem of the "Two Romes" became for the southern Italians the problem, as it were, of the "Four Romes." Not only did the Italian Catholics have to decide which Rome in Italy to follow in the confusion over nationalism, which they did not understand; they had to figure out which Catholic faith, traditional or American, to embrace in the United States. And the record is clear that they chose not the Irish or American-controlled Church but the traditional Roman Catholic Church of the *paese*. It was this Roman Catholic Church of the villages of southern Italy, its possible excesses notwithstanding, that one of the greatest of all popes saluted in his Marian Bull of 1904.[26]

The Festa and Its Afterglow

In his book *The Italians*, Luigi Barzini relates an anecdote passed down from the time of Garibaldi and the *Risorgimento* that reveals the practical common sense and hard-won wisdom of the southern Italians. It helps us to understand the Catholic realism of the *contadini*. We glimpse their loyalty to home and family (*domus*), village and *paese*, their distrust of Modern (Gnostic) individualism (*Gesellschaft*), and their personal, social, and religious traditionalism viz-a-viz Garibaldi's nineteenth-century romantic nationalism. It also throws light on the exquisite sense of marginality that enabled southern Italians over the centuries to survive on the peninsula apart from the many contenders for power.[27]

"The extended fingers of one hand," Barzini introduces the anecdote by describing a favorite southern Italian gesture, "moving slowly back and forth under the raised chin means: `I couldn't care less. It's no business of mine. Count me out.' This is the gesture made in 1860 by the grandfather of Signor O.O. of Messina as an answer to Garibaldi. The general, who had conquered Sicily with his volunteers and was moving on to the mainland, had seen him, a robust youth at the time, dozing on a little stone wall, in the shadow of a carob tree, along a country lane. He reined in his horse and asked him: `Young man, will you not join us in our fight to free our brothers in Southern Italy from the bloody tyranny of the Bourbon kings? How can you sleep when your country needs you? Awake and to arms!' The young man silently made the gesture. Garibaldi spurred his horse on."[28]

In the course of his survival, the southern Italian valued the family (*la famiglia*) and the home (*domus*) more than any other institution. Individualism, in the Modern sense of nominalism and antinomianism, was unthinkable to him. He possessed the authentic Catholic sense of life as *communio*, as *Gemeinschaft,* in the Church as the Mystical Body of Christ. So much so, that in his vocabulary to be educated (*ben educato*) meant not to acquire literacy and diplomas, but to interiorize the values of the *domus* and become *cristiani*.[29]

In the *contadini's* implicit understanding, there was no Gnostic opposition between these values which gave meaning to life, and the Church. There was no intellectualizing, no theologizing of Roman Catholic faith and family. The very icons of home and *festa*, probably Byzantine in origin, which cluttered his village Churches proclaimed the peasant's deep belief in the Incarnation and declared his loyalty to the Church Christ founded.[30] Sacred space and time, so important in man's natural religiousness—as Eliade, Bouyer, and others have shown—in their totality included home, village, and Church, with the *festa's* streets leading like so many *via crucis* to the God-Man's triumph on the parish altar. At *festa* time, truly a celebration of the *mirabilia Dei,* the wonders of God, parishes like Holy Rosary in Jersey City became radiant and strove to realize their ancient unity in the faith. The *paesani*, amid music and gaiety, crowded the streets decked out with brilliant colored lights while above in the black night sky Roman candles exploded in an orgy of transcendence. The very stones of Brunswick Street seemed to cry out that Jesus Christ is the Messiah and that all was right with the world!(Luke, 19, 40).

At the peak of southern Italian immigration into the United States, the country was undergoing the radical change to Modernity that we have already noted. In his "The Significance of the Frontier in American History," the American historian Frederick Jackson Turner discussed what he believed to be the critical role of the frontier in shaping American thought and institutions and the meaning of its passing. Like John Dewey and the other Pragmatists, Turner was a Gnostic thinker who in the American manner stressed one-dimensional, immanentist experience on the frontier—not Judaeo-Christian Revelation and Old World classical philosophy. Knowledge and truth came from experience, from *praxis,* from American experience, which necessarily must be different from European experience (relativism). This contracted view of reality was cut from the same cloth as the other Gnostic reductionism that imprisoned man in the opaque here and now. It had no place for the Catholic absolute, for any absolute, as it would soon turn out—even for the Natural Law of the Declaration of Independence on which the United States had been founded.[31]

Soon, like the afterglow of the *festa's* pyrotechnics in the great cities, the southern Italians' heightened Mediterranean sense of mystery and transcendence was to begin dissipating in the great wide-open spaces of surburban, bourgeois America. In the post-war decade of the 1950s, with the spread of doctrines of relativism, a former Marxist, i.e., Gnostic, and finally Orthodox Jewish sociologist of religion, Will Herberg, announced what anyone with historical perspective should have been able to see. New, largely secularized "religions of democracy," really a civil religion, was, in effect, replacing the three great historic religions of Protestantism, Catholicism, and Judaism in the United States.[32] Southern Italians, now in the second and third generations, were no exception to the rule. As American culture was transformed into commodity, religion—like marriage, sex, family, and practically everything else—was becoming a consumer product for them as well. The misrepresentations and betrayals of the Vatican Council (1961-1965) further weakened the Church in America, especially by eroding away even more the precious southern Italian heritage of transcendence, substituting Gnostic, world-immanent action (Pelagianism) for the Church's teaching of seeking first the Kingdom of God.(Matt. 6, 33-34).

But it is not for the historian to conclude pessimistically about anything in time, for as the first southern Italians in America would remind us, history belongs to God like everything else. There is, ultimately, no time or space apart from God (secularism). History too is sacred time, like the festa and the Church's spiritual year with its calendar of the saints' feast days. There is no Gnostic "contracted existence" for man here, no escape from the merciful God. In all mythologies, as van der Leevw has shown, the feast, the lucky day (*dies festus*), manifests "the powers which support, preserve, and even renew the world" with its ritual "carried out as a human activity in sympathy with the epiphany in the world of the divine energies upon which the very existence of man depends."[33]

And so every day, in Christian truth, the *paesani* teach us, is a *festa,* a celebration of our Resurrection with Christ and His saints. With the Holy Eucharist, the *Pasch,* it is the divine refreshment promised by Jesus Christ. "Come to Me, all you who are weary and find life burdensome, and I will refresh you." (Matt. 11, 28) This is the real meaning of the *festa*. It was made by God, like life itself, for "fun and frolic,"—in the words of one of the favorite songs of the *paese*. It will, as in the priest's words in the rubric of the Divine Liturgy, protect us from the sin of anxiety, never greater or more widespread than in today's neurotic society (*angst*).[34]

What else, as if there could be anything more, do these simple people of the *festa* have to say to us today? Out of the wisdom of their humility they teach us that we must be witnesses to the universal, to guard against those false particulars, those lies against God and man, that Modern ideologies tend to absolutize in imprisoning men in Gnostic "contracted existence." Here again, no one has said it better than Jacques Maritain. "There is no other authentic and truly supranational universalism than Catholicism. The minds of men can only readjust themselves to the present needs of the world by adjusting themselves to the Catholic Absolute."[35] We can learn from them too to see man as he really is, as God created the human person—man, woman, and child—in His Image and likeness, and therefore of infinite value. This great truth alone, in the fulness of its implications, can restore the family and the community after the devastations of Gnostic Modernity (antinomianism, *Gesellschaft, anomie*).

But the people of the *festa* teach us even more, that "everything now bears the mark of the almost inconceivable exaltation of humanity brought about through the Incarnation of God and through Baptism which implants in man a new principle of life, participation in the life of Christ and the Holy Trinity." Dietrich von Hildebrand continues in his *Liturgy and Personality:*

> To the extent that every baptized person develops this life himself (or, more accurately, lets this life be developed in him), to the extent that he gives himself up to Christ and follows Christ, living from Christ, with Christ and in Christ—he lives no more but Christ lives in him. He thus participates in the unlimited breadth and fullness of Christ. He who is immersed in the life of Christ, he in whom Christ is truly imitated—the saint—becomes a personality no matter what his essential endowments are.[36]

In the *festa* as sacramental, as symbolic action, but above all in its fulfillment in absolute transcendence, in the Divine Liturgy and Holy Eucharist, the Father's plan—that greatest of miracles— is realized as men, women, and children become personalities, become saints!

This deep Catholic faith explains why the southern Italians in America were a people of hope, of "hope against hope." It is hope, they would remind us, that is the "true enfranchisement of human life....a deliberate will to hope." It is our "historic duty, a duty to our brothers, and to future generations to keep hope firm....It is a work of courage and hope, of confidence and faith, which must begin with an effort of the mind determined to see clearly at all cost, and to rescue from the errors which disfigured them the great things in which we have believed and in which we believe, and which are the hope of the world." "This hope is holy in itself; it corresponds to the deepest and most ineradicable desires of human nature; it places souls in a communion of pain and longing with all the oppressed and the persecuted; it calls for heroism; it has a divine power for transforming human history."[37] The *paesani*, heroes of the Modern Age, are now gone. But they have set us an example by fulfilling their "historic duty," and have in Jacques Maritain's stirring words, kept "hope firm." We their descendants and fellow human beings must do the same.

Finally, and most dramatically, the southern Italians themselves tell us in their very words and example what their message is to the world. As a rule, they came to America not for land, not even for money. They were decidedly not materialists, they did not lust for property; nor did they come here to make a great figure among men. They came, they said over and over again, so they could live as *cristiani* (Christians), so they would no longer have to exist as beasts of burden. Most of them came to America to work in order that they might earn that modicum of dignity they knew in their Catholic faith was owed to all men and women, and that would enable them to return to the *paese* to live in the land they loved—as real Christians. The point is that they knew, as so many of us do not, what dignity is owed to men and women. What this meant to them, and what this means today to us their descendants and fellow-human beings, is the greatest part of their legacy.[38]

To be *cristiani,* to be Christians, meant to the southern Italians to be more worthy participants in the *festa* of life, truly believing what they as sinful men and women professed to believe as Catholics about Christ, the Madonna, and the saints. As a living catechism of men and women, of colors and lights, the *festa* proclaimed to a skeptical world that the saints were once sinners like the *paesani*, were flesh-and-blood men, women, and children; but now by the mystery of divine grace they were with Christ and Mary in the Communion of Saints. To be *cristiani*, meant to be saints, new men, to break through a darkening, opaque, Gnostic anti-world to transcendence. Jesus Christ Himself had commanded His disciples, men, women, and children, to be saints: "In a word, you must be perfect as your heavenly Father is perfect."(Matt. 5, 48)

The faith and the Holy Sacraments of the Catholic Church, especially the sacred bread of the Mass—broken like the toil-weary bodies of the *contadini*— made men saints, "one bread, one body," in the words of St. Paul (1Cor. 10, 16-17). These were the infinite gifts, the gifts of the divine life of the Second Person of the Blessed Trinity, of Jesus Christ in His passion, death, and Resurrection. The southern Italians sought to live this life every day with the intensity of the *festa*, as a risen people, at last having escaped from the degradations of *la Miseria*, whether in Italy or in America. And the final degradation, the ultimate *la Miseria*, is not physical, but Gnostic as we have seen. The "dark valley" has grown even darker. (Psalms 23,4) It is, as Gabriel Marcel warned us against after World War II, the acceptance by man himself of a degraded conception of himself.[39]

We must learn from the southern Italians in America—and they can teach us—what we might call Incarnational realism, the courage to escape from Gnostic non-being, to transcend this misery of the spirit and self-degradation, this all-embracing "contraction of existence" in our day. They can teach us to intensify our contact with Incarnational reality, with Christ, that "the light shines on in darkness."(John 1,5) We must, with them in their Franciscan littleness and poverty of spirit, break through the opaqueness of things to God, to the "Father of the heavenly luminaries, Who cannot change and Who is never shadowed over."(James, 1,17) We must, with them "break into song, sing praise."(Psalms 98, 1,2-4) We must join ourselves to Jesus Christ, to the Church, and *truly* become *cristiani,* the people of the *festa*.

Donald J. D'Elia

---

[1] C. S. Lewis, *Screwtape Letters*, No. 25, in Walter Hooper, ed., *The Business of Heaven: Daily Readings from C.S. Lewis* (San Diego: Harcourt Brace Jovanovich, Pub., 1984), pp.28-29. Cf. Gilbert K. Chesterton, *The Victorian Age in Literature* (London: Oxford University Press, 1944), p. 45. An excellent general discussion of *la festa* in Italy and its many foods is Carol Field, *Celebrating Italy* (New York:William Morrow & Co., 1990). I would like to dedicate this essay to my Mother, Francesca Maria Santello, the Santellos and the D'Elias, and all the "People of the *Festa*" of Holy Rosary Roman Catholic Church, Jersey City, New Jersey (St. Joseph's *Festa*, New Paltz, New York, July 26, 1997). My thanks to Rev. Fr. Peter Polo of the Missionaries of St. Charles for helping me locate this quotation from Bishop Scalabrini.

[2] Emmanuel LeRoy Laduire, *Carnival in Romans*, trans. Mary Feeney (New York: George Braziller, Inc., 1979), p. 370. For the carnival or *festa* as relic, ibid., pp. 340-341; idem., *Montaillou; The Promised Land of Error*, trans. Barbara Bray (New York: George Braziller, Inc., 1978), pp. 32-33. Of classic importance is Josef Pieper, *Leisure, The Basis of Culture* (New York: Pantheon Books, 1963), *passim.*; Rudolph J. Vecoli, "Cult and Occult in Italian-American Culture; The Persistence of a Religious Heritage," in *Immigrants and Religion in Urban America*, ed. by Randall M. Miller and Thomas D. Marzik (Philadelphia: Temple University Press, 1977),pp. 28-34. Classic in its defense of Italian-American ethnicity and indispensable is Richard Gambino, *Blood of My Blood: The Dilemma of the Italian-Americans* (New York: Doubleday, 1974).

[3] See Louis Bouyer, *Rite and Man; Natural Sacredness and Christian Liturgy,* trans. M. Joseph Costelloe, S.J. (Notre Dame, Indiana: University of Notre Dame Press, 1963), on the degradations of liturgy to theater and amusement in Catholic Europe. But what always saved, and saves the *festa,* is its union with the Church in the Holy Eucharist. On the meaning of sacrifice as "essentially a meeting with God in a sacred meal," *ibid.*, 88-90. On "The Impact of Italian Migration and American Catholicism," see Francis X. Femminella's article by that title in the *American Catholic Sociological Review,* 22 (Autumn 1961): pp. 233-241. Useful is Francsco Cordasco, ed., *Italian-Americans: A Guide to Information Sources* (Detroit, Michigan: Gale Research Co., 1978).

[4] "Strictly speaking, the past cannot be celebrated festively unless the celebrant commuity still draws glory and exaltation from the past, not merely as reflected history, but by virtue of a historical reality still operative in the present," Josef Pieper, *In Tune With the World; A Theory of Festivity,* trans. Richard and Clara Winston (Chicago: Franciscan Herald Press, 1963, 1973), pp. 19,14-15, 64-65 *et passim.* My thanks to Prof. Dominic A. Aquila for calling my attention to Dr. Pieper's essay. In the general analysis of Modernity I have used in this essay, I am indebted to Eric Voegelin and Msgr. Romano Guardini. See Voegelin, *From Enlightenment to Revolution*, ed. John H. Hallowell (Durham: Duke University Press, 1975), p. 21 *et passim* and other works cited below; Romano Guardini, *The End of the Modern World*, ed. with an Introduction by Frederick D. Wilhelmsen (Chicago: Henry Regnery Co.,

1968). On symbolic systems, esp. food metaphors—so important in the *festa*—, in 16th century French carnivals, etc., "a fundamental procedure of folk discourse," see Laduire, *Carnival*, pp. 316-317. On man's "recourse to sacramental rites that symbolize his desire to be at one with the powers to which he looks for his 'daily bread,'" see R.R. Marett, *Sacraments of Simple Folk* (Oxford: At the Clarendon Press, 1933), p. 22 *et passim*; Frances M. Malpezzi and William M. Clements, *Italian-American Folklore* (Little Rock, Arkansas: August House Publishers, 1992), ch.x, 221-245. On the "social role of food" as "key to the Italian-American family," see Salvatore Primeggia and Joseph A. Varacalli, "Community and Identity in Italian-American Life," in *The Ethnic Quest for Community: Searching for Roots in the Lonely Crowd. Research in Community Sociology*, eds. Michael Hughey and Arthur Vidich (Greenwich, Connecticut, JAI Press, 1993) vol. 3, pp. 43-72, 47. "The Incarnanation must not be reduced to the taking-on of the flesh alone. God has intervened even in the collective unconscious, that it may be saved and fulfilled. The Christ descended into hell. How, then, can this salvation reach into our unconsciousness without speaking its language and making use of its categories?" Mircea Eliade, *Images and Symbols; Studies in Religious Symbolism,* trans. Philip Mairet (New York: Sheed and Ward, 1961), p. 161, quoting Fr. Louis Beirnaert, S.J. Bernard McGinn has examined the distinctive "symbolic mode of presentation" of a great Medieval thinker from Calabria in *The Calabrian Abbot; Joachim of Fiore in the History of Western Thought* (New York: Macmillan Pub. Co., 1985). The Gnostics, not surprisingly, were consistently anti-Italian in regarding wine as evil, especially refusing to use it in their "Eucharist" for that reason.

⁵ *Images and Symbols,* 166;on sacramentals, see Romano Guardini, *Sacred Signs*, trans. Grace Branham (St. Louis, Mo.; Pio Decimo Press, 1956), pp. 85-91, et passim. Excellent on the Giglio Feast of Brooklyn and insightful into the festa in general, is Salvatore Primeggia and Joseph A. Varacalli,"The Sacred and Profane Among Italian-American Catholics: The Giglio Feast," *International Journal of Politics, Culture and Society*, Vol. 9, No. 3 (Spring 1996), pp. 423-449. See, Hobbie, ed., *Italian-American Material Culture: A Directory of Collections, Sites, and Festivals in the United States and Canada* (New York: Greenwood Press, 1992). Rich in detail is Mildred Urick, "The San Rocco Festival At Aliquippa, Pennsylvania: A Transplanted Tradition," *Pennsylania Folklore* (1969):14-22. An example of a different perspective is Barbara Corrado Pope, "The Origins of Southern Italian Good Friday Processions," in *Italian-Americans Celebrate Life: The Arts and Popular Culture*, ed. Paola A. Sensi and Anthony Julian Tamburri (Selected Essays from the 22nd Annual Conference of the American Italian Historical Association, 1990), pp. 155-168.

⁶ Mircea Eliade, *The Sacred and the Profane: The Nature of Religion*, trans. Williard R. Trask (New York: Harper & Brothers, 1961), pp. 116-118 et passim. Of great importance also are Rudolf Otto, *Das Heilige* (The Idea of the Holy), 1917; Baron Friedrich von Hugel, *The Mystical Element in Religion* (1908); and Evelyn Underhill's many works. See Bouyer, esp. ch.iii, "Recent Developments in Psychol-

ogy," pp. 38-52. "A pagan," wrote G.K. Chesterton, "is a person who can do what hardly any person from the last two thousand years could do: a person who can take nature naturally," *The Victorian Age in Literature*, p. 139.

[7] Mircea Eliade, *A History of Religious Ideas* (3 Vols; Chicago, University of Chicago Press, 1978-) I: *From the Stone Age to the Eleusinian Mysteries*, Introduction, p. xvi; Leonard Covello, *The Social Background of the Italo-American School Child; A Study of the Southern Italian family Mores and Their Effect on the School Situation in Italy and America*, ed. with an Introduction by Francesco Cordasco (Leiden: E.J. Brill, 1967), ch. v, "Religious Concepts and Practices," pp. 103-145; Eliade, *A History of Religious Ideas*, II: *From Gautama Budda to the Triumph of Christianity*, p. 404; Bouyer, ch. viii, "Pagan Mysteries and Christian Sacraments," pp. 123-150. No one has laid bare the conceits of the late nineteenth-century "scientific" mind better than Viktor E. Frankl: "One of the most commonly quoted statements of Freud is that the narcissism of mankind has suffered a severe shock on three occasions: first, through the teaching of Copernicus; second, through the teaching of Darwin; and third, through that of Freud himself. We can easily accept the fact of the third shock. But of the other two we cannot understand why an explanation of the 'where' (Copernicus) or the 'where from' (Darwin) of humanity should have been a shock. The dignity of man does not suffer in the least from the fact that he inhabits the earth, a planet of the sun, and is not the center of the universe....Why should the fact that man is not the center of the universe affect the worth of man?...It is obvious that anything like the dignity of man depends on grounds other than his location in the material world. In brief, we are confronted here with a confusion of different dimensions of being, with a neglect of ontological differences. Only for materialism are light-years a measure of greatness," *Psychotherapy and Existentialism: Selected papers on Logotherapy* (London: Souvenir Press, 1967), p. 114. On scientism, also see John Wellmuth, S.J.,*The Nature and Origins of Scientism* (The Aquinas Lecture 1944) (Milwaukee: Marquette University Press, 1944), esp. pp. 1-5.

[8] Covello, *ibid.* Also, see Phyllis H. Williams, *South Italian Folkways in Europe and America; A Handbook for Social Workers, Visiting Nurses, School Teachers, and Physicians,* Introductory Note by Francesco Cordasco (New York: Russell & Russell, 1969), esp. ch. ix. 135-159. "'Time' and the ' Spirit of the time' were the great shocks for Catholicism in the nineteenth century," Friedrich Heer, *The Intellectual History of Europe*, trans. Jonathan Steinberg (2 vols.; Garden City, New York: Anchor Books, 1968), II: *The Counter-Reformation to 1945*, p. 313. For "pagan literature, philosophy, and mythology, properly understood" as "but a preparation for the Gospel," see John Henry Newman's *Apologia Pro Vita Sua: Being a History of His Religious Opinions,* ed. with an Introduction by Martin J. Svaglic (Oxford: At the Clarendon Press, 1967), p. 36.

[9] Werner Stark, *Sociology of Religion; A Study in Christendom* (2 vols.: London: Routledge & Kegan Paul, 1966) and *idem., Sociology of Knowledge: An Essay in Aid of Deeper Understanding of the History of Ideas* (London: Routledge & Kagan

Paul, 1958).

   [10] See, especially, *WOP!; A Documentary History of Anti-Italian Discrmination in the United States*, Edited with an Introduction by Salvatore J. LaGumina (San Francisco: Straight Arrow Books, 1973); Silvano M. Tomasi, *Piety and Power; The Role of the Italian Parishes in the New York Metropolitan Area, 1880-1930* (Center for Migration Studies, 1975), ch. iii, 43-60. It is remarkable how naively many writers today, who should know better, accept as reliable typical anti-Catholic, Protestant, and anti-papal commentaries of the late nineteenth century on the religious condition of the southern Italians. On looking at these materials, commendably assembled by Prof. Salvatore LaGumina, a co-editor of this present anthology, the historian must not forget that publications at the time invariably reflect an American Protestant understanding of "church" and other key organizing concepts of religion. Even Catholic publications at the time often had an Americanistic and anti-Catholic bias. An important study "On the Changing Nature of the 'Italian Problem' in the Catholic Church of the United States" by Joseph A. Varacalli, appears in *Faith & Reason* Vol. XII, No. 1 (1986), pp. 38-73; cf. Stark, *The Sociology of Religion,* passim.

   [11] Voegelin, *The New Science of Politics,* p. 131, 129, ch. iv, "Gnosticism—The Nature of Modernity,' pp. 107-131; Hans Aufricht, "A Restatement of Political Theory: A Note on Voegelin's *The New Science of Politics*," in Stephen A. McKnight, ed., *Eric Voegelin's Search for Order in History* (Baton Rouge: Louisiana State University Press, 1978), pp. 50-52; Voegelin, *From Enlightenment to Revolution*, p. 21, ch. vi, "The Apocalypse of Man: Comte," pp. 136-159; Bruce Douglass, "A Diminished Gospel: A Critique of Voegelin's Interpretation of Christianity," in McKnight, p. 142; Bouyer, p. 58. On the ecclectic nature of Gnosticism—the fact that even the different sects could not agree—see St.Irenaeus, *Adversus Haereses* (1.11.1).

   [12] Voegelin, *The New Science of Politics*, p. 131; idem., *From Revolution to Enlightenment*, pp. 301-302; Eugene Webb, *Eric Voegelin:Philosopher of History* (Seattle: University of Washington Press, 1981), p. 236 *et passim*; Douglass, p. 139. On similarities between Marxist and American thought, see Michele Federico Sciacca, *Philosophical Trends in the Contemporary World*, trans. Attilio Salerno, with an Introduction by A. Robert Caponigri (Notre Dame, Indiana: University of Notre Dame Press, 1964), p. 438 et passim; Aufricht, p.50.

   [13] Voegelin, *From Enlightenment to Revolution*, pp. 301-302; idem., *The New Science of Politics*, pp. 188-189; Webb, pp. 79-80, 235-236. Cf. Christopher Dawson, "Christianity and the New Age," in Christopher Dawson and J.F. Burns, eds., *Essays in Order* (New York: The Macmillan Co. 1931), p. 226.

   [14] Voegelin, *The New Science of Politics*, pp. 188-189.

   [15] *From Enlightenment to Revolution*, p. 231.

   [16] Pp. 52-60, *et passim*.

   [17] On this strange custom, *lingua strascinuni* (dragging tongue), see Robert Anthony Orsi, *The Madonna of 115th Street; Faith and Community in Italian Harlem, 1880-1950* (New Haven: Yale University Press, 1985), pp. xiii-xiv; Vecoli, " Cult

and Occult," pp. 32-33; and Peter Burke, *The Historical Anthropology of Early Modern Italy; Essays on Perception and Communication* (Cambridge: Cambridge University Press, 1987), p. 199. This hierophantic quality of the *contadini,* this child-like humility and poverty of the spirit, which recognizes man's absolute dependence upon God by glorifying the Father, is Franciscan in character. In the *Fioretti,* the "Little Flowers of Saint Francis," the story is told that Francis, accusing himself of a lack of charity toward Brother Bernard, commanded him under obedience to "put one of you feet on my throat and the other on my mouth. and thus to step over me three times from one side to the other," saying "Lie there, you country lout, son of Pietro di Bernardone!...How is it you have so much pride, since you are such an extremely worthless creature?" (ed. Raphael Brown; Garden City, New York: Image Books. 1958), pp. 47-48. Traditional *feste* often included prayers for family and community, e.g., street processions to the Church by women on their knees. In the time-honored practice of ascending on one's knees the Scala Santa (Holy Stairs) in Rome, the Sacraments of confession and communion are required by Catholic Church teaching for a papal indulgence. Although perhaps they might not have been able to articulate it, the southern Italians in their deep humility would have agreed with John Henry Newman that Holy Church's "mysteries are but the expressions in human language of truths to which the human mind is unequal," *Apologia Pro Vita Sua; Being a History of His Religious Opinions,* ed, with an Introduction, by Martin J. Svaglic (Oxford; At the Clarendon Press, 1967), p. 37. On "St. Francis and Franciscan Spirituality," Evelyn Underhill, *Mixed Pasture; Twelve Essays and Addresses* (Freeport, N.Y.: Books for Libraries Press, 1968), pp. 147-168, 95. For a brief and excellent discussion of Italian spirituality, see Jordan Aumann, *Christian Spirituality in the Catholic Tradition* (San Francisco: Ignatius Press, 1986), pp. 207-211.

[18] Voegelin, *From Enlightenment to Revolution,* ch. vii, "The Religion of Humanity and the French Revolution," pp. 160-194.

[19] *Summa Theologica* I, Q43, a5; Voegelin, *The New Science of Politics,* p. 130. Ladurie and Orsi use the richly explanatory term "domus" (building and family), which suggests to the present writer that it may not be inappropriate to describe the festa as an extended *domus,* Orsi, pp. xix-xx, *et passim.* It cannot be developed here, but it is most interesting that St. Anthony of Padua, a great favorite of the *paesani* in *feste,* was in his day known as the "Hammer of Heretics"; and is honored by the Church with the title of Doctor because of his holiness and great learning.

[20] *On the use of Philosophy; Three Essays* (Princeton: Princeton University Press. 1961), p. 10. We must leave to the theologian the distinction between those, devotees, who desire merely sanctity, and the saints, who seek God; See Raymond L. Bruckberger, O.P., *Toward the Summit,* trans. Sr. M. Camille, O.S.F. (New York: P. J. Kenedy & Sons, 1956), p. 137.

[21] Quoted in Orsi, p. 22. See Jacob Riis, "Feast Days in little Italy," in Wayne Moquin, ed., with Charles van Doren, Consulting Editor Francis A. J. Ianni, *A Documentary History of the Italian-Americans* (New York: Praeger Publishers, 1974), pp.

313-316.

[22] The mysteries of the rosary "accord with the sacred liturgy, are in some fashion derived from it, and lead the people to it," (Vatican II, On the Sacred Liturgy, 13). "The monotony of these repetitions clothes the poor old woman with physical peace and recollection," wrote J. Marechal, "and her soul, already directed on high, almost mechanically, by her habitual gesture of drawing out the rosary, immediately opens out with increasing serenity on unlimited perspectives, felt rather than analyzed, which converge on God....What does it matter, then, if the humble *orante* does not concern herself with living over again the exact meaning of the formula she is repeating?...often she does better, she allows her soul to rise freely into a true contemplation, well worn and obscure, uncomplicated, unsystematized, alternating with a return of attention to the words she is muttering, but building up in the long run *on the mechanical basis they afford* a higher, purified, personal prayer." (*Studies in the Psychology of the Mystics*, English trans. p.158) Quoted in Evelyn Underhill, *Worship* (New York: Harper& Brothers, 1957), p. 27. See Very Rev. Msgr. George W. Shea, "The Dominican Rosary," in Juniper B. Carol, O.F.M., *Mariology* (3 vols.; Milwaukee: The Bruce Publishing Co., 1961) 3: pp. 88-127. Many non-Catholics still mistake the veneration of St. Mary for worship. But even if the *paesani*, in their ignorance, "worshiped" the Blessed Mother (Nestorian heresy), it is easy to believe that her Son, true God and true Man, will forgive the excess, so great is His love for her. "Thus Catholic Christianity occupies an intermediate position between the two spiritual ideals and the two conceptions of reality which have divided the civilized world and the experience of humanity. To the West its ideals appear mystical and otherworldly, while in comparison with the Oriental religions it stands for historical reality and moral activity. It is a stranger in both camps and its home is everywhere and nowhere, like man himself whose nature maintains a perilous balance between the worlds of spiritual and sensible reality, to neither of which it altogether belongs,". Christopher Dawson, p. 226.

[23] Orsi, p. 106. On the "religious significance of the human dwelling place," Eliade, *The Sacred and the Profane*, pp. 56-57. "Exactly like the city or the sanctuary, the house is sanctified, in whole or part, by a cosmological symbolism or ritual, " *ibid.* For the Italian-American community as "not a place but a spiritual, emotional, or blood tie," Virginia Yans-McLaughlin, *Family and Community: Italian Immigrants in Buffalo, 1880-1930* (Ithaca: Cornell University Press, 1977), pp. 264-265.

[24] See, e.g., Joseph Husslein, S.J., *The Spirit World About Us* (Milwaukee: Bruce Publishing Co., 1934), p. 30. "Thus St. Bonaventure, recalling the lesson of Brother Giles (a *simplex etydiota* like Francis himself) says, 'the fact is that an old woman, with a little graden, but who possesses charity, derives more fruit from it alone than a great master with an extensive garden and a knowledge of the mysteries of nature,'" quoted by Etienne Gilson, *Christianity and Philosophy* (New York: Sheed and Ward, 1939), p. 57; Marco Caliaro and Mario Francesconi, *John Baptist Scalabrini; Apostle to Emigrants* (New York: Center for Migration Studies, 1977),

pp. 359-360.

[25] Essential is Stephen Michael DiGiovanni, *Archbishop Corrigan and the Italian Immigrants* (Huntington, Ind.: Our Sunday Visitor Publishing Division, 1994), esp. ch. ii, "Rome and the Catholic Immigrants," pp. 31-77; Feliks Gross, *Il Paese: Values and Social Change in An Italian Village,* with a Preface by Prof. Vittorio Castellano (New York: New York University Press, 1973), ch. xiv, "Religion and Continuity," pp. 203-212. S. M., Tomasi, ed., *The Religious Experience of Italian-Americans* (American Italian Historical Association Proceedings, Nov. 17, 1973), "Research and Studies on the Religious Experience of Italian-Americans," pp. 5-9; Richard A. Varbero, "Philadelphia's South Italians and the Irish Church," ibid., pp. 33-52; Rudolph J. Vecoli has noted with deep insight, and Russo and other students have confirmed, that the Catholic mysticism of the first generation of the Italians in America could have enriched, and lent new depth to the Church in the United States, had it been appreciated and nurtured at the time, "Cult and Occult," pp. 25-47, esp. 42.; *idem.,*" Prelates and Peasants: Italian Immigrants and the Catholic Church," *Journal of Social History,* vol. 2 (Spring 1969), pp. 217-268; That the Italians were deeply Catholic but in need of good priests in America, see Humphrey J. Desmond, *The Neglected Italians: A Memorial to the Italian Hierarchy* (Milwaukee, September 30, 1899), cited by DiGiovanni, p. 95. One American priest wrote: "What good Catholics these people would be if they only had the qualities fitting them to be good Americans,"quoted in DiGiovanni, p. 91. In an audience with a visiting German bishop in 1929, Pope Pius XI insisted that "the right of a people to Christian instruction and pastoral care in their mother tongue was a natural right," Barry J. Colman, *The Catholic Church and German Americans* (Milwaukee: The Bruce Pub. Co., 1953), p. 265n. On Americanized Italians and other citizens' complaints about "Italian religious celebrations" in Newark, New Jersey, as a desecration of the Sabbath, see S. M. Tomasi, *Piety and Power,* pp. 123-125. Shortly after her arrival in America, Mother Cabrini wrote of the plight of her fellow Italians, that they were "abandoned and very much looked down upon by the English public," June 12, 1889, quoted by her biographer, Sister Mary Louise Sullivan, M.S.C., "Mother Cabrini: Missionary to Italian Immigrants," *U.S. Catholic Historian,* vol. 6 (1987), p. 267.

[26] Orsi, ch. iii, "The Origins of the Devotion to Mount Carmel in Italian Harlem," pp. 50-74; DiGiovanni, pp. 69-70, 74, *et passim.* As for later developments, see Nicholas John Russo, "Three Generations of Italians in New York City: Their Religious Acculturation," in *The Italian Experience in the United States,* ed. by S.M. Tomasi and M.H. Engel (Staten Island, New York, 1970), "Conclusion," p. 209; and Femminella, pp. 240-241.

[27] Luigi Barzini, *The Italians* (New York: *Atheneum,* 1964), p. 63; Joseph A. Varacalli, "What It Means to be an Italian-American: Initial Reflections," ms, a paper read at the Annual Meeting of the American Italian Historical Association, Chicago, Illinois, November 13, 1987, pp. 11-12.

[28] On the "Dual Loyalty" and "Complex of Canossa" of *Il Paese* in the end, see Gross, pp. 204-206.

[29] Orsi, pp. 79-83, iii, xx, 18-20, 86 . On the importance of "blood-sharing" and "blood bonding"—so much so that "many in the first generation believed that a mother's blood was mixed in with the milk her child suckled," see *ibid.*, 82; Bouyer, 88 *et passim.*

[30] Jaroslav Pelikan, *Imago Dei: The Byzantine Apologia for Icons* (Washington, D.C.: Princeton University Press, 1990), pp. 7-8.

[31] See the discussions of Natural Law in Donald J. D'Elia and Stephen M. Krason, eds., *We Hold These Truths and More; Further Catholic Reflections on the American Proposition; The Thought of John Courtney Murray, S.J., and Its Relevance Today* (Steubenville, Ohio: Franciscan University Press, 1993). Also see Joseph A. Varacalli's "The Contemporary Culture War in America: Whither Natural Law, Catholic Style?" *Faith and Reason*, Vol. 21, No. 4 (Winter, 1995). For an interesting discussion of *feste* on Malta, and their religious and political implications, see Jeremy Boissevain, *Saints and Fireworks; Religion and Politics in Rural Malta* (London: University of London, The Athlone Press, 1965). For "Carnival on the Island of Pantelleria: Ritualized Community," see the study by Anthony H. Galt in *Ethnology* Vol. 12, No.3 (July 1973). On the procession and the return to Paradise, (and my extension of this image to the sacred space of the streets of the *festa*), Eliade, *Images and Symbols*, p. 166.

[32] *Protestant, Catholic, Jew: An Essay in American Religious Sociology* (Garden City, New York: Doubleday, 1955).

[33] Bouyer, "Sacred Time," ch. x ,pp.189-205, esp. 191.

[34] Excellent on the Divine Liturgy is Johannes Pinsk, *Divine Worship* (Collegeville, MN: The Liturgical Press, 1931), esp. pp. 7-9; Alan Keenan, O.F.M., *Neuroses and Sacraments.* (New York: Sheed & Ward, 1950), *passim.*

[35] *The Things That Are Not Caesar's*, trans. J.F. Scanlan (London: Sheed and Ward, 1930), p. 69.

[36] *Liturgy and Personality; The Healing Power of Formal Prayer* (Manchester, N.H.: Sophia Institute Press, 1960), p. 25.

[37] Jacques Maritain, *Christianity and Democracy*, trans. Doris C. Anson (London: Geoffrey Bles, The Centenary Press, 1945), pp. 10-11, 14, 36-37.

[38] Orsi, pp. 191-192, et passim. The Italian peasants, like the French peasants, wrote G.K. Chesteron, "fell on their knees before the Crucifix," not because they were slaves (as Swinburne wrote in his poem *Before a Crucifix*). They fell on their knees before the Crucifix because they were free men! (*The Victorian Age in Literature*, p.183).

[39] *Man Against Mass Society* (Chicago:Regnery, 1963), pp. 18-20 *et passim.* Another brilliant analysis along similar lines is that of the French Protestant writer, Jacques Ellul, *Propaganda: The Formation of Men's Attitudes* (New York: Knopf, 1965). The Christian," writes Josef Pieper, "is convinced that no destructive action,

no matter how thorough going, even if it is fervently celebrated as a gruesome 'antifestival,' can ever corrode the substance of Creation," *In Tune With the World*, p. 65.

Part V

The Saints March On

CHAPTER 12

THE SAINTS IN THE LIVES OF ITALIAN-AMERICAN CATHOLICS: TOWARD A REALISTIC MULTICULTURALISM

Introduction: Italian-American Catholic

This chapter of the volume deals with both a cognitive and normative issue.[1] Cognitively, the general issue revolves around the question of how individuals who came out of Italian and Catholic backgrounds and have historically resided in the United States have related these three attachments. More specifically, the cognitive issue is how have Italian-American Catholics, in both thought and behavior, historically related themselves to the saints? Normatively, the general issue is how *should* individuals who are simultaneously, in some sense, Italian, Catholic, and American, relate these commitments to each other? The more specific normative question, as such, is how *should* Italian-American Catholics have embraced the issue of devotion to the saints?

Given that an official, institutional Catholicism never became a deeply entrenched reality in the pre-modern, *gemeinschaft*, village settings of a turn-of-the-century southern Italy, it should come as no surprise that the Italian immigrant to American shores was considerably more influenced by a pre-modern, pre-Christian southern Italian culture—*la via vecchia* (the old way)—than he was by the Catholic faith, correctly understood. As such, the southern Italian immigrant who reached the shores of the United States was primarily shaped by his village culture, less so by his Catholic faith, and only incidentally—through word of mouth, written correspondence, and by his previous and occasional trips as a "bird of passage"—by the vision of America. Speaking of the immigrant generation, Rev. Nicholas John Russo observed that:

> The Italians manifested a casual attitude toward religion, which was often interspersed with what seemed to some Americans to be 'magic and superstition.' Creedal tenets were not taken very seriously. Instead there was an intense devotion to the warm personages of Mary and the saints. Southern

231

Italian Catholicism was a personal, parochial type of religion. The clergy as well as the people were poorly instructed. Formal religious instruction was absent, and adherence to Catholicism ranged from indifference to great devotion. However, most immigrants remained nominally loyal to the Church, albeit in their own way.[2]

Correlatively, for the most part, the immigrant apprehended the saints in a manner consistent with a natural and basically healthy paganism, a paganism whose edges may have been refined and perfected, to some smaller or larger degree, by an official Catholic understanding. Correspondingly, the southern Italian immigrant rejected the more abstract and barren cosmology of the typical American and Protestant worldview that he encountered in the New World; witness the generally failed attempts of Protestants to convert the Italian-American immigrant. For many southern Italian immigrants, devotions to the saints *were* infused by magic, *were* used in a very "world-affirming" way to fight against an oppressive social and physical environment, and they *were* seen as more important than the doctrinal issues, sacramental participation, civil concerns, and magisterial authority constitutive of an official Catholicism. Indeed, the concept of the saint as a personal contact to the supernatural *was* more important to the immigrant than was the concept of the Church herself as the living Mystical Body of Christ. The immigrant utilization of the saints, then, was part and parcel of the general "Italian problem" in the Catholic Church of the United States, viewed from an official Church perspective.[3] As noted by the social historian Henry J. Browne, "...racial antipathies, political-religious conceptions brought from Italy, inadequate churches, Protestant proselytizing, immigrant priests of poor quality, and over and above all a woefully unstructured people—these elements went to make up the 'Italian problem' for the Church in the United States."[4] Rudolph J. Vecoli's analysis is worth quoting at length. Regarding anti-clericalism, Vecoli states that:

> Anticlericalism may have been the most notorious aspect of the 'Italian Problem,' but it was not its most significant dimension. The great majority of the immigrants from Italy were not free thinkers or socialists; rather they were *contadini* (peasants) from the *Mezzogiorno*. Modern notions of nationalism and radicalism had not penetrated the isolated villages of southern Italy.[5]

For Vecoli, southern Italian religion was decidedly "folk" or what is now commonly referred to as "popular":

> In their religion as in all else, the peasants were intensely parochial and traditional. While nominally Roman Catholics, theirs was a folk religion, a fusion of Christian and pre-Christian elements, of animism, polytheism,and sorcery with the sacraments of the Church. 'Even the ceremonies of the Church,' Carlo Levi observed 'become pagan rites, celebrating the existence of inanimate things, which the peasants endow with a soul, and the innumerable earthy divinities of the Village.' Dominated by a sense of awe, fear, and reverence for the supernatural, the peasants were profoundly religious. However, their beliefs and practices did not conform to the doctrines and liturgy of the Church.[6]

Furthermore, this folk religion was intensely personal, communal, and practical:

> The religion of the *contadini* was enclosed within the spirit of *campanilismo*. Each village had its own array of Madonnas, saints,and assorted spirits to be venerated, propitiated, or exorcized. There was no turn of fortune, for good or for ill, that was not due to the benevolence or malevolence of these supernatural beings. God, like the King, was a distant, unapproachable figure, but the local saints and Madonnas, like the landlords, were real personages whose favor was of vital importance. With a mixture of piety and shrewdness, the supplicants bargained with their patrons, offering gifts, sacrifices, and praise, if their petitions were granted. The feast day of the patron saint or Madonna was the highpoint in the life of the village. With panegyrics, processions, brass bands, and fireworks, these communal celebrations exalted the miraculous powers of the patron and invoked his protection upon the village. Since to *fa bella figura* was assumed to be a common aspiration of spiritual as well as human beings, the statue of the saint clothed in fine robes and adorned with jewels was paraded through the streets followed by the throng of admirers.[7]

That this folk religion was saturated with a heavy mixture of non-Catholic elements was undeniable:

> Among the spirits of the villages were some not to be found in the calendar of the Church. The *contadini* lived in dire fear of the evil eye

(*malocchio* or *jettatura*). Spells cast by witches could destroy crops, bring sickness and death, or arouse forbidden passions. To combat these malevolent forces, the peasants had recourse to sorcerers (*mago* or *strega*) to break spells, exorcize spirits, and divine the future. These black arts were an essential element in the folk religion of Southern Italy. Particularly for the peasantry, amulets, potions, and magical rites were at least as important as the sacraments of the Church in coping with the terrors of the supernatural.[8]

Regarding the world-view of most southern Italians toward an "official," institutional Catholicism, Vecoli notes that:

For the Church as an institution the South Italian peasants had little sense of reverence. Historically it had been allied with the land-owning aristocracy and had shown little sympathy for the misery of the *contadini*. Although surrounded by a multitude of clergy, the people by and large were not instructed in the fundamental doctrines of the Catholic faith. Toward their village priests, whom they regarded as parasites living off their labors, the peasants often displayed attitudes of familiar contempt. Clerical immorality and greed figured largely in the folk humor of Italy. The parish priest appeared to be regarded as a functionary who performed the necessary rites of baptisms, marriages, and funerals. Other than on these occasions and feast days, the *contadini*, especially the men, seldom set foot in church. The fact that the priests rarely accompanied their parishioners to America reflected the lack of reciprocal affection between the clergy and people.[9]

Finally, Vecoli makes clear that southern Italian religiosity and American Christianity, whether Catholic or Protestant, were mutually viewed as uncongenial:

The Italian peasants, to be sure, thought of themselves as *cristiani*; not to be a Christian was to be a Turk, a racial memory of the Saracens. Their brand of Christianity, however, had little in common with American Catholicism. An observer noted in 1888: 'The fact is that the Catholic Church in America is to the mass of the Italians almost like a new religion.' Those Italians who ventured into Irish or German churches found them as alien as Protestant chapels. The coldly rational atmosphere, the discipline, the attentive congregation, were foreign to the Italians who were used to behaving in church as they would in their own house. Nor did the poorly dressed, sometimes unwashed, Italians find a ready welcome in the churches of other nationalities. Often they were turned away or seated in the rear with Negroes. Sometimes they heard themselves denounced as 'Dagos' from the pulpit and told that they were not wanted.[10]

However, the southern Italian immigrant appropriation of the saints could also legitimately be seen as a precursor to a fully and more authentic participation into the Catholic faith and as an efficacious mode of prayer to the One God. As practitioners of the natural law, "written into their hearts," southern Italian saint worship and manipulation of the saints could be, and in many cases was, perfected and purified (in the America of the mid-twentieth century). Such a development was by no means inevitable, but required the transformation of *la via vecchia* into a legitimate variation of the Catholic religion. Such a transformation itself presupposed the development of an intact and internally consistent Catholic "plausibility structure" or set of mutually interlocking and supporting social institutions geared to successfully socializing individuals and groups into an authentic Catholic way of viewing and living in the world.[11]

Where one stands normatively on the related issues of one's general religious orientation and stance to the saints obviously depends on what is one's ultimate frame of reference. For many traditional southern Italian peasants and first generation immigrants that ultimate frame was a holistic attachment to a basically pagan-informed *la via vecchia*. Things Catholic and American, as such, were either ignored or selectively incorporated to buttress or supplement traditional practices, the worshipping/ manipulating of the saints included. For many contemporary Italian-Americans what is of "ultimate concern" (in Paul Tillich's terms) or what constitutes their "sacred" cosmos (in Emile Durkheim's phrase) is their acceptance of what Will Herberg referred to as "the American Way of Life," although, perhaps, lived out *la dolce vita style*.[12] Again, as such, elements of *Italianità* or Catholicity are accepted as long as such an incorporation in no way threatens a full and unqualified acceptance into the mainstream of what is now clearly a quite materialistic American society. Many times such an accommodation entailed, if not outright banishment, the pushing of the saints to the periphery of both consciousness and household.

This essay is written from a perspective of someone whose primary and overriding allegiance is to a Catholic worldview whose ultimate arbiter is the Church's Magisterium. From such a perspective, there *is* much that can be accepted from both an Italian and American worldview as long as such an acceptance is either compatible with or, better yet, enlivens and energizes the Catholic faith. Inculturation, after all, is intended to further the goals of evangelization. Conversely put and more concretely, such a perspective does *not* allow one to divinize the saints or make them more central than an allegiance to Christ or to His Church. Neither does it allow one to deny the reality or efficacy of sainthood or, conveniently, to privatize such a conception. The reality of the communion of saints and the imperative for all individual Christians to strive for sainthood, properly understood, is a non-negotiable, constitutive, but not solely defining, feature of the Catholic religion.

The Catholic Church as a Multicultural Institution

There are few institutions in the United States that are as complex and pluralistic as is the American branch of the Catholic Church. This complexity is the result of both external and internal forces. Internally, the Catholic tradition was shaped over a 2,000 year period allowing individual Catholics and Catholic groups to choose from a wide range of differing philosophical and theological outlooks, liturgical and devotional styles, and religious orders, apostolates, and organizations. Theoretically, this internal complexity is supposed to be organically related, non-contradictory, and given coherence and supervision by Magisterial authority. In reality, a good deal of this pluralism is unchecked and is quite selectively appropriated by the individual or subgroup on the basis of some other non-Catholic allegiance that is ultimate.

Externally, there are numerous social sources of differentiation in the Church: regional variations, generational and age differences, divergent male versus female perspectives, a wide-range in background socio-economic status, opposing ideological commitments, and differing racial and ethnic subcultural traditions. Again, these various social sources of pluralism can be, theoretically, harnessed and energized under a distinctive Catholic worldview; historically, many times they take on a life of their own supplanting Catholicism as ultimate concern. Empirically speaking, and for better or worse, there is more than a grain of truth to James Joyce's observation that Catholicism means, "here comes everybody" (and everything).

Obviously, although perhaps superficially, it is the significant ethnic and racial pluralism that is considered to be the defining characteristic of the Catholic Church in the United States as a multicultural institution. This is superficial, perhaps, because one's socio-economic class background or ideological commitment may be a far better indicator of pluralism in the post-Vatican II Catholic Church than is either ethnic or nationality affiliation. Nonetheless, in the popular as well as academic mind, multiculturalism is associated most readily with ethnicity and race.

Unlike some other American religious denominations which are more neatly associated with one specific ethnicity or race, historically the Catholic Church mirrors the vast ethnic and racial complexity that made so telling the insight of historian Oscar Handlin to the effect that "the history of America *is* the history of her immigrant groups." Ten percent of African-Americans are Catholic as is the overwhelming percentage of Filipino-Americans. A not insignificant percentage of the current immigration from India and from some "Third World" nations also share in this designation. The ethnic complexity of Catholicism generally followed the successive waves of immigrants to American shores. First, in the colonial era, there were British and French Catholics; then around the 1820s-30s, Irish and German Catholics started to arrive; followed by the turn-of-the-twentieth century influx of Slavs and Italians; and, now, the "new" post 1965 immigration of Filipinos, Haitians, Arabs, and, most importantly in a numerical sense, the various "Hispanic" groups.

While the Catholic religion has been very ethnically and racially pluralistic, it would be historically incorrect and romantically naive to assume that each ethnic and racial group was equally imbued with an authentic sense of the Catholic faith or that they equally contributed to everyday Catholic life, either within the institutional routines of the Church or as a leaven in American society. The standard sociological set of "variables" or factors were and are operant: some groups came over to America earlier than others, thus affording a better opportunity to establish themselves in the new land; some groups were numerically larger; some groups came to America with a more viable and potent set of Catholic traditions; some groups were more inclined toward internal ecclesiastical affairs; some groups came over, relatively speaking, with more education, wealth, and social status; and some groups came over with more of an assimilationist, or what Andrew Greeley has referred to as an "Americanizer," mind set.[13]

These and other reasons explain the predominate status that the Irish historically have been accorded in the Church in America, at least until the last
few generations. Some ethnic groups (e.g. the Germans and Poles) actively
resented and contested the Irish near monopoly while others (e.g. the Italians and Bohemians and, most recently, the Hispanics) have responded
more with an indifference indicative of not just a lack of power and social
organization but also a lack of interest in internal Church affairs. While the
Irish, so to speak, controlled the parish and the saints found within its walls,
the Italians were just so happy to control that region that most closely ap-
proximated their previous village existence, i.e., their homes and their
neighborhood streets, and to populate them with their own set of saints.
Thus existed not so much a battle of the saints, but saints marching, at least
in some cases and to some degree, to different drummers.

The overriding point to re-emphasize, however, is this: what differen-
tiates authentic from inauthentic versions of Catholic multiculturalism is
whether or not the cultural worldview/practice in question is subordinate
to, compatible with, energizes, and is organically related to the broader
tradition as given articulation by Magisterial authority. In terms of the
historical stance of Italian-American religiosity *vis-à-vis* Catholicism, the
general movement has been one from paganism (albeit, again, pregnant
with promise) to a legitimate pluralism/multiculturalism to various forms
of contemporary neo-paganism.[14]

Multiculturalism in the United States: The Historical Background

The contemporary concept of "multiculturalism" in our society not
only means divergent things to varying groups but is also actualized and
implemented very differently in intellectual work and social programs.
Theoretically speaking (as compared to its actual ideological functions), the
concept is meant to respond affirmatively to the justifiable (and abstract)
claim that the legitimate historical contributions and experiences of some
less-than-powerful groups in our nation's history have been either misrepre-
sented or grossly underreported.

Multiculturalism as a concept is useful in our analysis of the saints in
the lives of Italian-Americans for several reasons. First of all, it points to
the ignorant and, at times, malicious stereotyping against Catholics of the
concept and application of sainthood on the part of a dominant Protestant
elite that has held a religious, cultural, political, and economic hegemony

over most of American history. Secondly, it highlights the significant antipathy that existed between the "Irish Catholic" and "southern Italian Catholic' utilization of the saints from the turn to the middle of the twentieth century and brings up the issue of which modes of worship are legitimate *vis-à-vis* an official objective understanding of authentic Catholic tradition. Thirdly, it raises the issue of the attempt of current revisionist historical analysis to unfairly attack and bash the institutional Catholicism of the time by arguing that the Irish-Italian "battle over the saints" primarily was over power and privilege and not over truth and correct religious practice. Finally and fourthly, it brings to the fore the issue of the logical contradiction of at least one strand of multiculturalism—i.e., "multicultural relativism"—which puts forth the proposition that all forms of belief and practice deserve equal respect. In the specific case at hand, this absurdity translates into the proposition that both belief and non-belief in the saints (or, variously, that all differing modes of belief in the saints without qualification) simultaneously are legitimate positions to embrace.

However, before pursuing these foundational questions, it is perhaps useful to briefly outline historical developments that have led to the plausibility and development of the present array of multicultural variations. Given the Protestant hegemony that held sway in America until the post-World War II era, it comes as no surprise that the normative ideal of citizenship was that of "Anglo-conformity." The pervasiveness of this ideal made any pluralistic model of citizenship impossible to envision on any society-wide scale.

After World War II, however, Catholics and Jews were not only numerous enough but influential enough in terms of power, status, and wealth to stretch "Anglo-conformity" to the "triple-melting pot" ideal, i.e. "Protestant," "Catholic," and "Jewish" alternate routes to American citizenship, as discussed by Will Herberg.[15] The reality of the triple-melting pot did not threaten American unity because it simultaneously evolved and involved a common Judaic-Christian religious-cultural framework that sought out and meshed the very real commonalities existing within the world religions of the Biblical orbit. Sociologically, this common Judaic-Christian framework represented a variation of cultural and structural pluralism, of diversity within unity. However, contemporary multiculturalism—or more precisely, the two main variations of contemporary multiculturalism, i.e., "radical multiculturalism" and "multicultural relativism"—are incompatible within a society shaped by a Judaic-Christian framework because, respectively, they are primarily secular and relativistic.[16] These two multicultural variations, in other words, are shaped primarily by visions—Marxist, feminist, Freudian, deconstructionist, among others,— historically antagonistic to Western religion and that certainly deny the absolutist truth claims of Judaism and Christianity. "Radical multiculturalism" is directly threatening to American national unity because of its revolutionary nature: it precisely attacks the Western heritage upon which American civilization is based, portraying it was unhealthy, unnatural, and pathological and which must be replaced by some utopian (e.g. socialist, feminist) alternative. "Multicultural relativism" is also not a plausible option in a Judaic-Christian world because it falsely equates the importance of all differing groups and lifestyles in terms of the dimensions of truth, beauty, holiness, and utility.

Both major variations of contemporary multiculturalism had to await the conjoining of certain demographic movements and historical developments for them to become dominant social forces.[17] Demographically, the movement of large numbers of upper-middle-class youth, females, Afro-Americans, homosexuals, and other "minorities" into programs of higher education provided not only some of the leaders of the multiculturalist movement but also its (alleged) constituency. Relatedly, professed Marxists and feminists became the "tenured radicals" and administrators of colleges and universities. The historical occurrences of the anti-Vietnam War, Civil Rights, feminist, and homosexual movements created an atmosphere that energized these demographic movements and created, at worst, violent feelings of antipathy toward American civilization and its leading institutions and leaders—religious institutions and leaders most definitely included— to, at best, a paralyzing ambivalence about the meaning of life and the existence of truth and sound morality. Pilate's query, "What is truth?" became progressively diffused and institutionalized throughout American society as did the cultural anthropologist's belief that the very existence of multiple moralities made imperative the acceptance of "cultural relativism" as the guiding religious and philosophical worldview. A belief and practice in the saints became, for many middle-class Catholic religious or lay people, either an opiate to be discarded, something to be hid in the closet (or bedroom), or, at best, one path to searching—seemingly blindly—for something "on the other side" of natural reality.

There is, however, a third variation of contemporary multi-culturalism, i.e., "multicultural realism," that is both intellectually sound and consonant with Catholicism. Multicultural realism is ultimately based on the ever-present reality of the natural law, that there is a God-given reason and logic that is structured into each and every human being, into all rightly conceived human arrangements and civilization, into very creation itself. As such, multicultural realism grants both normative and cognitive respect to many cultural formations not obviously found within the structures of an institutional Catholicism or even to those previously alluded to in a broader and once common Judaic-Christian framework. Such respect is so provided given the qualification that these formations, in the words of Vatican II, "reflect the rays of Truth" that are compatible with and that serve to enrich and enliven the faith while at the same time themselves necessarily requiring the light of the Gospel, a sacred yet evolving Church Tradition, and Magisterial guidance to approach a fuller perfection. Evangelization and inculturation are always intended to be mutually supportive. Translated into the concern of this essay, the pre-modern, pre-Christian pagan southern Italian utilization of the saints was, at base, a healthy and sound practice founded on an irreducible element of reality that needed to be surrounded by and immersed within the totality of Catholic tradition and sensibility in order to flower and to develop its full potential. This salutary development, furthermore and concretely, took place within the context of both the Italian national and defacto Italian ethnic parish of mid-twentieth century Catholic America.

Returning now to the applicability of "multicultural realism" to this volume as previously alluded to, several points now can be argued and briefly pursued. First of all, the emaciated and barren, respectively, Protestant and secular cosmology of early and late, respectively, American history could not and would not acknowledge a reality, i.e., a body of mediators to the realm of the supernatural—that appear to be rooted anthropologically into the very nature of what it means to be human. The universal, in so many words, is inevitably broached through the lens and vehicle of the particular. To theologize Peter L. Berger's sociology, one can state that the Catholic veneration of the saints is an example of a necessary "praise of particularity."[18] With all of their too human limitations, the saints nonetheless assist us in helping to reach and imitate Christ. Secondly, while many Irish prelates, priests, and laymen *were* correct in acknowledging the obvious, i.e., the pagan, magical nature of a good deal of Italian religiosity, they must be held accountable for their own indefensible ethnocentrism. The Irish, by and large, simply did not appreciate the degree of truth, beauty, holiness, and utility to be found within the admittedly pagan Italian appropriation of the saints and for lacking the imagination and sensibility to envision the developmental possibilities of an essentially healthy and realistic orientation that links this world to the other side.

Multiculturalism and the Italian-American Community

Many in the contemporary Italian-American community can be classified as embracing multicultural relativism, radical multiculturalism, or multicultural realism in either their "high" or "low" tradition variations. Historically, many southern Italian immigrants and second-generation working class Italian-Americans have responded to the charge of an official Catholicism (as embodied in the utterances of many Irish prelates) that their religious practices were pagan by making recourse to a low tradition ver-sion of multicultural relativism. That is, the typical peasant/immi-grant/working class response to the Irish was to deny that the latter's ver-sion of the faith was any truer or more objectively valid than their own version. In this regard, Francis X. Femminella has spoken usefully of the major Italian-American response to an official Catholicism as one of "indif-ference."[19] That is, a typical southern Italian response to the Irish charge was not to actively contest the official definitions of religious reality but merely to ignore them and proceed merrily with "doing religion" their own way. Similarly, Paul McBride speaks of the subjectivist response of many members of the early Italian community to official Catholic teachings and practices as that of the "solitary Christian."[20] In the Introduction to his *The Madonna of 115th Street: Faith and Community in Italian Harlem, 1880-1950*, Robert Orsi relatedly observed that:

> The study of Italian-American religion must begin with the people themselves, and they invariably insisted that going to church was not so important to them but that they considered themselves good and faithful people and Catholics...My informants in Italian Harlem continually made a distinction between religion and church. A person could be a good man or women—a *cristiano* or *cristiana* in the language of the immigrants—in other words,

could be religious, without having anything to do with how often he or she went to church."[21]

An all-important caveat about the nature of the early southern Italian-American embrace of the low tradition version of multicultural relativism must be noted. That is, multicultural relativism was probably as much a *strategy* to check the Irish charge as it was a deeply held belief. There is, for one thing, no historical evidence supporting the contention that a primarily pre-modern worldview, southern Italian or otherwise, allowed for a sincere attachment to *any* form of relativism. Put another way, the southern Italian immigrant to American shores was as "ethnocentric," as unqualified in his embrace of *la via vecchia*, as were his Irish critics to the latter's "ultimate concern." While it is true, as the relevant literature suggests, that Italian-Americans have a high tolerance for ideas and practices that diverge from their own *as long as those ideas and practice don't negatively impact on them*, it would be romantic nonsense not to acknowledge that the typical early Italian-American saw his mode of religious practice as *superior* to that of the Irish. Nonetheless, the stated claim that "the Irish can be religious their way as long as they leave us free to be religious in our own way" most probably served as an effective political and emotional response for many early Italian-Americans.

Relatively speaking, a more subjectively authentic and deeply emotionally held attachment to multicultural relativism in its highly articulated high tradition, on the part of some substantial segment of the Italian-American community, would have to await the post-1960s emergence of the philosophy of moral relativism. Unsurprisingly, the Italian-American segment most committed to offering "no offense," in John Cuddihy's phrase[22], to non-Italian religious and cultural formations was the highly educated (in a formalized sense, at least), prosperous, suburbanized, and assimilated (into the current rad/chic) third and fourth generation. The acceptance of the philosophy of moral relativism on the part of a significant segment of the contemporary affluent Italian-American population, whether authentically held in consciousness or not, allows these "socially mobile" Italian-Americans, (as with all other Americans) to better get along with each other, following Alan Bloom,[23] even at the expense of truth and the acknowledgment of the obvious. It is precisely this bourgeois Italian-American segment that is most likely to "privatize," in the various ways as analyzed by David Halle[24], their devotion to the saints.

A feigned or, at best, highly selective (and therefore inauthentic) attachment to Italian ethnicity has been used ideologically by some Italian-Americans to attack, variously, an official institutional Catholicism and both Western and American civilization. The unstated and actual goal of radical multiculturalism among Italian-Americans, contrary to its claim, is not to promote and institutionalize a sense of *Italianità* within American society. Rather it is to use such a feigned or unauthentic attachment to undermine some of the key pillars of Italian-American (e.g. the Church) and American (e.g. democratic capitalism) life and to substitute for these, instead, some utopian alternative (e.g. socialism/Marxism, anarchism, classical liberalism, New Age, feminism, homosexuality, or some other neo-paganism) that constitutes, *sotto voce*, the operant attachment of the radical multiculturalist.

With the occasional exception of the radicalized and self-educated man on the street, radical multiculturalism is inordinately found in a high tradition version. Within contemporary society, it is housed within the university system, the mass media, the arts, Hollywood, the Democratic Party, the Rockefeller wing of the Republican Party, and other important progressive organizations and movements. While mostly a post-1960s phenomenon, it can be traced, among Italian-Americans, to the heirs of *Il Risorgimento* that sought refuge and an alternative field of proselytization in the New World.

What is attacked by any specific radical multiculturalist naturally flows from what actually constitutes his/her ultimate allegiance. Socialist oriented Italian-American intellectuals argue the exploitation of Italian-Americans in a democratic capitalist setting, and ignore the dramatic material success of Italians in America. Feminists argue against the patriarchal nature of much of Italian-American family life, ignoring how constitutive this is of the tradition of which they nonetheless claim to be a part. Lesbian Italian-American women promote the superiority of women over men, ignoring the obvious complementary and loving relationship that has existed between men and women in Italian history. Italian-American New Agers deny the Church, her doctrine, her sacraments while trying to convince Italian-Americans of the utility of crystals and the reality of reincarnation. Libertarians and anarchists who are Italian try to convince their people of the authoritarian nature of Catholicism and of any governmental agency. Italian-American Marxists inform their fellow Italian-American citizens that the "worship" of the saints is retrograde and that their efforts must solely be re-channeled to the pursuit of this-worldly programs of social justice, presumably along socialist/statist lines. In all of this, a thin veneer of *Italianità* is applied in the attempt to get the unsuspecting off the scent of what is really cooking. The attempt is made, in other words, to push the Italian-American population from an essentially pre-modern paganism to that of a post-modern neo-paganism with no time to stop and contemplate what the Italian tradition was, and could be, surrounded by and immersed within, Catholic and pre-18th century, albeit updated, Western traditions.

Multicultural realism, finally, has been embraced by that portion of the Italian-American population who simultaneously affirm several propositions. The first is the existence of absolute truth and of an objective moral order. The second is that the ultimate author of this order of truth and morality is the triune God. The third is that God established his divine Church through the institutionalization of the Catholic faith and that the integrity of the Catholic faith is guaranteed through the exercise of Magisterial authority. The fourth is that truth is institutionalized in earthly form through Revelation (or Divine Law) and through revelation grounded in the human condition, i.e., the natural law as the human participation in the Eternal Law. The fifth is that the religious and cultural practices of pre-modern Italy that form the foundation of much of early Italian-American thought and practice (*la via vecchia*) is consonant, for the most part, with the natural law. The sixth is that *la via vecchia* required the introduction of Catholic elements to-be-purified, molded, and moved toward perfection. The seventh—and supported at least indirectly by studies by Gerhard Lenski, Rev. Silvano Tomasi, Nathan Glazer and Patrick Moynihan, and Rev. Nicholas Russo[25]—is that the evangelization of Italian-Americans into the Catholic faith was proceeding smoothly from the turn of the last century though to the early 1960s. This successful evangelization involved, furthermore, the inculturation of *la via vecchia* into the faith. The eighth is that a combination of internal Church developments involving a false reading of the Second Vatican Council and external cultural and societal developments including the rise of materialistic and relativistic philosophies in the 1960s onwards, and the strong desire of Italian-Americans for upward social mobility and acceptance into the elite circles of America, reversed much of this successful evangelization. Put another way, the general contours of the historical movement of Italian-Americans *vis-à-vis* Catholicism has been from paganism to Catholicism to various contemporary neo-paganisms.

Toward a Realistic Italian-American Catholic Multiculturalism

In one of his many insightful essays on the Italian-American experience, Rudolph J. Vecoli notes with sadness and regret that Italian-American religiosity, complete with its devotion to the saints, has undergone over its years in the New World what can variously be termed a Hibernization, Protestantization, and Americanization.[26]. The typical Italian-American no longer perceives that he lives in a dense, richly populated universe but now inhabits what is perceived to be a cold, abstract, and impersonal one. Vecoli sees the alternatives to be stark: either embrace the vividness and sensuality of *la via vecchia* or the abstractness and impersonality of the secularized modern world. This author presents a third possibility: that an authentic Italian-American multiculturalism can and must be rooted in the Catholic faith. Utilizing the widely accepted work of Charles Glock and Rodney Stark[27], one can posit five basic dimensions or aspects of religion in general: the *ritualistic, ideological, experiential, intellectualistic*, and *consequential.* Roughly speaking, one can say that the religious orientation associated with *la via vecchia* was strong experientially and ritualistically, if not necessarily shaped by the Catholic tradition. The pre-modern Italian religious orientation was, conversely, weak ideologically (or doctrinally), intellectually in its ability for self-reflection, and consequentially in the necessary demand to address systematically the social question and participate fully in civil society.

The mid-twentieth century immersion of southern Italianness into Catholicism redirected the experiential dimension from saint worship to a more correct devotional practice and broadened Italian rituals to include those of a 2,000 year old international community, including most importantly, a more active participation and appreciation of the sacramental system. Furthermore, Italians were simultaneously exposed to the rich doctrinal and scholarly traditions of the Catholic faith while coming to a far greater appreciation of the Catholic reality that a concern for justice is a constitutive element of the preaching of the Gospel. (Italian-Americans have historically demonstrated much charity to friends and neighbors but the Catholic vision necessarily extends the range to all fellow human beings made in the image of God, and adds justice to charity.)

As I have argued recently, Italian-Americans, for their part, have brought to, or variously supported, the Catholic faith with their emphasis on such values as familism, work, traditionalism, personalism, and indifference to worldly pretensions and claims.[28] Relatedly, Nicholas J. Russo, writing in 1977, implies that Italian-Americans have provided a balance to an Irish-dominated institution that was, among other things, Jansenistic, too clerically controlled, overly imbued with an emphasis on the active virtues, and too nationalistic.[29] Writing *before* the exaggerated forces of social change affected greatly both Church and society, Francis X. Femminella described the Italian-American impact on American Catholicism as follows:

> American Catholicism is becoming more fully American. It is becoming a little less conservative and formalistic. Laymen are developing some mature independence from the clergy. There seems to be a greater emphasis on depths of spirituality than on the laws of fast.[30]

The potentially positive and mutually beneficial relationship between the southern Italian and Catholic traditions come to an unfortunate end with the decomposition of Catholicism in the U.S. in the post-Vatican II years. Rebuilding the institutional integrity of Catholicism, recovering accurately the eternal truths found incarnate within the traditions of south Italy, and more fully appreciating the naturally positive dispositions and contributions of the Italian immigrants and their sons and daughters to American shores are the prerequisites for the development of a realistic Italian-American Catholic multiculturalism.

JOSEPH A. VARACALLI

---

[1] The cognitive and normative issues dealt with in this chapter have been previously and generally addressed by myself. See Joseph A. Varacalli, "Italian-American-Catholic: How Compatible?," *Social Justice Review*, (Volume 83, Numbers 5-6, May-June, 1992).

[2] Rev. Nicholas John Russo, "Three Generations of Italians in New York City: Their Religious Acculturation," in S. M. Tomasi and M. H. Engle (Editors), *The Italian Experience in the United States*, 1977, pp. 196, 198.

[3] Henry J. Browne, "The 'Italian Problem' and the Catholic Church of the United States, 1880-1900," *United States Catholic Historical Society, Historical Records*

and Studies, XXXV (New York, 1946), pp. 46-72. Also see Joseph A. Varacalli, The Changing Nature of the 'Italian Problem' in the Catholic Church of the United States," *Faith and Reason* (Volume 12, Number 1, March, 1986).

[4] Browne, *op.cit.,* 1946, p. 53.

[5] Rudolph J. Vecoli, "Prelates and Peasants: Italian Immigrants and the Catholic Church," *Journal of Social History* (Volume 2, Number 3, Spring, 1969), pp. 227-8.

[6] Vecoli, *Ibid.,* p. 228.

[7] Vecoli, *Ibid.,* pp. 228-9.

[8] Vecoli, *Ibid.,* p. 229.

[9] Vecoli, *Ibid.,* p. 229.

[10] Vecoli, *Ibid.,* p. 230.

[11] Joseph A. Varacalli, "A Catholic Plausibility Structure," *Homiletic and Pastoral Review* (Volume LXXXIX, Number 2, November, 1988).

[12] Paul Tillich, *The Courage To Be* (New Haven, Yale University Press, 1952; Emile Durkheim, *The Elementary Forms of the Religious Life* (New York: Collier Books, 1965); Will Herberg, *Protestant, Catholic, Jew* (New York: Anchor, 1960).

[13] Andrew M. Greeley, *The Catholic Experience* (New York: Doubleday, 1967).

[14] Joseph A. Varacalli, *op.cit.,* 1992.

[15] Herberg, *op.cit.,* 1960.

[16] Joseph A. Varacalli, "Multiculturalism, Catholicism, and American Civilization," *Homiletic and Pastoral Review* (Volume XCIV, Number 6, March, 1994).

[17] See the Introduction to the issue, "Does 'Multiculturalism' Debase the Curriculum?," in *Taking Sides: Clashing Views on Controversial Issues,* Eighth Edition, Kurt Finsterbusch and George McKenna (Editors), (Guilford, Connecticut: Dushkin, 1994), pp. 2-3.

[18] See Peter L. Berger's "In Praise of Particularity: The Concept of Mediating Structures" in his anthology, *Facing Up to Modernity: Excursions in Society, Politics, and Religion* (New York: Basic Books, 1977).

[19] Francis X. Femminella, "The Impact of Italian Migration and American Catholicism," *The American Catholic Sociological Review* (Volume 22, Fall, 1961).

[20] Paul McBride, "The Solitary Christians: Italian-Americans and Their Church," *Ethnic Groups* (Volume 3, Number 4, December, 1981).

[21] Robert A. Orsi, *The Madonna of 115th Street: Faith and Community in Italian Harlem, 1880-1950* (New Haven, Connecticut: Yale University Press, 1985, pp. xvi-xvii.

[22] John Cuddihy, *No Offense:Civil Religion and Protestant Taste* (New York: Seabury, 1978).

[23] Alan Bloom, *The Closing of the American Mind* (New York: Simon and Shuster, 1987).

[24] See Chapter Six, "The Truncated Madonna and Other Modern Catholic Iconography," in David Halle, *Inside Culture: Art and Class in the American Home* (Chicago: University of Chicago Press, 1993).

[25] Gerhard Lenski, *The Religious Factor,* (New York: Doubleday, 1961); Rev.

Silvano Tomasi, *Piety and Power* (Staten Island, New York: Center for Migration Studies, 1975); Nathan Glazer and Daniel P. Moynihan, *Beyond the Melting Pot* (Cambridge, Massachusetts: M.I.T., Press, 1963); Rev. Nicholas John Russo, *op.cit.*, 1977.

[26] Rudolph J. Vecoli, "Cult and Occult in Italian-American Culture," in *Immigrants and Religion in Urban America* (Editors, Randall M. Miller and Thomas D. Marzik) (Philadelphia, Pennsylvania: Temple University Press, 1977).

[27] Charles Glock and Rodney Stark, *Religion and Society in Tension* (Chicago: Rand McNally, 1965).

[28] See Varacalli, *op.cit.*, 1992.

[29] See Russo, *op.cit.*, 1977, p. 197.

[30] See Femminella, *op.cit.* 1961, p. 241.

CHAPTER 13

THE SAINTS IN EVERYDAY THOUGHT AND PRACTICE: AN EXPLORATORY SOCIAL PSYCHOLOGICAL INQUIRY

The purpose of this chapter is to suggest the outlines of a systematic social-psychological inquiry on the subject of the saints in the everyday thought and practice of contemporary Italian-Americans.[1] Hopefully, this outline can be critiqued, further perfected, and eventually satisfactorily implemented by researchers from scholarly organizations like the American Italian Historical Association and the Society of Catholic Social Scientists. The inquiry is psychological in that it attempts to get into the consciousness of contemporary Italian-Americans in a way that avoids the oft-times superficial and misleading conclusions produced by research based solely on positivistic methods. It is social in the sense of accepting the sociological claim that human consciousness is in a dialectical relationship with cultural and historical forces.[2]

Such a social-psychological study would have to correlate or associate answers to some basic cognitive and normative questions about the saints with a range of background sociological variables. The three most basic cognitive questions asked of individual contemporary Italian-Americans would ascertain 1) their *fundamental knowledge of*, 2) their *belief in*, and 3) the *impact on their lives by*, the saints. Relatedly, the most fundamental normative question to be addressed is to tap to what degree contemporary Italian-Americans *want* to see their tradition of the veneration of saints preserved and strengthened. The basic background sociological variables asked of respondents would be: 1) strength of subjective identification as an Italian-American, 2) strength of subjective identification as a Catholic, 3) acceptance of the Magisterium (or teaching authority of the Pope and those Bishops in union with him), 4) formal educational background, 5) age, 6) gender, 7) generation within the United States, 8) history of family intermarriage, 9) subjective class identification, and 10) occupation.

A useful secondary purpose of such a social-psychological inquiry would be to check the subjective opinions of the respondents to the host of issues discussed by the various authors of the essays contained within this volume. If the saints are marching out of the lives of Italian-Americans, why is this the case? To what degree was the worship of the saints infused with superstition? Is the rejection of the saints coterminous with an expanded or limited vision of life? What was the American Protestant, Irish-Catholic, and northern Italian response to the southern Italian style of worship of the saints? Can belief in the saints and modern science be reconciled? Can the saints come marching back into the hearts and minds of Italian-Americans? If so, what has to be done? Understanding the sometimes sharp distinction between objective truth and subjective opinion, the responses of the individuals queried can nonetheless be of value to the researcher in addressing these key issues.

Methodology

This initial, exploratory study utilized the results of six in-depth interviews lasting approximately one and a half hours each. The authors feel strongly that only such an intensive interview approach (apart, of course, from the complementary method of participant-observation) is capable of generating the subtlety, nuance, depth, and authenticity of response necessary to produce a worthwhile study. Ideally, at least fifty such interviews should be conducted to better guarantee a fair representation of responses and in order to conduct meaningful statistical comparisons. The six interviews conducted are intended, obviously, to be merely suggestive and insightful; hopefully they can be of use as "leads" for future researchers to more fully explore. Believing in the principle of triangularization in research, the authors do not eliminate either the necessity or desirability of having a national, random sample survey conducted after the results of the more comprehensive, systematic and intensive interview study have been intellectually digested. The argument, however, is that the qualitative method must precede the quantitative.

The Basic Questions

To ascertain the respondent's degree of fundamental knowledge about the saints, the following questions should be asked: 1) name as many saints as you can that have an appeal to Italian-Americans 2) what are their respective "specialties?" 3) why do they appeal to Italian-Americans? That is, explain the basis for the attachment in terms of such things as tradition, spiritual and emotional needs, or as a reflection of human nature. To determine the issue of the depth of the respondent's attachment to the saints, the following questions should be put forth: How many times a day, a week, a month do you seek the intercession of a saint (saints)? When and why is there such an intercession? How do you visualize your attachment to the saints *vis-à-vis* God/Jesus Christ? Explain the role of the Blessed Virgin Mary in your personal life. Regarding the issue of consequences, what impact have the saints (or any particular saint) made in your life? What impact have the saints made in the life of your family, friends, and society? Finally, the normative question should be broached: Should the saints be venerated? Under what conditions? Why or why not?

Hypotheses

Based on the few empirical studies[3] available and on a general understanding of Italian-American history and culture, the following *pre-interview hypotheses* about the role of the saints in the lives of Italian-Americans are being proposed. The first is that the stronger the subjective identification of being an Italian-American, the stronger should be the attachment to the saints. The second is that the stronger the subjective identification of being Catholic, the stronger should be the attachment to the saints. The third is that the greater the acceptance of the Catholic Church's Magisterial authority, the stronger should be the attachment to the saints. Fourth, those with less formal education would be expected to have a stronger attachment to the saints. Fifth, older Italian-Americans should empirically evince more support for the concept of sainthood. Sixth, women should be more open to the reality of the saints than are men. That the first and second generations of Italian-Americans are stronger in their devotion to the saints than are the third and fourth generations would constitute the seventh hypothesis. That those Italian-American families who have a history of not marrying outside of the Catholic faith would have a greater acceptance of the saints than those who do would represent the eighth hypothesis. The ninth hypothesis posits that those with a lower subjective class identification would have a stronger relationship with the saints than those with a higher subjective class identification. Finally, the tenth hypothesis would expect those from lower status occupations to favor the saints more than those from more prestigious fields of work.

Hypotheses in Light of the Exploratory Interviews

Interview Number One - Monsignor David L. Cassato[4]

Monsignor Cassato is a middle-aged priest (50 years of age), trained and ordained in the post-Vatican II climate, who is formally educated (a Masters in theology), and who identifies himself as middle-class in socio-economic status. Cassato, of Sicilian heritage, considers himself to be unquestionably loyal to the Church's Magisterium and is fiercely proud and knowledgeable of southern Italian tradition. His interview, which the authors would expect to be atypical of the general third and fourth generation Italian-American population and even for the priest cohort of his time, is nonetheless notable on several counts. First of all, his knowledge of the saints in general and with specific appeal to Italian-Americans was exceptional, even for a priest who is expected to be seriously acquainted with the religious and cultural tradition. It was also clear that whatever may or may not be the case for other "post-Vatican II" priests, the veneration of the saints was centrally important to him in his public vocation as a pastor, in his personal interpretation of what constitutes the faith, and in his private existential and emotional needs as a human being. His public and private life give testimony to the fact that a strong knowledge of, and positive attachment to, the saints is not necessarily incommensurate with being a full participant in modern, American life.[5]

The interview was revealing in other respects. For one thing, Monsignor Cassato sees a special attraction to the saints on the part of many Italian-Americans because of the latter's earthy, concrete, and emotional bent. Italian-Americans, historically at least, are an expressive people who seek out not abstract, intellectual truths but the warm, personal, and immediate reality of the saints. For another, Monsignor Cassato acknowledges both positive and negative aspects to the historic attachment of Italians to the saints. Positively, they can be a pathway to God and can serve legitimate therapeutic functions in the this-worldly lives of individuals. Negatively, they can take one away from the triune God by serving as idols to be worshipped in their own right or as agents to be magically bargained with. The key issue, for this priest, is the issue of whether the veneration of the saints is placed within a proper doctrinal framework: "Without effective catechesis, the worship of the saints can lead one outside of the Church." Regarding the controversial issue of the priority and location of the saints in the post-Vatican II parish, the interviewee sees three reasons for the seeming attenuation of the tradition: the Church's decision to retract the official status granted to some saints (e.g. St. Christopher, St. Filomena); legitimate liturgical redesign (i.e., to clear the altar to better focus on the worship of Christ); and, for radicalized and "extremist" clergy, to misuse the issue of liturgical redesign as a method to modernize and secularize the parish. Monsignor Cassato regretfully acknowledges that devotions to the saints on the part of younger generations of Italian-Americans who have assimilated too uncritically to secular culture is seriously on the wane, especially for young men. Without such devotions, he follows, "Italian-American religiosity becomes bland and loses something indispensable and vital." This is both sad and ironic for the priest because he believes that "if you perform devotions to the saints and do them well, you will bring people into the Church; they are great tools for teaching and evangelization."

Interview Number Two - Marco Pezzano[6]
    Marco Pezzano proved to be an intriguing individual who provided an insightful interview but represents yet another case study that the authors strongly suspect is atypical in many respects. A thirty-six year old municipal employee with a high school education who identifies with the working class, Marco evinces a strong sense of solidarity with both the southern Italian and Catholic tradition. He is accepting of Magisterial authority but reserves the right to disagree with it on certain issues. While less knowledgeable about official Church history and tradition than is Monsignor Cassato, Marco was even more knowledgeable about the southern Italian veneration of the saints. Indeed, his knowledge about the role of the saints in Italian and Italian-American history is nothing less than phenomenal.
    Marco, who has an intense personal devotion to St. Anthony of Padua "who has never failed him," grants top priority to Mary, Mother of God and "mediatrix of all graces," in the lexicon and panoply of saints. Asked whether the saints are primarily a folk religious or Catholic reality, he

shrugs and answers that the reality of the saints is self-evident: "They are part of the truth about what makes up the world." As such, Marco provides evidence for the claim that it is possible to construct a "natural law," i.e. "written into the heart of all," defense of the concept of sainthood: "The saints humanize your religion." Asked whether it's legitimate to barter with the saints, Marco again shrugs, "It's like human nature...it's like dealing with a family member." Although not making explicit reference to the Catholic idea of the "communion of saints," the saints, for the interviewee, "make you aware that you have friends in heaven." He adds, "without being connected to the other world, this world is a hard and harsh one." Asked whether the veneration of the saints detracts from the worship of Jesus Christ, Marco strongly demurs: "take the saints out of your life, you take Christ out, too."

Marco stressed that his strong knowledge about and devotion to the saints is indebted, in large part, to the effort his grandparents (in South Jamaica, New York) expended on him in imparting the tradition. He notes that one could expect only three agencies to be able, across the generations, to successfully pass on knowledge of the saints: the Italian family and community and the Catholic Church. Given that Marco feels the former two have succumbed significantly to assimilation to an American secular culture, it is up the Catholic Church to promote and revive the veneration of the saints. However, he is not sure that the contemporary Catholic Church can accomplish this vital task. This is so because of a fundamental division in the Church body: "There are actually two Catholic Churches," he muses, "the true Church of someone like Mother Angelica who represents tradition" and an accommodationist Church "overly afraid to lose parishioners." Regarding the latter, Marco believes that "some modern priests actually don't believe in the saints while others are afraid to set high standards or talk about old fashioned things." This is a tragedy, for Pezzano, because "there are plenty of people out there who are starved for the truth." In addition, as he continues, "there are many Italian-Americans who are not happy with the saints being pushed to the sides or outside of the parish." However, as he finally cautions, in order to bring back the veneration of the saints, the priests "must not scold or condemn" but "preach and teach in a lovingly way."

Interview Number Three - Nick LaBella[7]

This exploratory research project brought us into contact with yet another fascinating individual. Sixty-three years of age, Nick LaBella, of Neopolitan heritage, is a retired Catholic high school teacher (with thirty years of teaching experience) and landscaper. The interview suggests an individual with a broad and deep philosophical bent who is entrepreneurial, self-reliant, and, in part, self-made. He takes deep pride in both his Italian and Catholic heritages; a strong defender of Magisterial authority he considers the Catholic Church "to be the vortex of his existence." Like many second generation Italian-Americans, Nick worked his way through his higher education, going to school in the evenings and eventually earning an M.A. degree.

Nick has a special attraction to three saints "who I call on whenever I feel spiritually threatened—which means often." Of primary importance is Mary, mother of God, who "is like an older sister to me." Then there is St. Maria Goretti who Nick refers to as "the original Cinderella" and who represents "purity in an impure world." Finally, for Nick there is St. Rocco. Nick is drawn to St. Rocco because he represents the Christian individual willing to risk and offer his life to serve others; "St. Rocco didn't have to do what he did.. (in taking care of those afflicted by plague)...; his greatness lies in the overt consciousness of his act of self-sacrifice."

Asked what he thought was the single greatest consequence for him of venerating the saints, Nick responded that it has helped him be a faithful and better husband for his wife and father for his seven children. His belief in the saints has also shaped one of Nick's favorite activities, that is, the writing of short stories. He has both written stories about the saints and about individuals who, in their daily struggles, have been influenced by the saints. When asked about his perceptions of the change in the nature and quality of the veneration of the saints between the older and younger Italian-American generations, Nick offered several intriguing hypotheses. The first was that "the contemporary generation has within its vocabulary a broader range of saints than earlier generations who were familiar with only their local, village-oriented saints." However, he continued, "there is, at present, less depth, appreciation, and 'need' for the saints." Additionally, he observes that "the contemporary apprehension of the saints is fraught with less superstition and, in a sense, is more reasonable." However, the current utilization of the saints has its own abuses: "the young today want results immediately which is a reflection of today's society in which everything has a short shelf life; the young today don't understand that God works in his own way and sometimes that means getting a 'no' or 'not now' in response to a petition."

Nick feels that the contemporary Catholic Church in the United States is short-changing parishioners by not adequately preaching and teaching about the saints; "the saints provide the role models we all need, especially the young." When asked why this is the case, Nick responded that this was because too many Catholic leaders want a more "American, ecumenical, and streamlined" Church. When asked about the degree to which Italian-American institutions are carrying on the tradition of the veneration of the saints, Nick responded "mainly through the feasts but even there one sees a thinning out." Nick also emphasized that a major reason for the attenuation of the tradition was "to be found in the constant lampooning of the saints in the movies, television and the mass media." Regarding the future, Nick just shrugged, "I don't really have a feel for what will happen. I certainly hope, however, that there will be a return to the saints and God. There really is no way else to go!"

Interview Number Four - Anthony Ricci[8]

For this interview, the authors consciously sought out an American of Italian descent from a younger generation. Anthony Ricci is an articulate, twenty four year old professional graphic designer with a B. A. in Fine Arts from New York City's Parsons School for Design (which is a component of the New School for Social Research). Defining himself a member of America's "middle-middle" class, Anthony considers himself an active Catholic who nonetheless admits that his religion was more important to him at an earlier stage of life. He neither consciously seeks out an understanding of official Catholic dogma and doctrine nor necessarily concurs with all elements of it. Anthony, however, clearly declared an intense allegiance to his Italian heritage, making clear that he considers himself more Italian than Italian-American. Anthony's parents migrated from the town of San Tommaso in the Province of Pescara (a three hour car ride east of Rome) to Brooklyn's Italian Williamsburg at the age of twenty and eventually moved to their present location in Mineola, New York. The

Ricci family has other extended family members that also participated in the chain migration from San Tommaso to Brooklyn to Mineola (and neighboring Williston Park). The Ricci family is in active contact today with their relatives in San Tommaso; Anthony, for instance, recently made the trip to Italy for the marriage of one of his cousins.

Uncovered during the interview was Anthony's great, but singular, devotion to San Tommaso, (the "Doubting Thomas" Apostle of Christ). San Tommaso is the patron saint and protector of the town named after him in the Province of Pescara. *La festa di San Tommaso* takes place in the town the day after every Easter; the Ricci family and Anthony are actively involved in honoring, as an extended family affair, St. Thomas on this side of the Atlantic. The Ricci family, both nuclear and extended, pays for Masses said in honor of St. Thomas, food is prepared, and the family meets in celebration.

Several important observations about the nature of his devotion emerged. First, it occurred in the absence of any wide-ranging knowledge of, or devotion to, other saints. Other than St. Thomas, Anthony indicated a love for Mary and respect for his namesake, St. Anthony, and a vague awareness of another local Italian saint, Nunzio Sulprizio, Santo di Pescosansonesco. Secondly, St. Thomas was never, for Anthony, a vehicle of intercession. St. Thomas was to be honored and respected but when crises occurred that affected Anthony and the Ricci family, Anthony "went straight to Christ." (This is in contradistinction to the rest of the Ricci family who employ the wider panoply of saints to reach Christ. Anthony's mother, for instance, prays to St. Thomas daily.) Finally, the impact of his devotion to St. Thomas was primarily in strengthening his attachment to Italy and family and only secondarily on his religious faith. Indeed, Anthony sees St. Thomas as a spiritual and cultural force, not as a supernatural-related entity. Indeed, Anthony is quite clear in stating that the single biggest and most immediate impact of his recent visit to the parish of San Tommaso in Italy was "a dramatic increase in interest in all things Italian" and "enrollment in Italian language courses." For Anthony, what is of ultimate importance "is anything that keeps the family together...from tomato sauce to celebrating holidays to going to Mass." However, it may also very well be the case that Anthony's increased cultural attachment may serve, secondarily, as a carrier for the rebirth of his tie to Catholicism and the saints. As he states, "This past year has been a transition period in my life. After returning from Italy, religion has, once again, become part of my life." Anthony fervently hopes that, someday, he will be able to pass on his love of Italy and St. Thomas to his own children. Anthony does not see, however, any great veneration of the saints among the contemporary younger generation of Italian-Americans.

Interview Number Five - Dennis Starr, Ph.D.[9]

The next interview proved to be crucial because the individual in question turned out to be someone knowledgeable about the saints but, at the same time, provided a purely secular humanistic, and politically left-wing, perspective on the tradition. Dennis Starr, a 1979 Rutgers University Ph.D., is a Professor of History at New Jersey's Rider College and a leading figure in Italian-American studies. Interestingly, Dennis does not consider himself to be Italian-American despite living his whole life in an Italian-American household and neighborhood and being intimately involved, since childhood, with the famous Italian-American community of Chambersburg, located in Trenton, New Jersey. Dennis' mother considered herself very much an Italian-American and his mother's maternal parents migrated from Perugia. He is perfectly clear about his rejection of the Italian-American identity: "It's political. There's simply too much racism in the United States among all groups, including Italian-Americans; this must be transcended." Similarly, Dr. Starr admits to being raised in a Catholic milieu. As he states, "I know the Catholic faith as well as most informed, believing Catholic laymen do. I do not, however, consider myself to be a practicing Roman Catholic; I think I have been able to incorporate the universalizing thrust of the Catholic religion without adherence to any belief in the supernatural or Church dogma and doctrine." Apart from his obvious rejection of the content of the Catholic faith, Dennis rejects what he considers to be the authoritarianism of a religion based ultimately on the hierarchical authority of the Church's Magisterium: "I'm simply a free-thinker on all matters." As someone coming authentically from a democratic socialist orientation, he strongly identifies himself as a "member of the working class."

In the interview, Dr. Starr offered evidence that he possesses above-average knowledge about those saints who have a strong appeal to the

Italian-American population. As a secular humanist, however, he stated frankly that he has no personal belief in the concept of sainthood as understood by either an official Catholicism as an intercessor and imitator of Christ or by a southern Italian peasantry as a supernatural entity unto itself. However, he evinced great respect and admiration for a figure like St. Francis of Assisi, who gave up a life of privilege to serve the poor. "If all Catholics lived up to the role model of St. Francis," Dr. Starr stated, "the world would be a better place to live. He personified the best in the tradition of the saints." Indeed, he continued in this vein, arguing that the saints owe their historic place of esteem among the Italian people not for religious reasons but because they were perceived to be of practical assistance to the populace.

While the tradition of the veneration of saints has made no substantial impact on him personally, Dr. Starr was quite aware that this tradition historically has had strong consequences in both thought and action for Italians on both sides of the Atlantic. Furthermore, Dr. Starr's understanding of the nature of this impact is complex: sometimes this belief can serve as an opiate or illusion that helps maintain an unjust social order or, in other cases, can serve as a vehicle of social protest as a series of peasant revolts in southern Italy demonstrates.

Dr. Starr concluded his interview by offering the observation that the tradition of cult of the saints among Italian-Americans is in the midst of a serious attenuation. "The new religion," for most Italian-Americans he declared, "is popular and mass culture." Dr. Starr regrets this serious attenuation. "The decline in the cult of the saints," he asserts, "is a good yardstick to assess the degree of an uncritical acceptance by Italian-Americans of a capitalist, bourgeois culture with its manufacture of false needs and wants." Dr. Starr interprets the culture and values of the immigrant Italian-American population to be basically sound ("a healthy paganism"), while the movement into a mass culture in which Italian-Americans (as well as all other Americans) are manipulated by the megastructures of the State and the corporations is a deleterious one. "The cult of the saints" was an "important counter-cultural institution once empowering Italians and Italian-Americans from the clutches of ruling classes with near monopoly power." Finally he noted that the historic emphasis that Italian-Americans placed on the saints was not reinforced by the dominant Irish faction in the Catholic

Church of the United States which only accelerated the decline of what he considered to be a functional tradition.

Interview Number Six - Roseann Aiosa[10]

Before concluding this initial set of exploratory examinations, the authors wanted to interview at least one other young Italian-American. Ms. Roseann Aiosa, a lively and charming twenty-year old junior at Adelphi University, considers herself to be a member of the "upper-middle" class. Ms. Aiosa, with a strong identification as an Italian-American, is of Sicilian heritage. Both of Roseann's parents were born in Sicily—her mother from Castellammare and her father from Valdomo—and then immigrated to the United States in their youth. The Aiosa family, now residing in Long Island's Oceanside community, had previously lived in the East New York section of New York City. Admitting that "religion was more important to me when I was young," Roseann's attachment to the Catholic faith has been attenuated to somewhere between "weak" and "moderate." Her faith suffered appreciably when, at age eight, her grandfather died; Roseann believed that her petitions to God were, at the time, unheeded. Regarding Catholic rituals and Mass attendance, Roseann today "only does the biggies: Easter, Christmas, weddings, baptisms, funerals, etc." Much like the Italian-Americans who Robert Orsi reported on in his *The Madonna of 115th Street*,[11] Roseann appears to be a very *domus* or "family" centered Italian-American whose support for Church rituals coincides with those activities that are seen, simultaneously, as central to maintaining family life. Indeed, for Roseann, "family values are, for me, the most important values." Roseann gave evidence of being familiar with a few saints that are important to Italian-Americans; her knowledge in this area, conversely put, was not extensive. Personally speaking, she declares that "her prayer life is sporadic"; when she does pray "it is to God, Mary, and occasionally, St. Joseph." (St. Joseph is actually celebrated in the Aiosa family, with Roseann's brother being named after the husband of the Virgin Mary.) Roseann indicated that, in her youth, "she prayed to get stuff;" now she prays not for intercession but "to communicate to her deceased relatives in heaven that she and her family are O.K." She has Rosary beads in her car, "not to pray but for security and safety." While Roseann is not a strong participant in the tradition of the veneration of the saints, neither is she accepting of any of the "old world" superstitions regarding concepts like *il_mal'occhio* (the evil eye) or the wearing of *il corno* (the Italian horn) to ward off malevolent forces. Rather, Roseann is significantly secularized and modern, but with a decided Italian and Italian-American accent. Like many other Italian-Americans, Roseann believes that individuals "can be quite religious without going to Church." The essence of religion, furthermore, is not doctrine, dogma, and rules "but doing good for other people." She stopped going to confession at age twelve: "I'm much more likely now to go for assistance to my mother with my deep problems that I have to confront." One should never forget, Roseann reminded us, "that one's family is the biggest part of your life." Roseann took a course on the Italian-American experience at Adelphi University to learn more about her national/ethnic heritage of which she is fiercely proud. Ideally, she would like to marry a man who, first, is of Italian heritage and, second, is of the Catholic religion. Furthermore, she would ideally like to raise her future children in a world that, at least, includes some southern Italian and Catholic traditions: "from cooking the seven fishes on Christmas Eve to sending her children to Catholic schools which teach respect more than do the public schools." In Ms. Roseann Aiosa, one sees an abundance of active signals of *Italianità* and the vague residues of a Catholic past. She acknowledges, in conclusion, that "the saints are not nearly as important to my generation of Italian-Americans as they were in the generations of my parents and grandparents."

Concluding Note

Obviously, the six interviews conducted do not represent a random sample of the relevant population. Among other glaring imbalances, the elderly, the young, women, and nominal Italian-Americans are either not represented or underrepresented. Nonetheless, the authors do believe that this initial effort points in the right direction: toward a fuller understanding of the complex roles that the saints play in the lives of Italian-Americans.

SALVATORE PRIMEGGIA
JOSEPH A. VARACALLI

[1] Co-editors Primeggia and Varacalli include this chapter as a way to hope fully encourage further and systematic research on the subject.

[2] Both Primeggia and Varacalli on this count have been influenced by sociologists Peter L. Berger and Thomas Luckmann, *The Social Construction of Reality: A Treatise in the Sociology of Knowledge* (Garden City, NY: Doubleday, 1966). The authors have applied the Berger-Luckmann framework to the case of the dialectically related issues of Italian-American community attachments and identity maintenance in our study, "Community and Identity in Italian-American Life" in *The Ethnic Quest for Community: Searching for Roots in the Lonely Crowd* (edited by Michael Hughey and Arthur Vidich) Greenwich, Connecticut: JAI Press, Inc., 1993.

[3] Two such widely cited empirical studies are those by Nicholas John Russo, "Three Generations of Italians in New York City: Their Religious Acculturation" in *The Italian Experience in the United States* (edited by Silvano M. Tomasi and Madeline Engel) (Staten Island, New York: Center for Migration Studies, 1970) and David Halle, *Inside Culture* (Chicago, Illinois: University of Chicago Press, 1993).

[4] Monsignor/Pastor David L. Cassato, personal interview at the Rectory of the Shrine Church of Our Lady of Mount Carmel, Williamsburg, Brooklyn, New York, on March 17, 1997.

[5] The religious style and beliefs of Monsignor Cassato are manifest in the ways he has shaped the *Giglio* feast that annually takes place at the Shrine Church of Our Lady of Mount Carmel. See Salvatore Primeggia and Joseph A. Varacalli's analysis of the feast and interview with Monsignor Cassato in their "The Sacred and Profane Among Italian-American Catholics: The Giglio Feast," *International Journal of Politics, Culture, and Society* (Volume 9, Number 3, Spring, 1996).

[6] Marco Pezzano, personal interview at his residence in Bethpage, New York on September 5, 1997.

[7] Nick LaBella, personal interview at the Breaker's Restaurant, Bayville, New York, on February 13, 1998.

[8] Anthony Ricci, personal interview at his home in Mineola, New York, on March 19, 1998.

[9] Dennis Starr, Ph.D., phone interview conducted on March 21, 1998.

[10] Roseann Aiosa, personal interview at Adelphi University, Garden City, New York, on April 2, 1998.

[11] See Robert A. Orsi, *The Madonna of 115th Street: Faith and Community in Italian Harlem, 1880-1950* (New Haven: Yale University Press, 1985). See also the review of the book by Joseph A. Varacalli, *Sociological Analysis*, (Volume 49, Number 1, Spring, 1988).

Chapter 14

The Saints in the Lives of Italian-Americans: A Bibliographic Essay

The bibliography of materials on Italian-Americans and their saints has been building since Acts 6:8-7:60 recorded the story of Saint Stephen the proto-martyr. New devotions continue to appear; see, for example, Chris Doyle, "Thousands in Louisiana Field Look for Apparition of Mary," *National Catholic Reporter* XXV:22 (March 24, 1989), 3, a news item on an Italian immigrant's apparitions. There are already enough citations to fill a book, specifically, Silvano M. Tomasi and Edward C. Stibili, *Italian Americans and Religion: An Annotated Bibliography*, second edition, revised and enlarged (Staten Island: Center for Migration Studies, 1992). This essay identifies the major subtopics within the field of Italian-Americans and their saints, and suggests some further reading.

Biographies

In order to study saints, one has to be able to read the documents regarding them. This is more complex than literacy, or a command of ancient and foreign languages. Most early saints don't have solid scholarly biographies. The term for the literary genre is hagiography, which should not be taken as a synonym for "total fabrication." Hagiographies were written for different purposes than secular biographies. They emphasize different pieces of information about their subjects, they utilize conventions specific to the genre, and they do change over time. Help in understanding hagiography, at least in one period, comes from Pamela Gehrke, *Saints and Scribes: Medieval Hagiography in its Manuscript Context* (Berkeley: University of California Press, 1993); and Thomas J. Heffernan, *Sacred Biography:Saints and Their Biographers in the Middle Ages.*

Moving from hagiography to modern biography, the most basic level of information about the saints is a list of *The Who's Who of Heaven*, which was the actual title of one such compilation (by John P. Kleinz [Westminster, Maryland: Christian Classics, 1991]). The earliest such list biographical dictionary still in regular use is *The Lives of the Saints*, first published by the Reverend Alban Butler in London between 1756 and 1759. The most recent scholarly edition is Paul Burns, ed., *Butler's Lives of the Saints*, new full edition (Turnbridge Wells, Kent: Burns and Oates; Collegeville, Minnesota: Liturgical Press, 1995). The biographical dictionary which makes the greatest effort to be scholarly is the *Acta Sanctorum*, published periodically by the Bollandists of the Society of Jesus. *The New Catholic Encyclopedia*, published in 1967, of course, includes biographies of saints among its subjects. Shorter biographical dictionaries that focus specifically on the saints are Donald Attwater, *The Penguin Dictionary of Saints*, second edition, revised and updated by Catherine Rachel John (Harmondsworth, England, and New York: Penguin, 1983); James Bentley, *A Calendar of Saints: The Lives of the Principal Saints of the Christian Year* (New York: Facts on File, 1986); John J. Delaney, *Dictionary of the Saints* (Garden City, New York: Doubleday, 1980); David Hugh Farmer, *The Oxford Dictionary of Saints* (Oxford and New York: Oxford University Press, 1987).

The aforementioned are general biographical dictionaries, although biographical dictionaries written in English do have a tendency to emphasize saints from the English-speaking world, or familiar to it. There are other kinds of biographical dictionaries suitable for people with special needs. For example, art critics and historians who need to know how to identify the saints in pieces of art might consult Tom Morgan, *Saints: A Visual Almanac of the Virtuous, Pure, Praiseworthy and Good* (San Francisco: Chronicle Books, 1994); Clara Erskine Clement Waters, *A Handbook of Christian Symbols of Stories of the Saints as Illustrated in Art* (Boston: Ticknor, 1886; reprinted in Detroit: Gale Research Company, 1971); or Caroline Williams, *Saints: Their Cults and Origins* (New York: Saint Martin's Press, 1980). For geographers, there is Helen Roeder, *Saints and Their Attributes, With a Guide to Localities and Patronage* (London: Longmans, Green, 1955). For educators of all sorts, there is Mary Reed Newland, *The Saint Book: For Parents, Teachers, Homilists, Storytellers, and Children* (San Francisco: Harper and Row, 1979). Some religious orders have their own biographical dictionaries, an example being Joseph

N. Tylenda, *Jesuit Saints and Martyrs: Short Biographies of the Saints, Blessed, Venerables, and Servants of God of the Society of Jesus* (Chicago: Loyola University Press, 1984). Given that this is a volume on Italian saints, mention ought to be made of Christine Morhrmann, ed, *Vite dei santi: dall III al VI Secolo* (Milan: A. Mondadori, 1985), a reprint of a 1974-1975 book which translates from Greek and Latin to Italian a number of early hagiographies. Another Italian-language volume based on the liturgical calendar is Fausto Masante, *I Santi dell'anno: Calendario onomastico; significato dei nomi; prottetori di attività e malattie; notizie storiche; curiosità;brani per la meditazione*, second edition (Turin: Gribaudi, 1987).

Biographies of individual saints are more common for well-known or modern saints than they are for the early ascetics, martyrs, and holy men and women who attracted the devotion of the Italian laity. However, there are a few surprises; for example, Angelo Menucci, *San Paolino, Vescovo de Nola*, second edition (Siena: Cantagalli, 1989). And, of course, there is some overlap between the kind of saints who get biographies and the kind venerated by common people. Devotion to Saint Francis of Assisi, or Saint Anthony of Padua, to cite two examples, was widespread among Italian-Americans.

Rather than read biographies about them, it is possible to read the words of the saints themselves. There are numerous translations of classics by Saint Augustine of Hippo, Saint John of the Cross, Saint Theresa of Lisieux, Saint Thomas Aquinas, and others. In fact, rather than list the saints who wrote, it might be useful to mention two publishers who specialize in printing English-language translations. Doubleday Image books has published numerous short spiritual classics by the saints, such as a translation of Saint Benedict's rule for his monks, Saint Ignatius Loyola's spiritual exercises, and *The Interior Castle* of Saint Theresa of Avila. Paulist Press concentrates on selections from saints with large bodies of writing, and includes religious writings from outside the Catholic tradition. For one book on using the saints' writings to achieve theological understanding, see William M. Thompson, *Fire and Light: The Saints and Theology: On Consulting the Saints, Mystics, and Martyrs on Theology* (New York: Paulist Press, 1987).

The Variety of Scholarship

Theology

The earliest academic discipline to study sanctity was theology. It has been a subject for diverse writers, from Karl Rahner and Johan Baptist Metz, *The Courage to Pray*, translated by Sarah O'Brien Twohig (New York: Crossroad, 1980); to Elizabeth Stuart, *Spitting at Dragons: Towards a Feminist Theology of Sainthood* (London and New York: Mowbray, 1996). Of particular concern to the Church is the integrity of the process of identifying a saint. For books on this subject, see Michael Freze, *The Making of Saints* (Huntington, Indiana: Our Sunday Visitor, 1991); E.W. Kemp, *Canonization and Authority in the Western Church* (London and Oxford: Oxford University Press, 1948); and Kenneth L. Woodward, *Making Saints:How the Catholic Church Determines Who Becomes a Saint, Who Doesn't, and Why* (New York: Simon and Shuster, 1990).

All Christian denominations have some concept of sainthood, but not all have the same concept. As indicated in Edmund S. Morgan's *Visible Saints:The History of a Puritan Idea* (New York: New York University, 1963), seventeenth-century New England Puritans used the word "saint" differently from Catholics of any time or place. An example of how discussion of one aspect of sainthood, the belief that saints can intercede with Christ and God the Father on behalf of those on earth, can affect ecumenical relations is H. George Anderson, J. Francis Stafford, and Joseph A. Burgess, eds., *The One Mediator, the Saints, and Mary* (Minneapolis: Augsburg, 1992), which discusses Catholic and Lutheran doctrine on these subjects.

Psychology

A good place to begin the psychological study of sainthood is Michael P. Carroll, *Catholic Cults and Devotions: A Psychological Inquiry* (Montreal: McGill-Queen's University Press, 1989). Carroll takes up the saints and others who practiced devotions such as the wearing of the scapular and the holy hour before the Blessed Sacrament, adds what is known about the historical periods in which they developed or reached a peak of popularity, and uses the information to get at the inner world of the devout. He is careful to outline the steps by which he reaches his conclusions. And although the conclusions have to do with practicing devotions that ease some psychic tension, they aren't necessarily incompatible with having a spiritual dimension for the same devotion.

Regarding the psychology of those devoted to the saints, the best place to start is with Robert A. Orsi, *Thank You, Saint Jude: Women's Devotion to the Patron Saint of Hopeless Causes* (New Haven:Yale University Press, 1996). Again, Orsi is sensitive to the historical circumstances under which devotion to Saint Jude developed, but like Carroll he is primarily interested in the inner world. He points out the dangers of the cult of the saints, particularly Saint Jude: the devout might develop an unrealistic sense of their helplessness, and, paradoxically, an unrealistic sense of their personal power, their ability to call on an otherworldly figure who could restore hope to the most hopeless causes. At that same time, he points out that the women who actually practiced the cult weren't psychotic or even neurotic. They had integrated their veneration of Saint Jude into their lives in a way that helped cope with reality, not run away from it.

Sociology

Sociologists have studied Italian-Americans and their saints from a number of perspectives. Early efforts focused on studying the devotions for what they revealed about community values. An example is Leonard Covello, *The Social Background of the Italo-American School Child: A Study of the Southern Italian Family Mores and Their Effects on the School Situation in Italy and America* (Leiden:E.J. Brill, 1967). Covello was himself an immigrant from the southern party of Italy to Harlem in New York City. He relied extensively on Frazer's *The Golden Bough* for descriptions of Italian folk religion (he himself left Italy before he entered school, and as an adult was not a Catholic). He then used those descriptions to buttress his argument that the Italian outlook on life was composed of a large dose of fatalism mixed with the sense that only access to a powerful patron could affect one's life, not a view which predisposed them to provide their children with extensive education. An example of the same sort of approach, but from the world of medicine, is Phyllis Williams, *South Italian Folkways in Europe and America: A Handbook for Social Workers, Visiting Nurses,*

School Teachers, and Physicians (New Haven: Published for the Institute of Human Relations by Yale University Press, 1938). Williams also recounted numerous anecdotes regarding Italian religious practices, especially those involving applying a relic to a sick person to obtain relief, or using an image of the afflicted body part in a ritual of intercession with a patron saint. She used this information to alert her readers to the disparity between Southern Italian concepts of health, illness, and healing, and American concepts of the same.

Sociology can also illuminate how devotions function in community life. Robert Orsi, "The Religious Boundaries of an In-between People: Streete *Feste* and the Problem of the Dark-Skinned Other in Italian Harlem, 1920-1930," *American Quarterly* XLIV:3 (1992), 313-347, shows how one group used its feast to draw a symbolic line separating the community from those outside it. Interestingly, the same location Orsi used for his research has also been used to show how a *festa* can function in the process of creating a more multicultural community; see Maria Lurineo, "*La Dolce Festa*," *Village Voice* XXXIII:30 (July 26, 1988), 12.

Sociology combined with psychological insight can explore what devotions have meant to the people who practiced them. A pioneer in such research is Robert A. Orsi, *The Madonna of 115th Street: Faith and Community in Italian Harlem, 1880-1950* (New Haven:Yale University Press, 1985). Orsi built up to a grand conclusion demonstrating how the ritual for the feast of Our Lady of Mount Carmel in East Harlem portrayed women as terribly powerful, but also terribly responsible when things went wrong in family life. Salvatore Primeggia and Joseph A. Varacalli, "The Sacred and Profane Among Italian American Catholics: The *Giglio* Feast," *International Journal of Politics, Culture and Society* IX:3 (Spring 1996), 423-449, have more varied conclusions about the role the feast played in the lives of the men who took the most active roles in it.

Feminist Studies

A sexual division of religious labor characterized the cult of the saints in Italy. Analysis of the intersection of women, sanctity, and devotion to the saints is a creative part of the general study of Italian-Americans and their saints. An especially pertinent example for this volume is Daniel Bornstein and Roberto Rusconi, eds., *Women and Religion in Medieval and*

Renaissance Italy, translated by Margery J. Schneider (Chicago: University of Chicago Press, 1996). A fair amount of work has been done on one particular element of the history of female sanctity, the kind of self-denial, even extending to life-giving food, that some female saints practiced. In this regard, see Rudolph M. Bell, *Holy Anerexoria* (Chicago:University of Chicago Press, 1985).

Italian History

Historians have also contributed to the store of knowledge on Italian-Americans and their saints. Historians' work is usually divided regionally, in this case, into research into Italy and into the United States. It is then subdivided into different periods of time. Historical periodization for Americans tends to emphasize events that bring out the importance of the Reformation. Christianity marks the beginning of a new era. By the fifth century, the Roman empire had collapsed, and the papacy had replaced it as giving some sort of order to society in central Italy. A new era was underway, but one that ultimately led to a Reformation in the sixteenth century. Thus the period between the fifth and sixteenth centuries, between the high points of the beginning Christianity and its reform, became the Dark, or Middle, Ages. From the point of view of the study of the saints, though, that thousand-year period breaks into at least two periods. One extends from the fourth to the twelfth centuries, that is, from the establishment of monastic communities in Latin Christendom to the development of the new mendicant orders such as the Franciscans. The second goes from the twelfth century to the sixteenth, and is sometimes called the High Middle Ages. Students of the arts will know that the period of the Reformation and Counter-reformation also goes by the name Baroque.

One of the better books on sanctity covers the earliest period, Peter Brown, *The Cult of the Saints: Its Rise and Function in Latin Christianity* (Chicago: The University of Chicago Press [The Haskell Lectures on History of Religions, New Series, No. 2], 1981. It was Brown who first put into a short, simple book an explanation of how early Christians came to think of the sufferings of their martyrs and holy persons, the death of these special souls, and then to re-conceptualize respectful treatment of the body and the connection between the saints already in heaven with the Christians still on earth. There are other, more specialized monographs that are relevant to the study of Italian and Italian-American saints, such as Nicola` Ferrante, *Santi italogreci in Calabria* (Reggio Calabria: Edizione Parallelo-38, 1981).

Probably the best-known book among English-language readers for the early part of the Middle Ages is the Venerable Bede's *Ecclesiastical History of England*, with its stories of miracles and monks. There are, though, more recent scholarly works, such as Eleanor Shipley Duckett, *The Wandering Saints of the Early Middle Ages* (New York: Norton, 1959), Benedicta Ward, *Signs and Wonders: Saints, Miracles, and Prayers from the Fourth to the Fourteenth Centuries* (Brookfield, Vermont: Gower Publishing Company, 1992); and Diana Webb, "Saints and Cities in Medieval Italy," *History Today* XLIII (July 1993), 15-21. Titles for the High Middle Ages include: Richard Kieckhefer, *Unquiet Souls:Fourteenth Century Saints and Their Religious Milieu* (Chicago:University of Chicago Press, 1984); Pierre Jounel, *Le Culte des Saints dans les Basiliques du Lateran et du Vatican au douzie`me sie`cle* (Rome: E`cole franc~ais de Rome, 1977); or articles such as Jerydene Wood, "Perceptions of Holiness in Thirteenth-Century Italian Painting: Clare of Assisi," *Art History* XIV:3 (September 1991), 301-328. Of special mention is Donald Weinstein and Rudolph M. Bell, *Saints and Society: The Two Worlds of Western Christendom, 1000-1700* (Chicago: University of Chicago Press, 1982). Weinstein and Bell took all the biographical material on the saints in this period that they could find and then developed a way of coding the information. They used the coded data to produce statistical tables regarding the saints' birthplaces, the centuries of their births and deaths, their social class, their occupations, and their family relations. From the statistical tables they were able to draw up profiles of what was typical for male and female saints, and how the typical image changed over time. It is the antithesis of the intensely personal psychoanalytic approach of some other scholars.

The Baroque period presents an interesting juxtaposition. On the one hand, traditional hagiography diminishes after the High Middle Ages. On the other hand, the saints themselves begin to produce the kind of writing hagiographers used to supply. Works such as Saint John of the Cross's *Dark Night of the Soul*, despite that title, were intended to provide spiritual direction and guidance, and functioned as a substitute for the hagiographer's holding up a saint for the devout to pray to and to emulate.

Saint Theresa of Avila picked up on a genre already developed by her colleague as a Doctor of the Church, Saint Catherine of Siena, and replaced the miracles hagiographers attributed to saints with a saint's own account of miraculous-seeming mystical experiences. It was at this point that Italy developed a two-track history of holiness. Popular celebrations, especially in rural areas, continued to focus on saints' intercessory powers and their miracles, and on a demonstrative acting out of personal and communal sentiment. The saints Italy actually produced during this period continued to draw on this tradition but also participated in the intellectual world of the times. Saint Alphonsus Liguori wrote devotional pieces such as *The Glories of Mary* and works of moral theology that emphasized the workings of both reason and what the psychology faculty of the day called the "affections." One can start studying this time period, and the concept of a time period, with William V. Hudon, "Religion and Society in Early Modern Italy—Old Questions, New Insights," *American Historical Review* CI:3 (June 1996), 783-804, and continue with Jean-Michel Salemann, *Naples et ses saints a` l'a~ge baroque: 1540-1750* (Paris: Presses Universitaires de France, 1994). Perhaps the most famous incident in Italian Baroque religion was the condemnation of Galileo, a subject that is covered in Mario Biagioli, *Galileo, Courtier: The Practice of Science in the Culture of Absolutism* Chicago: University of Chicago Press [Science and Its Conceptual Foundations], 1993.)

The nineteenth century had a similar paradox. The Italian government made mighty efforts to become a modern, secular state, yet Italy maintained a tradition of popular devotional culture and also produced a new generation of saints who developed new ways of practicing personal holiness and also serving God in the world. A collection of essays that speaks to this issue is Sofia Boesch Gagano and Lucia Sebastiani, eds. *Culto dei santi, istituzioni e classi sociali in eta` preindustriale* (Rome: L.U. Japadre, 1984). There are many descriptions of devotional practices among rural Italians, Southerners particularly, in the late nineteenth century; perhaps the largest compendium is Sir James George Frazer, *The Golden Bough: A Study in Magic and Religion*, first published in 1906. Descriptions of contemporary Italian devotional practices include Lucia Chiavola Birnbaum, *Black Madonnas: Feminism, Religion, and Politics in Italy* (Boston: Northeastern University Press, 1993); Lucia Chiavola Birnbaum, "Women and

Italian Easter Folk Rituals," in Joseph V. Scelsa, Salvatore J. LaGumina, and Lydio Tomasi, editors, *Italian Americans in Transition: Proceedings of the XXI Annual Conference of the American Italian Historical Association* (Staten Island: American Italian Historical Association, 1990), 105-113; and Barbara Corrado Pope, "The Origins of Southern Italian Good Friday Processions," in Paola A. Sensi Isolani and Anthony Julian Tamburri, eds., *Italian Americans Celebrate Life: The Arts and Popular Culture: Selected Essays from the Twenty-Second Annual Conference of the American Italian Historical Association* (New York: American Italian Historical Association, 1990), 155-168. Of particular interest is James Randi, "Investigating Miracles,Italian-Style,"*ScientificAmerican* CCLXXIV:2 (February 1996), 136ff., this is an account of a recent upsurge of interest in the miraculous in Italy akin to that which produced the original cult of the saints, and the issue of defining the miraculous in the modern age.

United States History

Historical works on the piety of Italian-Americans begins with the first Italian in the Western Hemisphere. See Luciano G. Rusich, "Columbus's Religiosity and the Millennium," in Richard N. Juliani and Sandra P. Juliani, editors, *New Explorations in Italian American Studies:Proceedings of the 25th Annual Conference of the American Italian Historical Association* (Staten Island: American Italian Historical Association, 1994), 19-34, and Pauline Moffitt Watts, "Prophecy and Discovery: On the Spiritual Origins of Christopher Columbus's 'Enterprise of the Indies,'" *American Historical Review* XC (February 1988), 73-102. During the colonial, revolutionary, early republic, and Jacksonian periods, a steady stream of individual Italians came first to the Spanish, French, and English colonies and then to the United States. Some came in a religious capacity, as missionaries in various religious congregations. The work of Giovanni E. Schiavo, available in many editions and reprints, is still the best way to begin identifying names and dates. The relevant titles are *Four Centuries of Italian-American History*; *Italian-American History*, volume 2, *The Italian Contribution to the Catholic Church in America*; *The Italians in America before the Civil War*; and *The Italians in America before the Revolution*.

The forerunners of the mass migration out of Italy began to arrive in the United States in the 1850s. These were the working poor, whose lives were being disrupted by the unification movement and the development of a global economy. They no longer seemed to fit into Italy, but they didn't seem to fit in the places to which they migrated, either. They remained marginalized economically and culturally. An example of their marginalization in the religious culture of the United States is in Charles Loring Brace, *The Dangerous Classes of New York, and Twenty Years' Work Among Them*, third edition, with addenda (New York: Wynkoop and Hallenbeck, Publishers, 1880; reprinted Montclair, New Jersey: Paterson Smith, 1967). Brace depicts the Italians as marginalized even within Catholicism. They weren't being cared for by their own clergy, which provided him with an opening to the community. He hired a bilingual Italian man to teach an evening class, with the idea of also introducing the Italians to Protestant Christianity. At this point, an Italian priest turned up, claimed to be starting a Catholic church and school, collected money among the Italians, and then disappeared with the money. The Italians themselves didn't seem to have any religious life independent of their clergy: there is no description of lay devotions or the cult of the saints.

The "chain" feature of most international migrations is especially noticeable in the Italian case. People followed their relatives and friends, so that town disassembled in Italy and reassembled in some particular spot in the United States. This allowed the migrants to bring their specific religious devotions with them. By the 1880s, the devotions were more noticeable than they had been to Brace. Photographs of them are quite rare; one appears in Jacob A. Riis, *How the Other Half Lives: Studies Among the Tenements of New York* (New York: Charles Scribner's Sons, 1890; reprinted New York: Dover Publications, Inc., 1971), p. 42. Verbal descriptions begin in the 1880s, and increase in number in the 1890s and 1900s. A number are cited in the aforementioned Tomasi and Stibili bibliography. Perhaps some descriptions are still in manuscript form, and need to be located, transcribed, translated, and annotated as necessary, and brought to scholars' attention. For an example of a recent discovery, see Giacomo Gambera, *A Migrant Missionary Story: The Autobiography of Giacomo Gambera* (Staten Island: Center for Migration Studies, 1994), 157-158. Students with the patience to look under multiple possible index words will find study of the early twentieth century *New York Times* indexes rewarding, as these contain citations to newspaper articles on *festa* celebrations and parish activities in Italian communities.

Italian-American devotions figure in the class historical surveys of Italian-American religiosity: Henry J. Browne, "The 'Italian Problem' in the Catholic Church in the United States, 1880-1900," United States Catholic Historical Society *Records and Studies* XXXV (1946), 46-72; Rudolph J. Vecoli, "Prelates and Peasants:Italian Immigrants and the Catholic Church," *Journal of Social History* II (Spring 1969), 217-268; and Silvano M. Tomasi, *Piety and Power: The Role of the Italian Parishes in the New York Metropolitan Area, 1880-1930* (Staten Island: Center for Migration Studies, 1975). To these might be added a more recent, detailed account of the pastoral care of Italian immigrants, Stephen M. DiGiovanni, *Archbishop Corrigan and the Italian Immigrants* (Huntington, Indiana: Our Sunday Visitor, 1994). Despite the variety of books in the field, Vecoli's article has been widely cited and is very influential; echoes of it appear in other words such as Paul W. McBride, "The Solitary Christians: Italian Americans and Their Church," *Ethnic Groups* III:4 (1981), 333-353.

Much of the book-length work on Italians focuses on big cities. Chicago has Humbert S. Nelli, *Italians in Chicago, 199-1930: A Study in Ethnic Mobility* (New York: Oxford University Press, 1970); and San Francisco has Deanna Paoli Gumina, *The Italians of San Francisco* (Staten Island: Center for Migration Studies, 1985). Most of these books have chapters on religious life, and these generally include descriptions of parishes that began as a community gathered around the cult of a saint. New devotions are still being discovered in these cities. Lynn Ames, "Shriners," *New York* XIX (June 16, 1986), 30ff., is a picture article showing how Italian-Americans in the New York area venerate their saints in their yards at home. Anthony D'Angelo, "Italian Harlem's Saint Benedict the Moor," in Mary Jo Bona and Anthony Julian Tamburri, editors, *Through the Looking Glass: Italian and Italian/American Images in the Media: Selected Essays from the 27th Annual Conference of the American Italian Historical Association* (Staten Island, New York: American Italian Historical Association, 1996), 235-240, traces the history of a little-known cult in the heart of a large Italian enclave. However, it is also important to cover the smaller cities and the villages, even though it may be more difficult for scholars to visit them and to gather materials from them. The smaller the city, and the fewer the social institutions that can be used to form communities, the more important the parishes, and the cult of the saints, becomes. Howard Gillette, Jr., and Alan K. Kraut, "The Evolution of Washington's Italian-American Community, 1890-Present," in Joseph L. Tropea, James E. Miller, and Cheryl Beattie-Repetti, *Support and Struggle: Italians and Italian Americans in Comparative Perspective: Proceedings of the Seventeenth Annual Conference of the American Italian Historical Association* (Staten Island: American Italian Historical Association, 1986), 171-187, describes a community centered on Holy Rosary in Washington, D.C. Salvatore J. LaGumina, *From Steerage to Suburbs:Long Island Italians* (Staten Island: Center for Migration Studies, 1988), recounts the histories of many Long Island Italian communities, most of which can be identified at least in part by the churches in the area.Ethelyn Orso, *The St. Joseph Altar Traditions of Southern Louisiana* (Lafayette: Center for Louisiana Studies [Louisiana Life Series No. 4], 1990), is a 35-page pamphlet but irreplaceable in noting specifically the varied customs connected with this largely Sicilian observance. Donald E. Byrne, Jr., "Maria Assunta: Berwick's Religious Festival," *Pennsylvania Folklife* XXX:3 (1981), 123-141; and Louis M. Vanaria, "St. Anthony's Day in Cortland: *La Fiesta* in Central New York," *New York Folklore* VI:3-4 (1980),161-170, both preserve descriptions of devotions that take place far away from scholarly centers and thus unlikely candidates for visits from field researchers.

Economics

DiGiovanni's aforementioned *Corrigan and the Italian Immigrants* is interesting for pointing out that the cult of the saints shaped the economy of the local parish, and that the presence of Italian parishes had economic implications for territorial parishes in the same area. It stands to reason that such an important component of Italian life had an economic impact, if only in creating jobs providing articles for veneration, as is explored in Regina Storia, "*I Figurinai*: Lucca Plaster Figurine Makers in USA," in Remigio

U. Pane, ed., *Italian Americans in the Professions: Proceedings of the Twelfth Annual Conference of the American Italian Historical Association* (Staten Island:American Italian Historical Association, 1983), 265-273. Mary Elizabeth Brown, *The Scalabrinians in North America (1887-1934)* (Staten Island: Center for Migration Studies, 1996), contains examples of how Italian interest in devotions shaped parish financial life; the salient information is reused in "The Network of Community Life" in *U.S. Catholic Historian* XIV:3 (Summer 1996), 31-57. William Bastone, "Saints Alive," *Village Voice* XLI:35 (August 27, 1996), 13, 17, is an account of a long struggle to organize New York City's San Gennaro *festa* in such a way as to ensure profits went to local churches and charities, not into the pockets of the organizers.

Literary Studies

The creative arts have also explored the relations between Italian-Americans and their saints. Italian-Americans works of fiction in all genres use devotion and religiosity as motifs. This is explored in works such as Anthony LaRuffa, "Madonna and Mafioso: A View of Mythopoeia in Practice," in Frank J. Cavaoli, Angela Danzi, and Salvatore J. LaGumina, eds., *Italian-Americans and Their Public and Private Life* (Staten Island: American Italian Historical Association, 1993), 180-185; and Francesco Mulas, "Religion in John Fante's Novels," in Mary Jo Bona and Anthony Julian Tamburri, eds.,*Through the Looking Glass:Italian and Italian/American Images in the Media:Selected Essays from the 27th Annual Conference of the American Italian Historical Association* (Staten Island: American Italian Historical Association, 1996), 135-147; and Francesco Mulas, *Studies in Italian-American Literature* (New York: Center for Migration Studies, 1995). There has been some expansion of the definition of creative arts to include film; see Robert Casilli, "Catholicism and Violence in the Films of Martin Scorcese," in Joseph L. Tropea, James E. Miller, and Cheryl Beattie-Repetti, *Support and Struggle: Italians and Italian Americans in Comparative Perspective:Proceedings of the Seventeenth Annual Conference of the American Italian Historical Association* (Staten Island: American Italian Historical Association, 1986), 283-304. The definition of creative arts has been applied most broadly in Denise Mangione Di Carlo, "The History of the Italian *Festa*: 1880s to the Present" (Ph.D., New York University, 1990). The dissertation discusses the *festa* as community ritual, the most elemental communication among people who do not read and write or do highly trained musical, dance, or dramatic performances.

Beyond the Research Monograph
        Perhaps the most common reason for a specialized biographical dictionary is for personal devotion. There are numerous books of the type exemplified by Christian Feldman, *God's Gentle Rebels: Great Saints of Christianity*, translated by Peter Heinegg (New York: Crossroad, 1995); Anne Freemantle, *Saints Alive: The Lives of Thirteen Heroic Saints* (Garden City: Doubleday, 1978); Augustine Kalberer, *Lives of the Saints: Daily Readings*, second edition (Chicago: Franciscan Herald Press, 1983); John P. Kleinz, *Profiles in Faith: Following the Commandment of Christ* (Westminster, Maryland: Christian Classics, 1991); Mary Neill and Ronda Chervin, *Great Saints, Great Friends* (Staten Island: Alba House, 1989)—these present brief biographies for people interested in finding examples to emulate, or patrons to whom to pray. Some of these devotional aids are coordinated with the liturgical year. Examples include: Christine Chaundler, *A Year Book of Saints*, revised by Brother Kenneth (London and Oxford: Mowbrays, 1978); John J. Delaney, ed., *Saints for All Seasons* (New York: Doubleday, 1978); and Joseph N. Tylenda, *Saints of the Liturgical Year: Brief Biographies* (Washington, D.C.: Georgetown University Press, 1989). Regarding the general issue of the place of the saints in post-Vatican II Catholic rites, see Pierre Jounel, *Le Renouveau du culte des Saints dans la liturgie Romaine* (Rome: C.L.V.-Edizione liturgiche, 1986).
        There are also many authors ready to provide guidance as to what the saints can teach the modern reader. A modern classic in this field is a Phyllis McGinley, *Saint Watching* (New York: Viking Press, 1969), which is something of a personal account. An effort to make the saints relevant to modern society, but written from a less personal and more issues-oriented angle, is Lawrence Cunningham, *The Meaning of the Saints* (San Francisco: Harper and Row, 1980). It is a bit easier to guess the viewpoint

from the subtitle of Patricia Treece, *Nothing Short of a Miracle: The Healing Power of the Saints* (New York: Doubleday [Image Books], 1988).

Besides personal devotion at home, persons use books on the saints to travel to religious sites and feast days. This has spawned a genre of writing that in turn contributes to scholarship by collecting still more examples of Italian-American devotional life. Samples of this genre include timely articles such as Carol Field, "Twelve Italian Celebrations," *The New York Times Magazine* (October 10, 1993), 12Aff., and one solid reference book, Margaret Hobbie, *Italian-American Material Culture: A Directory of Collections, Sites, and Festivals in the United States and Canada* (New York: Greenwood Press, 1992).

Scholars' research into Italian-Americans and their saints has been used as a framework for understanding other issues. An example of this is Timothy M. Matovina, "The Italian 'Problem' and the Hispanic Opportunity," *America* CLXV:15 (November 16, 1991), 362. There might be some debate among scholars of Italian-American religiosity regarding some of the statements in the article, but its real purpose is to launch a discussion of Hispanic Catholics and how their particular devotional style relates to the universal Church. In this case, study of Italian devotions is one component of a larger project of comparative studies done with an eye to using the material gathered to take action.

Italian-Americans' religiosity is used to frame another sort of discussion in Joseph A. Varacalli, "The Changing Nature of the 'Italian Problem' in the Catholic Church of the United States," *Faith and Reason* XII:1 (1986), 38-73, which uses the historical debate over an Italian model of religiosity as a starting point for discussion of more contemporary clergylay relations. Another approach is exemplified by the work of Michael James Eula, "Between Contadino and Urban Villager: Italian-Americans of New Jersey and New York, 1880-1980. A Comparative Exploration into the Limits of Bourgeois Hegemony" (Ph.D., University of California at Irvine, 1987); Anthony Mansueto, "Blessed are the Meek. . . . Religion and Socialism in Italian-American History," in Jerome Krase and William Egelman, editors, *The Melting Pot and Beyond: Italian-Americans in the Year 2000: Proceedings of the XVIII Annual Conference of the American Italian His-*

torical Association (Staten Island: American Italian Historical Association, 1987), 117-136; the dissertation on which Manuseto's article is based, which was done at the Graduate Theological Seminary in 1985; and the aforementioned works by Lucia Chiavola Birnbaum. These interpret devotions as a manifestation of a comprehensive commitment to human equality and to the care of the poor and powerless.

Continuing Studies

Even non-historians tend to use historical material when they research Italian-Americans and their saints, as they must start with the customs the first generation brought with them. However, it is important to see how the customs fare over the generations in the United States. Edythe Quinn Caro, "Celebration, Conflict and Reconciliation at Saint Anthony's," in Jerome Krase and William Egelman, eds., *The Melting Pot and Beyond: Italian-Americans in the Year 2000: Proceedings of the XVIII Annual Conference of the American Italian Historical Association* (Staten Island: American Italian Historical Association, 1987), 249-258. is a pioneering work in this regard. Caro describes how one parish, founded for Italians, fared after the era of migration ended and the Archdiocese of New York, in which the parish was located, reorganized to create parishes more responsive to a younger generation that had less of an ethnic identification. Another effort to track the transition from the cult of the saints to the stable parish is Mary Elizabeth Brown, *Churches, Communities and Children: Italian Immigrants in the Archdiocese of New York, 1880-1950* (Staten Island: Center for Migration Studies, 1995).

Most of the work on the second generation deals not with particular parishes but with general populations. In Valentine J. Belfiglio, "Cultural Traits of Italian-Americans which Transcend Generational Differences," *The Italian-Americans Through the Generations* (Staten Island: American Italian Historical Association, 1986), 212-225, the authors explain that one trait that persists across generations of Italian-Americans is an identification with Roman Catholicism. In Nicholas John Russo, "The Religious Acculturation of the Italians in New York City" (Ph.D., Saint John's University [Queens, New York], 1968), the point is made that one of the traits that does not persist across generations of Italian-American Catholics is devotion to the saints, especially when it comes to participation in feast day, lighting candles before saints' statues, and having mass said in gratitude for favors received from a patron saint. However, it might be pointed out that the conclusion is a time-bound one, based on a survey taken right at a point at which the third generation of Italians still consisted primarily of very young adults, and also at a point at which lay Catholics were coming to terms with the mandates of Vatican II. Perhaps if the survey could be repeated at different points in history, it might indicate that the same people had picked up some personal devotions as they aged, as they matured in their faith, and as parishes combined old and new in post-Vatican II worship. Another useful entry into this field is Louis John Gesualdi, "The Religious Acculturation of the Italian-American Catholics: Cultural and Socio-Economic Factors" (Ph.D., Fordham University, 1974).

Italians and Italian-Americans are still being raised to the honors of the altar, and the style these days is not to write a panegyric but to write a solid, scholarly biography. Examples include Mary Louise Sullivan, M.S.C., *Mother Cabrini: "Italian Immigrant of the Century"* (Staten Island: Center for Migration Studies, 1992); and Marco Caliaro, C.S., and Mario Francesconi, C.S., *John Baptist Scalabrini: Apostle to Emigrants* (Staten Island: Center for Migration Studies, 1977). Such biographies have a double value. Not only do they add to the knowledge of Italian sanctity, they add to the knowledge of the world of Italian immigration and, ultimately, Italian-American spirituality.

MARY ELIZABETH BROWN

INDEX

Abbreviations: IA for Italian-American
　　　　　　　RC for Roman Catholic (s)
　　　　　　　RCC for Roman Catholic Church
　　　　　　　USA for United States of America
　　　　　　　SI for Southern Italian

SI, and Grace, 209, 212
Arabs, RC, 238
Areopagus, 172, 187
Aristotle, 207
Army of the Holy Faith, 96
Aryanism, 211
Ascoli, Max, 124
Assimilation, Assimilationist, 1, 8ff, 93ff, 118ff, 238ff; 122, 191
Astrology, 17
Athenians, 172, 187
Austria, 108
Avellino, Italy, 139

Bacon, Francis, as Gnostic, 206ff
Baltimore, MD, Third Plenary Council, 98
Baptism, 216ff
Barla, Pauline, 45
Baroni, Gino, and "unmeltable ethnics," 122-123
Barry, Ronald, Rev., on *festa*, 143
Barzini, Luigi, *The Italians*, 213
Batule, Robert J., Rev., 172-189, 12n
Beatification, *beati,* 37, 60ff
Beecher, Lyman H., Rev., 155, 157
Beirnaert, Louis, S.J., Rev., 220n
Bellport, Long Island, 144
Berger, Peter L., and "praise of particularity," 242ff; 12n

Bianco, Carmine, 145ff
Bible, 204, 240; and saints, 107, 123, 191-192
Biographies (saints), 264-266, 279-280
Black Hand, 167
Blessed Sacrament and Rosary, 210, and Tabernacle, 210, 224n *See also Eucharist, Sacraments*
Blood, 15, 224n, 226n
Bloom, Alan, 244
Blue Point, Long Island, 145
Bohemian (Czech) National RC Parish, 109
Bollandists, 62n
Bornati, Gabriella, 45
Boston, Massachusetts, 112
Bourgeoisie, 11ff, 159ff, 203ff
Bourne, Randolph, 165
Bouyer, Louis, Rev., on "opaqueness," 206
Modern man's blindness to the the the transcendent 206ff; and sacred space and time, 214; on the Eucharist, as saving the Divine Liturgy, 219n; on sacrifice as sacred meal, 219n; on paganism, 221n Bragdon, Claude, attempt to create secular "spirit of the *festa*," 165ff; and occult, 165
Brescia, Italy, 45
Briggsville, Wisconsin, 108
Brogan, D.W., 154

Episcopalianism, 115 *See also Anglo-conformity, Capozzi, Culture*

Erastianism, 212 *See also Civil Religion, Church and State, Americanism*

Ethnicity, 6, 59, 112ff, 133ff, 138ff, 167ff, 175ff, 185, 238ff, 242ff *See also Culture, Novak, Baroni, Assimilationism*

Ethnocentrism, 243, 244 *See also Irish-American RC, Church, Anglo-Conformity*

Eucharist, Holy, RC, and *Sacrosanctum Concilium*, 181ff; and IA, 204ff; with Pentecost, greatest gift of Christ, 210, 218; Sacrament of Sacraments, 200; 215; and *Festa*, 215; and becoming saints, 216; and Gnostics, 220n *See also Sacraments, Catholicism, Church, Mass, Jesus Christ, Magisterium, Altar; Evangelii Nuntiandi* (1975), RC Apostolic Exhortation, Pope Paul VI, and popular religiosity, 187; and well-oriented popular piety as "rich in values," 187 *See also IA, Evangelization, multicultural realism, Irish-American RC, Anglo-Conformity, Saints*

Evangelization, and the challenge of the IA Catholicism, 180, 225n; and inculturation, 242, 237ff; and failure of Church in the USA, and reversal of IA, 237ff, 172ff, 177, 187 *See also IA, SI Americanization, Modernism, Saints*

Evolution, as Gnostic, 205 *See also Voegelin, Immanentism, Opaqueness*

Ex Voto, 75, 100

Family, la *famiglia*, (Familism), as blood-tie, 224n; as IA value, 248; no IA theologizing of, 214 ; as consumer product in Modern society, 215

Farley, John Cardinal, 177

Far Rockaway, Long Island, 135

Feminist Movement, 241, 245

Feminist Studies (bibliography), 269-270

Femminella, Francis X., on impact of IA on Church in USA, as less formalistic, more fully American, less conservative and less dependent upon clergy, more spiritual, 248; 123, 176, 243 *See also Church, Irish-American RC, Americanism*

IA piety, 154; why repulsive to Protestants, 155ff; as opposed to church in Protestant and Irish-American RC understanding, 157ff; and criticism of *connazionali,* 159; "theatrical vulgarity of," 159; "the world is hung with banners" (C.Field), 159; as "mere entertainment for money,"160; as "amusements," 162; appeal to Progressive intellectuals like Jane Addams, Lewis Mumford, Randolph Bourne, Jacob Riis, and Claude Bragdon, 165ff; as "rallying-point" of IA civil and domestic life (Riis), 165; "wholeness" of, "organic experience" of, 165ff; Bragdon tries to recreate as unifying but secular events, participatory, democratic, 165ff; and intermingling of public and private spheres, 166; answers the question, "Who is my neighbor?," 167; seen by US hierarchy as transitional to a more American Catholicism, 177ff ; 7, 10, 29, 41ff, 58, 68, 84-88, 93, 102, 135, 175; Marian, 75ff

Also see Feasts, Fireworks, Incarnation, Bouyer, Voegelin, Processions, Saints, Eucharist, Irish-American RC, Church, IA, SI, Eliade,Agape, Cristiani

Field, Carol, 159, 219n
Finney, Charles Grandison, and Second Great Awakening, 155
First Fridays, 46
Fitzpatrick, Joseph P., 118
Foerster, Robert F., 120
Folk religion, and IA, 79ff, 89, 97ff
Food metaphors and *festa,* the social role of food, 219-220n
France, 108; and carnival as relic, 219n
Franch, Beniamino, Rev., 54
Franciscan Order, RC, 50, 52, 56, 64n
Frazer, Sir James G., *(The Golden Bough); Study in Magic and Religion*, 35, 205ff
French National Catholic Parish, 109
French Revolution, as Gnostic, 208; 96

Gable, Clark, 200
Gaeta, Frank, Rev., 137

Gambera, Giacomo, Rev., 47, 52

Gambino, Richard, 10, 70, 84, 219n

Gans, Herbert J., 112

Gay rights, 59

Gemeinschaft (community), 14n, 166, 178, 199ff, 215

German-American RC, 47, 100ff, 176; rise in divorce rate, 103; decline in Mass attendance, 103, 193; 225n

Gesellschaft (association), 14n, 213, 215

Giglio Festa, 86ff, 86ff, 102, 58, 205ff, 177ff, 40-41, 58, 7, 220n; by mid-1950's controlled by clergy, 102

Glen Cove, Long Island, 139ff

Glock, Charles, on five dimensions of religion, ritualistic, ideological, experiential, intellectualistic, and consequential, 247ff

Gnosticism, defined, 206, 208; and The Enlightenment, 207, 209; "dream" in the West, 209; and Docetism, 209, 214; and relativism, 215ff; and true history, 215, 216; hopelessness of, 217; "anti-world" of, 218; wine as evil, 220n; different sects of, 222; 9, 164, 205ff, 215ff
See also Voegelin,

Modernism, Hans Jonas, Guardini, Bouyer, Eliade, The Enlightenment

God, percentage of Americans who believe in, 191; Yahweh, 193; 198; and saints, 289; 203, 205ff; as *capax Dei,* 209; no escape from His mercy, 215; man created in His image, 216; SI dependence upon, 222n

Goffman, Erving, 83

Good Friday Processions, 42, 63n

Gospel, 221n, 247ff

Grace, and psychology, 199ff; and true culture, 207ff; 209; and St. Thomas Aquinas, 209

Gramschi, Antonio, and idea of studying culture, 168

Great Awakening, The, 155

Great Depression, The, 142

Greek myths, 196

Greek Rite (Ruthenians), 108

Greeley, Andrew, Rev., 12-13nn, 14n, 238

Greenpoint, Long Island, and RC, 82

Greenwich Village, New York, 58, 60, 66n, 87, 112, 153, 159

Gross, Feliks, on "Canossa Complex" of SI, 225n

Guardini, Romano, Msgr., *The*

292

End of the Modern World
(1968 ed.). Intro. Frederick
W. Wilhelmsen, 208, 219n
See also Modernity,
Voegelin, Culture, Man,
Nature, Relativism
Guardian Angels, 211
Guanella, Don Luigi, 160
Gubbio, Italy, 86

Hadrian's Tomb, 25
Haitians, RC, 138, 238
Hagerman, Long Island, 143
Halle, David, 7-8, 12-13nn, 82
Handlin, Oscar, 238
Hansen, Marcus (Hansen's
Law), 59
Heaven, 211
Heer, Frederick, 221n
Hennessey, James, S.J., Rev.,
146
Herberg, Will, *Protestant,*
Catholic, Jew: An Essay in
American Religious
Sociology (1955),
and "religions of
democracy," (civil
religion), 215, 236ff, 240;
112 *See also Civil*
Religion, Americanism,
Erastianism.
Hibernization, 4, 7, 93, 143ff,
146-147, 196, 180, 247 *See*
also Irish-American RC,
Feste, Americanism, IA, SI
Hildebrand, Dietrich von,

Liturgy and Personality;
The Healing Power of
Formal Prayer (rev. ed.,
1960), 216 *See also*
Liturgy, Mass, Man,
Church
Hillenbrand, M. J., 179
Hispanics (Latino), RC, 138,
211, 238
Historicism, 203-204
See also History,
Immanentism,
Transcendence,
Incarnation, Voegelin,
Guardini
History, as sacred time, 215ff ;
hope as transforming (J.
Maritain), 217; Christopher
Dawson on, 224n;
Protestantization of, 240-
241 *See also Incarnation,*
Immanence,Transcendence,
J. Pieper
Holiness, 60
Hollywood, California, 244
Holy Family, 5,40
Holy Family RC Church, 113
Holy Guardian RC Church, 112
Holy Hours, 46
Holy Rosary RC Church (Jersey
City, N.J.), early national
Italian parish (c. 1860's),
109, 209; and *festa*, 214,
219n *See also Feste,*
Incarnational Realism,
Brunswick Street

Holy Spirit RC Church, 55
Homo religious, 204
Homosexuals, 241, 244
Hope, J. Maritain on the will
  and duty to hope, 216-217;
  as holy, 217; its divine
  power, 217 *See also*
  Maritain, Incarnation,
  Revelation, God, Church
Hungarian-American RC, and
  saints, 125n
Humility, St. Bonaventure on,
  224n
Hungary, 108

Iconoclasm, rejection by
  bishops, 94
Iconography (Christian), 7, 11,
  98-99, 119-120, 204ff, 214;
  J. Pelikan on, 226n
Ideology, 6, 216, 238
Il corno (twisted horn), 3, 84
Il malocchio (the evil eye), 3,
  83, 194
Il Sud (the South of Italy), 5ff
Immaculate Conception, 19-20,
  89
Immaculate Conception RC
  Church, 114-115
Immanence, immanentism,
  207ff; and universe of pure
  immanence, 208; John
  Dewey as philosopher of,
  208; Frederick Jackson
  Turner and "frontier thesis,"
  214ff; immanentism

opposed to Judaeo-
  Christian Revelation, 214;
  215 *See also*
  Transcendence, Modernity,
  Pragmatism
Immigration Act of 1924, 102
Immigration History, 59ff
Incarnation, The, 99, 212, 214ff,
  216; and collective
  unconsciousness, 220n
Individualism, Irish-American
  RC and Protestant, 157ff ;
  and division between
  private and public
  realms as a problem for IA,
  164ff; as Gnostic, 213
  See also Modernity,
  Nominalism,
  Bourgeoisie, The
  Enlightenment, Gesellschaff
Indulgences, 223n
Instrumentalism, 206; as
  Gnostic, 207
Inwood, Long Island, 134ff, 147
Irish-American RC, failure of
  hierarchy to develop
  "plausibility structures" to
  assimilate integrally
  SI Catholicism, 236ff ;
  definition of religious
  reality, 243; 239, 191, 203ff
  Clergy's ethno-
  centrism, 243; and SI
  strategy of multicultural
  realism to oppose Irish-
  American control of

US Church, 244ff ; and
Incarnation, 203ff ; rise in
divorce rate, 103; decline in
Mass attendance, 103;
narrowness on role of the
saints, 243; 153; like most
Protestants, repulsed by
festa, 155; their
Catholicism more external
than Protestants, 156ff ;
seen by Protestants as
subversives, 157; as the
"Locusts of Egypt" (L.
Beecher), 157 *See also
Church, Americanism,
Feste, Papacy, IA, SI*
Islam, 68, 204
Italian-American, SI, RC
their Incarnational
Realism, 203-227; opposed
to Modernity, 213; more
than 500 national parishes in
US by end of WWI, 101,
108ff; first National parish in
Philadelphia (St. Mary
Magdalene de' Pazzi, 1852),
109ff; 107ff, 132ff, 142ff,
175ff, 180; local saints'
cults, 108, 180;
strengthening effect of local
saints' cults on Churches in
USA, 180ff ; Vecoli and
Russo on local saints' cults,
225n; Humphrey J.
Desmond on local saints'
cults, 225n; and their

Gemeinschaft
neighborhoods, 111ff,
166ff,175ff, 199ff, 213;
their Church dedications,
1896-1960, 107ff ; three
stages of Church
dedications, 111ff;
opposition to French
Revolution, 97ff ; and Cult
of Jesus Christ, 76, 232;
and Irish-American RC, 44,
79, 107, 124, 132, 144; and
Irish-American Americanist
RC bishops, 97ff; 100,
175ff, 234ff; and RC
doctrine, 85, 232-236,
210ff; and *campanilismo,*
80; as pragmatist, 73, 89,
132; not materialistic, 217;
predicted assimilation, 122;
and health problems, 120ff;
complaints to Bishop on
Long Island, 137ff, 183;
festa as "most authentic
expression of SI culture" in
New World, 85; 159ff,
231ff; private devotions,
181, 146, 81ff; and *Domus,*
209ff, 82ff, 164ff 213; and
presepio, 82; religious
iconography and working
class, 82; and *festa,* 84ff ;
and name day, 88; their
enduring value system, 89;
and RC Church in USA,
232, 175ff, 93; 243; and rise

of divorce rate, 103; not anticlerical, 97ff , 225n; as anticlerical (Paul McBride), 105n, 235; need of evangelization, 175ff , 232, 225n; their "nobleness of soul," 179; St. Anthony of Padua, "Hammer of Heretics," as great favorite of, 23n; and opposition to nationalism, 97ff, 232ff, 139, 212; and "Canossa Complex," 225n; and institutional Church, 159-160, 175ff, 204ff, 213ff; complaints that they failed to contribute to their parishes, 99, 146; and role of priests, 225n, 235-236, 98ff; as deeply RC and orthodox,133, 158, 161, 209, 211-214,223n, 225n; their ignorance of Apostles Creed, 99, 158-160; as not instructed well enough to receive the Sacraments, 99, 179, 225n, 235; as "not humiliated by humiliation," 99, 216; their humility, 222n; failure to assist at Mass, 101ff; decline in Mass attendance after Second Vatican Council, 103; dependence upon God the Father, 222n; and secular ideology, 172ff, 187; and Protestantism, 177ff, 127n, 232ff; and Pentecostalism, 132, 137, 162-163, 234ff; educated *(connazionali),* in general, opposed to *feste,* 159, 225n; and RC folk religion, 131, 146, 159, 163, 175, 181, 214ff, 232; their religiosity, 153ff, 158ff, 233; rejected by Protestants and Catholics more for their external expressiveness than for Catholicism *per se,* 158ff, 165, 225n; and Italian mutual society, 139, 146; indifference to official Catholicism in U.S., 243; non-practice of RC Faith, 187, 234ff; expressiveness of, 153ff, 161-162; criticised for honoring saints more than Italian national heroes, 159-160; separation of religion and Church, 159-160, 177ff; and radicalism, 231-232; and problem of division of private and public realms in U.S., 164ff; on IA moving easily from private to public realms, 167, 231-232; as pre-modern, 207ff, 231ff; American Church's failure of sensitivity to, 180ff, 236; Church's failure to develop

297

212, 233; and Catholic realism, 213ff; opposed to Gnostic individualism, 213ff opposed to Gnostic Modernity, 213ff ; opposed to romantic nationalism, 213ff; opposed to nominalism and antinomianism, 213ff; and *la Famiglia*, 213; and *communio,* 213; and *ben educato*, 213; and interiorization of values of the *Domus,* 213-214; their purpose to become *cristiani,* more worthy participants in the *festa* of life, 213-214, 217ff; and theology, 214; and Byzantine influence on icons, 214; and Mediterranean sense of mystery, 215; and flight to suburbs, 215; and erosion of sense of transcendence, 215; their understanding of history as sacred time, 215; and no Gnostic "contracted existence," 215-216; and every day a *festa*, 215, 222n as witnesses to the universal, 216ff ; and Catholic Absolute, 216; their lessons for us, 216ff; as a people of hope, of the will to hope, hope against hope, 216-217 ; and holy hope, 217; on keeping hope firm, 217; as heroes of the Modern Age, 217 ; and dignity of human beings, 217; their historic duty to become saints, 217-218 ; Vecoli on mysticism of, 225n; Pope Pius XI on natural right of IA, to religious instruction and pastoral care in mother tongue, 225n; *festa* as ritualized community, 226n; Chesterton on RC peasants as free men, 226n; authentic RC way of life, 236ff; contemporary IA acceptance of (Herberg's) "American way of life" as today's civil religion, 236; and RC as "ultimate concern," 237; object of Irish-American RC clergy's ethnocentrism, 243ff ; and pagan appropriation of Saints, 243; truth, beauty, holiness, utility within their folk religion, 243; multicultural relativism as strategy not deeply held, 243; their ethnocentrism and *la via vecchia,* 243-24; their high tolerance for ideas and practices consistent with *la via vecchia*, 244; third and fourth generations, 243ff; prosperity of, 243ff;

and social mobility, 244; and privatization of devotion to saints, 244 ; and radical multiculturalism and *Il Risorgimento* roots, 244; IA feminists against patriarchal family, 244-245; IA socialists against capitalist exploitation, 244-245; IA lesbians against male exploitation, 245; IA heterosexual love and marriage, 245; IA New Agers, 245; IA libertarians, 245; IA strong desire for upward mobility and acceptance into elite circles, 247; reversal of evangelization,247ff; and a realistic IA RC multiculturalism, 247-249; *la via vecchia* vs. attractiveness and impersonality of secularized modern world, 247; authentic IA multiculturalism must be rooted in RC faith, 247; IA religious orientation, 247-248; and 20th century RC, 247-248; correcting IA saint- worship and encouraging active participation in sacramental system and deeper sense of social justice, 247-248;

values of familism, work, traditionalism, personalism, and indifference to worldly pretensions and claims, 248; religiosity—stance from paganism to pluralism, multiculturalism to contemporary neo-paganism, 239ff, 247ff; 6, 10, 159; historical relationship to saints, 231ff; and Sacraments, 232; and Magisterium, 232; and Mystical Body of Christ, 232ff; lack of good priests, 232; and clerical immorality, 235.
Italianità, x, 86, 236; on its institutionalizing with American society, 244-245; radical multicultural exploitation of, 244

Mazziotta, Richard, Rev., on
veneration of the saints, 125
Medford, New York, and RC,
82
Mediatrix, 38 *See also Mary
Marian Titles, Rosary*
Medicine, 8
Mexicans, 112
Michelangelo Buonarroti, 19
Middle Ages, 204, 212
Middle Class, 240 *See also
Bourgeoisie, Capitalism*
Mignone, Mario B., Foreword,
iv-ix
Miracles, 41, 46, 61, 72-73, 99
Miraculous Medal (RC
Devotion), 57
Mission, nature of Protestant
and Irish-American RC
understanding in 19th
century, 157
Modernism, 212ff, *See also
Modernity, Gnosticism,
Voegelin, Guardini*
Modernity, x; SI oppose, 213ff;
and "contracted existence,"
9; 203ff, 209, 246-247; R.
Guardini's three pre-
suppositions of, 208ff ; as
Gnostic, 216, 219n; 13-14,
199ff, 203ff, 206 *See also
Gnosticism, Modernism,
Voegelin*
Monarchy, 70
Montfort Fathers, of Eastport,
Long Island, 144

Montpellier, 26
Morality, objective and
multicultural realism, 246
Morelli, Felix, C.S., Rev., 54
Moreschini, Tomaso, Rev., 53
Morison, Samuel E., on
similarity between RC and
Puritanism, 157
Moroni, Marcellino, Rev., 65n
Morse, Samuel F.B., on RC
political conspiracy, 157
Most Holy Name of Jesus (RC
Devotion), 18
Most Precious Blood of Jesus
(RC Devotion), 18, 52, 56
Mother Theresa of Calcutta,
200
Moynihan, Patrick, 246
Multiculturalism, defined, 238-
240; reasons for usefulness
in analysis of saints in IA
life, 238-240
multicultural relativism as
self-contradictory, 239-240;
history of, 240ff ; radical
multiculturalism, xi, 10, 240,
244-245; and Marxism, 240;
and feminism, 240;
Freudian, 240;
deconstructionist, 240;
denial of Judaism and
Christianity, 240; and
demographic movements,
240; and minorities, 240;
and realism, 242ff, 246ff ;
true multiculturalism

303

weakened by false, radical, relativistic multiculturalism in 1960's and later, 246 *See also Multicultural Realism*

Multicultural Realism, 13n, 242ff; and IA, 246ff; and IA affirmation of absolute truth, objective moral order, the Triune God, integrity of RC Faith, Magisterium, Revelation (Divine Law), Natural Law, *la via vecchia* as consistent with Natural Law but in need of purification; founding of Church by Christ, 246ff; no authentic IA multiculturalism without Catholic Faith, 247; need to recover truths incarnate in traditions of Southern Italy for IA multicultural realism, 248 ; inculcation of *la via vecchia* required for evangelization of IA, 247-248; and mis-reading of Second Vatican Council, 247; post-counciliar materialism, relativism, 247; saints and a realistic multiculturalism, 231-250 *See also Multiculturalism, la via vecchia, IA*

Mumford, Lewis, 164

Mussolini, Benito, 24

Mystical Body of Christ (RC Dogma), 210, 232

Mysticism, 203ff, 223n, 224n; Vecoli on IA mysticism, 225n *See also Sacraments, Eucharist*

Naples, Italy, 15, 20, 23, 42, 72, 77, 97, 136, 144, 159

Napoleon Bonaparte, 24

Narbonne, France, 27

Narcissism, and U.S. culture, 209

Nassau Community College Center for Italian-American Studies, x

Nationalism, 97, 139, 233; and *connazionali*, 159ff, 212ff

National Socialism, and Gnostic superman, 207 *See also Voegelin, Gnosticism*

Native Americans, 17

Nativism, 211

Nativity of Our Blessed Lady (RC Devotion), 113

Nature, as autonomous, 208ff; Chesterton on, 220n *See also Gnosticism, Guardini, Voegelin*

Natural Law, defined, 242, 206, 214ff ; and John Courtney Murray, S,J., 226n; and SI, 236; and multicultural realism, 242, 246ff

Natural Religion, 205

Nazareth (Holy Land), 19

Neapolitan States, 99

Nelli, Humbert S., 111
Nestorianism (RC heresy), and
    Rosary, 224n
Neuroses, and Sacraments, 226n
Newark, New Jersey, 225n
New Age, 244-245
Newman, John Henry, RC
    Cardinal, 205; on pagan
    literature, philosophy,
    mythology, 221n; on
    mysteries of RC Faith, 223n
New Orleans, Louisiana, 107,
    136
New York City, New York, 7,
    21, 45-46, 56, 58, 82, 97ff,
    112, 121, 177
New York, archdiocese of, 111,
    121
Nicaea, Second Council of, 94,
    195
Nietzsche, Frederick, Eliade on,
    205; and Gnostic superman,
    207
Nihilism, 206
Nola, Italy, 136
Nominalism, 213ff
Novak, Michael, 60; and
    "unmeltable ethnics," 122ff
Novena (RC Devotion), 7, 85
    *See also Mary, Marian
    Hyperdulia*

Opaqueness, and Gnosticism,
    203ff ; 214ff, 218 *See also
    Bouyer, Eliade, Voegelin,
    Transcendence*

Orsi, Robert A., *The Madonna
    of 115th Street; Faith and
    Community in Italian
    Harlem, 1880-1950* (1985),
    48, 61, 82, 88, 100, 102; and
    St. Jude, 120, 159-160;
    criticism of Vecoli, 159-160;
    on institutional Church vs.
    People, 160-161; and
    theology of the streets, 160-
    161, 179; agreement with
    Carlo Levi, 160; agreement
    with Protestant criticism,
    160-161; opposed by
    Schiavo, 160-161; 177; on
    Domus, 223n; 243; on SI
    distinction between religion
    and Church, 243
    *See also Patrick Carroll,
    Quinn, IA, SI*
Otto, Rudolf, *Das Heilige* (The
    Idea of the Holy) (1917),
    220n
Our Lady of the Angels RC
    Church, 114
Our Lady of the Assumption
    RC Church, 53, 142
Our Lady of Charity RC
    Church, 113
Our Lady of Consolation RC
    Church, 118
Our Lady of Fatima RC Church,
    81, 139
Our Lady of Good Counsel RC
    Church, 63n, 77, 114, 134-
    135ff

ministers on IA piety, 162ff;
fin-de-siecle, 163;
conversion of IA through
senses, 164; misconception
of saints, 210; as Docetic,
210; and Papacy, 210;
misunderstanding of
veneration of Mary, saints,
224n; failure to convert SI,
232; elite control of USA,
240ff; hegemony in USA,
240; in 19th century USA
citizenship as anglo-
conformity, 240ff;
Protestantization of IA, 247;
42, 94ff, 122, 153, 182, 201,
205 *See also Beecher,
Capozzi, Anglicanism,
Episcopalianism
Protestantism and the Latin
School,* book by F.C.
Capozzi, 163
Psychology (bibliography),
267-268
Psychology, some modern
forms as Gnostic, 207; 2
Puritanism (New England), and
public rites, 155; as
"reformist religious
culture," 155ff; no
Christmas, Easter,
Ascension, 155ff; severance
from cycles of nature, 155;
lack of merriment, 155; and
Awakenings, 155; rejection
of saints as mediators, 242ff

*See also Protestantism,
Edwards, Calvin, Calvinism*

Queen of the Most Holy
Rosary, 20, 53
Queens, Borough of New York,
Long Island, 133
Quinn, John F., 93-106, 12n
Quigley, James E., Archbishop,
53

Racism, as Gnostic, 207; 211ff;
232
Radical Empiricism, 206; as
Gnostic, 207; 214
Radicalism, 232
Rationalism, 204; as Gnostic,
207-208 *See also The
Enlightenment, Modernity*
Rationalization, 203
Realism, 203ff ; 10, IA Catholic
Incarnational, 213ff *See
also St. Thomas Aquinas,
Maritain, Guardini, Marcel,
Voegelin, Transcendence,
Gnosticism, Natural law,
Incarnational Realism, IA,
SI*
Reality, and C. Dawson on
experience of humankind,
224n; and Natural Law, 242
*See also Natural Law,
Incarnational Realism, IA,
SI*
Redemption, 99, 207
Redemptoris Missio (1990), 174

310

311

space, 215ff; J. Maritain on mankind's need for, 209ff; not Gnostic angels, 210; and real IA men, 210; and domus, 210ff; legitimatization of, 240; norms for SI, 231ff; marginalization of, 236; and conflict with Irish-American RC clergy as ideological, 240; imperative to become, 237,243; and Bible, 191-192; and Biblical names, 107ff, 123; in Jewish thought, 211; more Italians than others, 72; exemplary vs. miraculous, 73, 94-95, 123; and Sacraments, 192; and Church Fathers, 94ff; types of Church patrons, 116ff; relics of, 94ff; and archeology, 126n; and Christ, 94-95, 173, 190, 195, 211ff; more influential than catechisms, 94; and Alan Butler's *Lives of the Saints*, 127n; and Councils, 93ff; pilgrimages to tombs, 94ff; St. Francis de Sales on their teaching to praise God, 94-95; as role models more than wonder-workers, 11, 94-95, 173, 190ff; and personality, 11; and evangelization, 173ff; and human consciousness, x;

and symbolic boundaries, 10, 14n; and nature and extent of IA assimilation, i; and *clientelismo*, 7, 122; and the relationship between folk and official RC religiosity, x, l; moved to periphery, 8; and the "Italian Problem," x; worship of, 1, 3, 5, 68ff, 89, 94, 172, 195, 224n, 236, 242ff; not Veblenian "social engineers," or Ph.Ds, 209; devotion to as patrons, 39, 59, 200ff; 6, 94-95, 123, 172ff, 182ff, 247; veneration of, x, l ,6, 7, 34, 42, 51, 56, 60ff, 94ff, 181ff, 195; as flesh-and-blood, real men, women and children, 217; and mediatorship, 243ff; privatization of devotion to by bourgeois IA, 244-245; and grace, 217; decline in devotion since Second Vatican Council, 183, 195; and psychological well-being, 190ff; as brothers and sisters of Christ, 209, 242-243; J. Maritain on, and purpose of life, 209, 243-244; as within the Church—not the Church, 210ff; neglect of, 242; relics to be honored, according to Second Vatican Council, 181-182; on Long Island, 129ff; and hibernization of IA RC, 4, 79, 107, 124; and RC doctrine, 4, 195; strongly defended by Second Vatican Council, 181ff; and the investigator, 4; increasing marginalization in IA religious consciousness, 186; and consequences of belief, 4; and Communion of Saints, 5, 14,192, 217; veneration of, as subordinate to celebration of paschal mystery of Christ, according to Second Vatican Council, 183; and Pope John Paul II's *Divinus perfectionis magister* (1983),60; as perhaps "most important medium for transmitting Christian Faith to SI, 93, 173ff, 232ff; distinction between *dulia* (veneration) and *latria,* (worship) in RC teaching, 94ff, 195; as "examples who draw all to the Father through Christ," according to Second Vatican Council, 181ff, 243; typology of devotions to IA saints, 122; local Italian Saint's Cult,

108ff; Universal Italian Saint's Cult, 108ff   *See also Festa, Sanctity, Sacraments, Grace, Eucharist, Saints' Names, IA, SI, Mary, Church, Renoff, DiGiovanni, Brown, Varacalli, LaGumina*

Salesians, The, Society of St. Francis de Sales (RC Order), 45, 50; Don Bosco, 45

San Colegero, 71

San Cono, 81, 136

San Cosimo, 72

San Damiano, 72

San Donato, 74, 81

San Gennaro, 36, 56, 58, 70, 72, 74, 204,

San Gennaro Society, 56

San Gerlando, 72

San Giuseppe (St. Joseph), 42, 72, 204; and "St. Joseph's Altar," 88

San Lorenzo, 72

San Marino, 108

San Marino Society, 140

San Michele, 70

San Onofrio, 71

San Pantaleone, 72

Santa Lucia (St. Lucy), 70, 102, 107

Santa Ninfa Society, 65nn-66

Santa Maria Addoratta RC Church, 113

Santa Maria Incoronata, 63nn-64, 113

CONTRIBUTORS

Dominic A. Aquila is the Chairman of the Department of History, Humanities, and Political Science at Franciscan University, Steubenville, Ohio.

Rev. Robert J. Batule is Adjunct Professor of Theology at St. John's University, Jamaica, Queens, New York.

Mary Elizabeth Brown, Ph.D., is affiliated with Marymount Manhattan College and the Center for Migration Studies, Staten Island, New York.

Monsignor Stephen M. DiGiovanni, Ph.D., is Assistant to the Chancellor in the Diocese of Bridgeport, Connecticut.

Donald J. D'Elia, Ph.D., is Professor of History at S.U.N.Y.-New Paltz.

Salvatore J. LaGumina, Ph.D., is Professor of History, Emeritus at Nassau Community College - S.U.N.Y., Garden City, New York.

Mario B. Mignone, Ph.D., is Director of the Center for Italian Studies, S.U.N.Y.-Stony Brook.

Salvatore Primeggia, Ph.D., is Professor of Sociology at Adelphi University, Garden City, New York.

John F. Quinn, Ph.D., is Associate Professor of History, Salve Regina University, Newport, Rhode Island.

Richard Renoff, Ph.D., is Professor of Sociology at Nassau Community College-S.U.N.Y., Garden City, New York.

Philip J. Scrofani, Ph.D., is a licensed psychologist in private practice in Fort Washington, Maryland and a member of the Catholic Institute for the Psychological Sciences, West Bethesda, Maryland.

Joseph A. Varacalli, Ph.D., is Professor of Sociology at Nassau Community College-S.U.N.Y., Garden City, New York.